LOVE AND ASPERGER'S:

JIM AND MARY'S EXCELLENT ADVENTURE

LOVE AND ASPERGER'S:

JIM AND MARY'S EXCELLENT ADVENTURE

A MEMOIR

MARY A. JOHNSON, PH.D.

atmosphere press

ISBN - paperback: 978-0-9962029-2-3
ISBN – hardcover: 978-1-63988-130-7
Mary A. Johnson, Ph.D., Albuquerque, NM

"Chance is a nickname for Providence."
Sébastien Roch Nicolas Chamfort – 1741-1794

"Chance is perhaps the pseudonym of God
when He did not want to sign."
Anatole France [Jacques Anatole François Thibault]
– 1844-1924

CONTENTS

INTRODUCTION   *iii*

PROLOGUE   1

PART I – MY
ADVENTURES BEFORE JIM

1 – My Early Years   5

2 – My Married Years   11

3 – I'm Alone   21

PART II – JIM'S
ADVENTURES BEFORE ME

4 – Jim's Early Years   27

5 – Jim's Married Years   43

6 – Jim is Alone   52

PART III – WE BEGIN OUR
ADVENTURES TOGETHER

7 – I Meet Jim Online   65

8 – Things Progress   69

9 – The Die is Cast   75

10 – Obama and Politics   77

11 – Prepping for the Visit   79

12 – We Meet in Person   83

13 – Dazed   97

14 – Seeking Another Opinion   99

15 – Prepping for My Visit   101

16 – A Rocky Arrival   105

17 – Some Family Plans   115

18 – A Better Airport Reception   120

19 – Always on My Mind   126

20 – Family Times, Plans, and Memories 129
21 – Visiting the Girls 133
22 – Round-Up Fun 138
23 – A Ticket and "Are You Sure?" 141
24 – Husband and Wife 145

PART IV – OUR INITIAL ADVENTURES AS WIFE AND HUSBAND

25 – Another Reception and a First Christmas 151
26 – Life Goes On 156
27 – Wheat Ranching and a House Change 158
28 – Learning New Rules 161
29 – Spring is On Its Way 164

PART V – A MIX OF ADVENTURES

30 – Criticisms 169
31 – Finding My Place 174
32 – Visitors 176
33 – Halcyon Days 178
34 – The Licensure Issue 185
35 – The Picnic 189
36 – Good Times 191
37 – Interrupting and Bluegrass 193
38 – Phone Book and Depression 195
39 – An Office, Balloons, A First Anniversary 198
40 – Hearing, Dressing, and Stress 203
41 – Birthday Celebrations 206
42 – Trip, Donut Holes, A Pump, and Bills 209
43 – A Fun Visit and A Licensure Development 217

PART VI – AN ADVENTUROUS RESOLUTION

44 – It Hits Me! 221
45 – The Revelation 223

46 – Jim is A Sponge   226

47 – Disclosure   236

48 – The Guiding and Learning Begin   238

49 – A Tragedy and A Learning Experience   243

50 – Evidence of Learning   245

51 – Wordless   248

52 – A Winning Surprise   249

53 – Weddings   250

54 – TV, Dancing, and A Visit   254

55 – Fun Times   258

56 – A Major Development   262

57 – New Baby, Construction, and A Memorial   265

58 – A Festive Anniversary!   267

59 – The Book, A Cancellation, and A Brief Visit   269

60 – A Top Hat, A Car Show, and Honesty   273

61 – A Dream Comes True   276

62 – House Hunting, Fright, and Hilarity   278

63 – The Move and A Sore Back   282

64 – Settling In   285

65 – Everyday Stuff and Health   287

66 – Visits and A Roadrunner   291

PART VII – ADVENTURES INTO THE UNKNOWN

67 – This Time He's Right   297

68 – Jim is Stoic; I'm Terrified   302

69 – Gathering Data   306

70 – We Get Help   310

71 – Toll Ticket, Visits, and Betrayal   313

72 – A Movie Scene   320

73 – Can't You Make It Go Quicker?   322

74 – The Palm of God's Hand   328

75 – Jim and Mary's Excellent Adventure Ends   330

EPILOGUE   333
A FINAL NOTE   337

PHOTO GALLERY   339
ACKNOWLEDGEMENTS   353
REFERENCES AND SUGGESTED READINGS   355
INDEX OF SOME COMMON TERMS   365
ABOUT THE AUTHOR   369

INTRODUCTION

This book is a love story. Yes, it is about Asperger's, but also about our life together, as Jim wished. Whatever else may be imparted to, or received by, the reader, I want the take-away to be love. Without love, there would be no story and no book.

As a Licensed Professional Clinical Counselor in the state of New Mexico and also Oregon, I developed expertise in counseling people with various problems – among them, couples who are having relationship difficulties that endanger their partnership or marriage, and persons who want help in learning to develop and maintain relationships. As a result of this focus, I encountered a number of clients with Asperger's Syndrome, a constellation of communication and social idiosyncrasies that are located on one end of the larger autism spectrum. The opposite end of the autism spectrum is populated by individuals who cannot communicate well or be comfortable in our larger society composed of "neurotypicals," that is, those who do not have autism. The brains of autistic persons and neurotypical persons are wired differently (Grandin & Barron, 2016, p. 105). Genetics play a large part in who has autism at birth (Falk & Schofield, 2018, pp. 111-112), and it is never "cured." Those who are born with it have it all their lives. They may learn to compensate, but it does not go away. "Asperger's is not a disease. It's a way of being" (Robison, 2008, p. 5).

Many persons with Asperger's – "Aspies," as some of them like to be called, considering it a "badge of honor" (Silberman, 2015, p. 399) – demonstrate high intelligence and, despite some idiosyncratic behaviors, by adulthood have learned to adapt to some of society's demands, hold responsible jobs, and excel in certain areas. They are referred to as "high functioning," but many of them dislike that term, as they have expended years of hard work to attain and maintain the skills that help them adjust to the neurotypical world, and high functioning seems to denote they've had it easier than others on the spectrum.

I diagnosed Jim Hanks with Asperger's soon after his seventh decade of life. In retrospect, I should have been alerted sooner. But Jim Hanks was not my client, and I was not looking to diagnose him. He was my husband, and I loved him. Because "love is blind," as the saying goes, it took me longer than usual to recognize Jim's traits and make the diagnosis. I'm not the only spouse or partner whose awareness was clouded. One wife said, "Slowly the condition revealed itself to us, one confusing situation at a time" (Finch, 2012, p. 230).

In the last weeks of his life and our marriage, Jim said, "I want you to write a book about our life together, so someone may read it and see themselves in it, and feel the relief I felt when I found out about Asperger's."

I asked him if I should omit some details.

He said, "My life is an open book. I don't care who knows about it. Write it the way it happened."

Many Aspies are open and honest. Lesko (2011, p. 83) says, "I'm a very 'what you see is what you get' kind of person," a phrase Jim also often used.

Not everyone with Asperger's likes to be called an "Aspie," but after Jim discovered Asperger's, he used the word Aspie as a term of endearment for himself, so I use it in this story. Because I am talking about Jim, I also use male pronouns when describing general traits, although females also can have Asperger's.

Though few persons have all the various traits of Asperger's, having a preponderance of them strongly suggests Asperger's Syndrome. Aspies are not all alike, and will have different traits (Tammet, 2009, p. 20; Willey, 2015, p. 132). The italicized paragraphs after some scenes will alert you to the traits I failed to recognize, with acknowledgements of the references listed in the back of the book.

It is no mystery that Jim was not diagnosed earlier in his life. Asperger's Syndrome is a condition recognized during the mid-1900s, and was named for an Austrian physician, Dr. Hans Asperger. Before the condition had a name, one of Dr. Asperger's team arrived from Austria in 1934, the year Jim was born. Dr. Asperger gave his first public lecture on autism in 1938, when Jim was four years old, and the condition was described by Dr. Asperger in 1944, when Jim was ten years old. One form of autism was considered a disorder of early infancy as late as 1957, when Jim was 23 years old, with no acknowledgement of undiagnosed adults' struggles with life. Dr. Lorna Wing introduced Asperger's Syndrome as a diagnostic label in 1981, when Jim was 47 years old. She noted that people with Asperger's were obviously highly intelligent, but seemed naïve, as if they couldn't pick up subtle social signals from the people to whom they were talking. The first international conference on Asperger's was held in 1988, and criteria to define the condition didn't emerge until 1989, when Jim was 55 years old (Silberman, 2015, pp. 221-222, 350, 352, 397). There are probably many other older adults who could be diagnosed with Asperger's, but it was not added to the DSM-IV (Diagnostic and Statistical Manual) until 1991, when Jim was 60 years old (American Psychiatric Association, 1994). In the later 2013 edition, the DSM-V subsumed Asperger's under the umbrella term of Autism Spectrum Disorder (American Psychiatric Association, 2013). However, many professionals, including me, prefer to distinguish between Asperger's and classic autism. While both classic autism and

Asperger's share some traits – social communication difficulties, narrow interests, and repetitive actions – they differ in two important ways. In classic autism, the child does not develop language normally, and intelligence varies widely. Asperger's differs from classic autism in that language develops normally and intelligence is at least average (Baron-Cohen, 2008, p. 1).

However, I add, and emphasize, a disclaimer: **This book is not a diagnostic tool. To be properly diagnosed, someone suspected of having Asperger's, or otherwise dwelling somewhere on the autism spectrum, will need to be seen by a licensed professional and examined in person.**

Creating this book has been an emotional journey involving reliving parts of our lives, while fulfilling my promise to Jim. At times I've had to lay it aside before I could continue. I'm fortunate to have kept many emails and other documents as source materials. I have searched my memory and filled the gaps as best I can, making this memoir as truthful and accurate as possible.

If you've never tried to condense over seven years of your life and a love relationship into a book of reasonable length, you cannot fathom what it's like – the details, the cutting, the choosing, the condensation. I can liken it to the process of making maple syrup – it takes 40 gallons of maple sap to make one gallon of maple syrup. What you will read are selections I chose from many, to illustrate the story Jim asked me to tell. I think you will fall in love with him, too.

To fully understand the story, it is necessary for you to know how each of us grew up and matured. Enjoy the journey, as you get to know us, and as I share our loving, delightful adventure. At some points, it did not seem loving, nor delightful, but, to get you started . . .

M.A.J.

PROLOGUE

On a clear, sunny morning in January 2006, in Albuquerque, New Mexico, I watched as the body of my husband of over 50 years, Paul, was driven away in the mortuary van. On that same morning, Jim sat at a meeting at the First Presbyterian Church in Pendleton, Oregon, discussing the prior year's annual fundraising Soup Supper. I know this, because of a penciled notation I found later on in his calendar. I can visualize that cold, foggy, and rainy morning in Pendleton – Jim, newly separated, and his fellow clam-chowder maker, Dale, sitting at a table listening to whomever is speaking. Jim surely had a cup of hot coffee in his hand, properly sugared and stirred, and, even though he listened, his private focus was on how to rebuild his life.

I didn't know Jim, and he didn't know me, as these disparate events took place on that same morning in January, over a thousand miles apart. My world, as I knew it, had stopped, and I couldn't imagine people going about their ordinary lives. Jim, alone after being married many years, was adjusting to his own upsetting and life-changing event.

On that morning, neither of us could have imagined how our lives would cross and how that crossing would involve many life changes for each of us – and for both of us.

PART I

MY ADVENTURES BEFORE JIM

CHAPTER 1

MY EARLY YEARS

My earliest memory is feeling abandoned by my mother. I say "feeling," because I was not abandoned. I was about 20 months old, standing inside our French front door on Giddings Street, looking out one of the panes at my level, watching as my mother walked away, across the wooden front porch and down the sidewalk. I can still see the gray painted boards of the porch and the cracks in the sidewalk. I don't know the whole story (and my mother seemed never to remember that event), but I felt I had done something bad to cause Mother to leave. I was alone, crying, feeling tears roll down my bare tummy, onto my panties. I'm sure Mother had a valid reason for stepping out of the house for a few minutes without me, but I was too young to realize that. I don't remember her returning, but, of course, she did. I only remember being left alone, and the fearful feeling of abandonment remains with me to this day.

Daddy said he would buy me a palomino pony and a rifle when we moved from north Texas out to west Texas cowboy country, in 1948. I was in the fifth grade. After a few years of being a Texas State Bank Examiner, Daddy decided to settle our family down to a more stable life, without travel and moving, and he took a job in the bank in the little town of Rankin.

Mother and I went with him to look at houses. There were not many to look at. There were not many in the whole town. The wind blew dust and tumbleweeds around. Everything looked brown. Mother said we were out in the middle of nowhere. We chose an older white, frame, two-bedroom house with a large front porch, on a paved street, and moved in. No grass in the yard, only dirt. I got the light and bright front bedroom, in the southeast corner. I couldn't wait to unpack my Nancy Drew books and my collection of horse figurines and arrange them in my bookcase. The room became mine. The move seemed exciting and adventurous.

I waited for the pony and gun, but realized that was not going to happen. However, Rankin soon felt like home.

"And how is your teacher?" Mother and Daddy asked, after my first day at school.

I said something I probably heard in a movie, "Well, she looks like she can hold her own in a swimsuit, but I'm not sure about a classroom."

They looked at each other and rolled their eyes. They never quite knew what to expect from me.

Movies were my thing. And with the move, western movies – the more cowboys, horses, covered wagons, and tumbleweeds, the better.

I made friends with a few girls whose families owned sheep ranches. I got to enjoy horseback riding, roundup time, and in my new custom-made boots with my initials inlaid, I thought I was a cowgirl! I was invited to one of the ranches in the summer. We girls had been out riding and were hot, so we went to the big rock house, got thick, red, juicy watermelon slices, and sat on the cool floor in one of the back rooms.

I said, "Let's cry."

My friends said, "Why?"

I said, "I saw a movie once where someone started crying and everybody joined in, so I'll start." I summoned all the sadness I could muster, as I imagined actresses did, and started mock sobbing. The others joined in. This caused the grown-ups to hurry from the front of the house to see what the commotion was about. The father got a broom and, towering over us, pushed us with the bristles, and pretended to sweep us out of the house. "Darn kids! Crying over nothing!"

Daddy assumed the role as treasurer of our Methodist church, I guess because he was a banker, and I heard about some lengthy, and sometimes heated, meetings of the board, on the budget and various other issues. Mother was a leader of our youth group. I played the piano for Sunday School and the organ for church.

My parents' best friends, Bob and Leah Johnson, were active in our church. They had a son, Paul, and we were thrown together a lot, having family dinners at each other's homes. As Mother and I washed and dried our yellow and green Fiestaware after one of those dinners at our house, I said, "Someday I'm going to marry Paul Johnson." Mother just smiled. I was 13, and Paul was in high school.

Seventh grade rolled around. I became interested in boys, leading to an interest in tennis – I even asked for a tennis racquet for Christmas. I didn't know a thing about tennis (and still don't!), but the school's tennis courts were beside the dirt road behind the school, and the boys drove their pickup trucks after school to watch the girls in their short shorts knock those yellow, fuzzy balls over the net. It worked – the boys noticed I was growing up! I begged for permission to date, but Mother said I was too young. Bah!

In spite of Mother's rule, I agreed to meet a boy and sit with him at a movie, only to be surprised by my parents, who also happened to be at the only theater in town. Out of the corner of my eye, I saw movement in the aisle, and it stopped at the end of our row. It was Daddy. He raised his hand, palm side up, crooked his index finger, and motioned me to come with him. We drove in silence. We got home. I was threatened with his leather razor strop, which hung on our screened-in back porch, and I received a stern talking-to about disobedience. Daddy no longer used a straight-edge razor, so I'm not sure why the razor strop was still with us, but it did serve as a symbolic deterrent.

I looked forward to the youth dances at the Community Park Building. I loved to dance – square dancing, folk dancing, slow dancing. We did the Bunny-Hop and the Hokey-Pokey, as well as couples' dances. Unbridled fun and happiness, with emotions energized by hormones. When the "bop" came into vogue, we all gyrated with abandon, until the adult chaperones said the "dirty dancing" was off-limits.

During my teen years, Mother and Daddy often said, "Let's go play golf!" They meant a miniature golf course in a nearby town. It was a great family activity, and kept my mind off of boys for a while, which may have been their point. Mother usually won, and I came in second. I loved avoiding all of the "traps" – streams, sand pits, and revolving, colorful, wooden windmill blades. Fifties songs whined forth from the loud-speaker. We'd play a couple of games, and afterward go for enchiladas and sopapillas at a nearby restaurant. The unique tangy smell of Mexican cooking whetted our appetites while we waited to be seated.

My teenage friends loved movies as much as I did, especially musicals. After a movie, we'd waltz out of the theater and dance down the sidewalk, laughing and singing as many of the songs as we could remember, imagining we were on stage. We tried to remember lines from the movies, to use in conversation, so we'd sound grown-up. We played my piano and sang "You Belong to My Heart," "Buttons and Bows," "Sweet Violets," and whatever else was popular at the time.

One weekend when I was 16, Paul Johnson hitchhiked home from Texas Technological College in Lubbock. After church, as we visited in the churchyard while our folks gabbed, he asked me to go to a movie with him that afternoon before he had to go back to school. I told him I had a date. He was incensed and stalked off. The next week I got a letter, saying, "Here are the weekends I'll be home the rest of the year, and I want you to save me a date on every day of these weekends." I couldn't have been happier.

When I was a junior in high school, Mother got a call from a younger girl's mother, who was prominent in Rankin, wanting to come by to talk to Mother and me. She arrived in a beautiful beige suit with a sheen, and the gist of it was that she was hoping to start a teen chapter of her sorority at our high school. She wondered if I'd be the sponsor, because she said all the younger girls looked up to me.

Mother was beaming. Her daughter, a sponsor of a sorority chapter!

I got the idea, as the woman shared details, that it was intended to be an exclusive, elite group of girls.

I asked, "Can any girl join who wants to?"

"Oh, no! Any girl can apply, but she would have to be approved by the rest of the group."

That did it for me. I was always for the underdog, and I could see her proposal wouldn't fit my belief system.

I said, "We have a small school. I don't think I can do that if some girls would be excluded. Their feelings would be hurt."

My mother was crestfallen, but I felt good about my decision. I was for inclusivity. I think the sorority chapter never got off the ground. If it did, I did not hear about it.

MARY A. JOHNSON, PH.D.

I was hired as a typist for the abstract office in the courthouse, after high school hours, making ten cents per legal page of perfect copy. I could, if I was very careful, produce six legal pages an hour, earning 60 cents. I also taught voice and piano to some younger girls, and charged a small fee.

I continued to take voice and piano lessons all through school. My schedule was full, with cheerleading practice, band, and dating. I had a classical guitar and took lessons, but I was never good at it, because I didn't make time to practice.

I was 17, and the summer after my junior year, Paul was the lifeguard at our city pool, a cool summer job for a college kid. He was a handsome tan hunk, sitting up in the lifeguard's chair, high above the crowd. I went swimming with my friends every day, flirted with Paul, and went on dates with him every night.

In midsummer, Paul came to pick me up one evening, pulled from his pocket a box that held a diamond solitaire, and asked me to marry him. I was on top of the world! I ran back into my parents' bedroom and showed them the ring. Even though I was young, I think my parents were relieved that I would marry a known entity, the son of their best friends. Paul and I joked about ours being an "arranged marriage." We were engaged all of my senior year in high school, and Paul came home from Tech on weekends to escort me to special events like homecoming and the prom.

I loved to learn, and I breezed through high school easily, graduating as valedictorian. Daddy was Class Orator of his graduating class decades before, and he helped me write my speech.

In three weeks, I'd marry Paul.

CHAPTER 2

MY MARRIED YEARS

Paul and I were married in the Methodist Church in Rankin, and moved into a tiny apartment close to campus, in Lubbock. Paul still had two years of college to go. I started to Tech in the fall.

By the middle of spring semester, I was pregnant. My doctor said I'd miscarry if I continued to climb stairs, so I withdrew from school.

One female professor looked at my withdrawal slip and said, "Why are you dropping the class?"

"I'm pregnant, and my doctor doesn't want me climbing stairs."

The professor curled her lip, and said, "Oh, I'm so sorry you got pregnant."

I said, "Oh, I'm married, and we're excited!"

The day Paul registered for his senior year, fifteen months and two days after our wedding, our first daughter, Nancy, was born.

I never heard politics mentioned in our house as I was growing up. I don't know whether my parents were Democrats or Republicans. I know they voted. There was a poll tax of $2.00 in Texas. Daddy would hand Mother her tax receipt and write down how she was to vote, and she put the list in her purse.

After Paul and I married, I registered as a Democrat, and Paul was a Republican. We voted, but we didn't talk politics, and it was never an issue.

When Paul graduated, he was offered a job in El Paso, and we added another daughter, Cathy, to our family.

We began a life of many moves. As Paul worked his way up the career ladder, we lived in several towns in Texas, Louisiana, New Mexico, Illinois, Michigan, and back to New Mexico in 1985. Our moves became legendary in the family. Paul was wise, and each move was better for his career and better financially for our family. I looked at moves as adventures, even as an adult.

When we lived in Houston, tragedy struck. Cathy, then four-and-a-half years old, died just after Halloween, from staphylococcus pneumonia. Alive and well on Thursday, she had a fever on Friday night and Saturday, was seen by the doctor, treated for a sore throat, then hospitalized on Sunday. She died Monday morning. Indescribable heartbreak and grief. Our family and our lives would never be the same. Devastation with a capital "D."

Nancy, then almost seven, wrote a note to Cathy on the day of the funeral, "Dear Cathy, Grammaw and Pawpaugh are here. Wish you were here. Love, Nancy."

Only those who have been through the loss of a child can possibly understand what we experienced. We were zombie-like for months. How would we survive? How would we go on from that point?

But we did survive, and life began to have a regularity to it. Seven months later, I got a call that Daddy had come home from the bank, telling Mother he didn't feel good. The local doctor sent Daddy to the hospital in San Angelo, where he died of massive internal bleeding. We buried him near Cathy's grave.

Paul was transferred back to El Paso, where our son, Paul, was born. Two and a half years later, our daughter, Julie, was born. Life was regaining some normalcy and happiness.

We moved to a suburb of New Orleans, soon after Julie's first birthday. We bought a house near Lake Pontchartrain.

In the summer of 1969, Nancy, 12, Paul, 4, and Julie, almost 2, piled with me into the car, and we headed toward the Mississippi River bridge to a birthday party in another suburb. The kids had on their party clothes, and each had a gift, wrapped in festive paper and bows. We were singing, and as we passed a commercial bakery on the freeway, the last thing I remember was the delicious smell of baking bread wafting into the car.

I woke with rain in my face. I looked up and saw the broken windshield. I heard voices.

"We're taking you to the hospital." I asked about the children. Someone said, "We have them in another car, out of the rain. They're all okay."

I breathed a sigh of relief as I was loaded into the ambulance.

My husband's boss got a message from the hospital saying I was dead, though he told Paul only that we'd been in an accident, and they drove to the hospital. I woke up on a gurney in the emergency room, with bright lights in my face, aware I was being worked on, but still in and out of consciousness.

I saw a woman in a white uniform cutting my clothes off, starting at the hem of my new green plaid dress. I said, "Oh, don't cut my dress. I just finished it this morning."

"Honey, you wouldn't want it now."

I heard someone say, "She has seven broken ribs, a concussion, a broken left shoulder, and a massive wound in her left upper arm." My left ear was reattached. I was wavering between wakefulness and sleep.

I woke up in a hospital room, unable to move my arms or legs. I felt the bandages tight around my chest, keeping my ribs in place. I didn't know yet, but I had tire tracks on the left side of my face, from the car that hit us as it was sent airborne on the rain-slick roadway.

In ten days, I was home again, but confined to bed and unable to take care of the children. Paul hired a woman to stay with us during his work hours. We watched the moon landing. The woman helping with the children said it was a hoax, that it was filmed in Arizona.

It was months before I was able to function normally. When I saw the photos of the car we were in, I was awed, knowing we emerged from that mangled metal and survived.

In a few weeks, I learned to drive again. However, even now, decades later, though I drive normally, the residual fear of being blindsided by another car still lies deep within me, and I am nervous driving or riding on a rainy roadway.

Life regained some normalcy. I engaged in my hobbies – oil painting, leather tooling, embroidery, and I sewed a lot – made quilts and many of the kids' clothes as they grew up. I did some writing, published several magazine articles, and hoped someday to publish a book. I was always an avid reader, enjoying memoirs, books on psychology, and novels. I read *The Bridges of Madison County* in one night, staying up until almost dawn. Paul also loved to read, so he and I often shared an evening without TV.

I was never the best cook, but I managed to keep my family fed and reasonably healthy. I was raised on meat, potatoes, and vegetables, so my cooking was along those lines. In lean times (and there were plenty over the years!), I occasionally fed my family pinto beans and cornbread, or vegetable soup made with whatever was available, so I knew what it was like to eat whatever was put on the table. I was always partial to Mexican food.

Music wove into and out of our lives. Over the years, I liked to listen to John Denver, Dionne Warwick, Rod Stewart, and Kenny Rogers. I liked Kenny G. on the sax. Paul and I both liked The Mormon Tabernacle Choir. On a trip to Salt Lake City, Paul and I were privileged to see and hear the choir rehearse in the tabernacle. One Christmas, we were treated to a Kenny Rogers concert in Detroit.

Paul took a job in sales related to his profession, and we moved back to Houston. Then more steps up the ladder, and later Albuquerque, where we were able to gorge ourselves on the best Mexican food – my favorite, enchiladas.

Paul's work later took us to Illinois and Michigan, where I learned some things about snow. What I learned was that I do not like being wet and cold, and I do not like shoveling snow, walking in it, or driving in it.

In Illinois, I worked part-time at a childcare center and did typing for our homeowner's association, at $3.50/hour. By now, Nancy was in her last year of college.

Paul was transferred to Michigan, near Detroit, and the two younger kids were in junior high and high school. I decided to enter The University of Michigan-Dearborn, majoring in psychology, and graduated with my bachelor's degree.

Paul's company agreed to move us back to Albuquerque and let him commute until he retired. Paul's traveling made me independent by necessity, since I had to deal with the household, plus raise the kids by myself during the week. We were in love with Albuquerque – the food and the culture, in which the diverse ethnicities all blended well. I began working at a nursing home, and entered The University of New Mexico part time, where I earned my master's degree and began studying for a doctorate. Even after my computer crashed, and I lost half of my dissertation, I said, "This will not defeat me."

I persevered, often watching the sun come up after a long night, and rewrote the lost half, earned the doctorate, and later became licensed as a counselor. My doctoral minor was Aging Studies, so I was recruited to manage assisted living communities in Albuquerque, while still keeping up with my private counseling practice on weekends. Soon all the kids were married; one family lived in Illinois, one in Morocco, and one in Michigan. Paul continued commuting, then retired. It was nice to have him home. He cooked enchiladas for me, as well as other wonderful meals!

Paul and I acquired a passion for genealogy. He found the record of his deceased baby brother, who had never been mentioned by his parents. I learned my paternal great-grandparents had come from Texas to New Mexico in 1898, in a covered wagon, with their three kiddos, including my 13-year-old grandmother. I found a photo of them, taken on the outskirts of Alamogordo, New Mexico, as the wagons rolled into town. I also found that my paternal grandfather's first wife had taken their two little boys and left to go back east. He filed for, and was granted, a divorce at age 34, citing abandonment (the only divorce I know of in my direct lineage), and married my grandmother, who was half his age. Her parents knew he was a good man, and they approved.

Paul and I did a lot of vacationing – Alaska, Hawaii, Aruba, St. Thomas, and many places within the continental U.S. In Hawaii, I got my first (and last) tattoo, a pink hibiscus on my right shoulder.

When I returned and told a friend about my adventure, she said, "What did your children say?"

"I haven't told them."

"Well, you'd better tell them – if something happened and they had to identify your body, they'd say, 'That can't be our mom, with a tattoo.'"

We laughed. I did tell my kids, and they approved.

In 1997, Mother fell in her bathroom and developed a subdural hematoma, from which she never recovered. We buried her beside Daddy and Cathy in Texas.

In 1998, my husband Paul and I visited our son Paul, who was teaching in Morocco. We travelled to colorful Casablanca, and I remembered the movie, which I love. Later we traveled to Spain and Paris for Christmas and New Year's. I will never forget coming up out of the Metro tunnel and seeing the Champs Elysees decorated, every tree along the long, wide avenue twinkling with white lights. The Arc de Triomphe was spotlighted. What a magical memory!

Husband Paul commemorated my doctoral graduation and New Mexico counseling licensure with a trip to Lake Tahoe, where he gave me 20 silver dollars to play the slots. I'd never played more than quarters and pennies. I put a dollar into the slot and pulled the lever. Bells rang, lights flashed, attendants started rushing to my machine, and I thought I'd done something wrong. This was the first jackpot I'd ever won, and the only time I'd played dollar machines. I'd always been used to making twenty dollars (2,000 pennies!) last a long time. I was thrilled to win $800.00!

Paul gave me a gift certificate for pilot's training one Christmas, and I registered for ground school. I love flying in general, but especially enjoy the exhilaration of flying in small planes. Before my classes started in 2002, Paul was diagnosed with acute myelogenous leukemia at age 69. I cancelled my pilot plans, resigned my job at an assisted living community, and cut my counseling practice to part-time, to be available when Paul needed me. He was given six to nine months to live, but with many bouts of chemo and much suffering, he continued past that prognosis. He was determined to make it to our 50th wedding anniversary in 2005. He was on a walker, but made the party our children hosted at our favorite Mexican restaurant. The kids showed a film they'd made of our lives. The best movie ever, resulting in few dry eyes among the 38 relatives who were present from all over the country.

Five months later, on Thanksgiving Day, Paul relapsed, and we were back in the hospital. As the oncologist came into the room, Paul managed a faint smile.

"Paul, you've put up a good fight, but I'm sorry to say, the leukemia is winning."

Paul's face sagged, and he looked over at me.

The doctor continued, "The blasts, the immature cells, are gaining on us, and we have no more treatments to try. I'm so sorry."

In January 2006, we were back home, with Paul on hospice. I committed to the caregiving role years ago when I pledged, "in sickness and in health," and I was glad I was able to do it, as I knew he would do the same for me.

In one of our many talks, we agreed on a private code word, not one I'd commonly see nor hear, and not shared with anyone, in case it would be possible for him to communicate with me after death.

He said he wanted me to marry again. I could not imagine loving anyone else.

"I don't want anyone else. I want you."

"But I don't want you to be alone."

One night, as I was administering Paul's medications, he asked me to "make it end sooner." He was so weary of being sick.

I could not, and would not, do that. "It's not my job to make that decision," I told him.

He asked me to play the Mormon Tabernacle Choir CD, "The Sound of Glory." It soothed both of us.

Early the morning of January 25, 2006, I woke with a start, alert to the absence of Paul's noisy breathing. I was in our king-size bed about three feet away from his hospital bed. I jumped up, turned on the lamp, and hoped I was wrong. He was covered with a quilt his grandmother had made, orange with small blue flowers. The blossoms were not moving.

"Paul . . . Paul, please breathe."

I watched, wanting to see movement, but no more breaths came. I said his name again, but there was no response.

I cried, kissed him, and said, "I love you," but he was gone. Looking at his thin body, which was so muscular and strong in our youth, I sat for a surreal span of time. Even though I'd known death was inevitable, I was not ready for it, and although I didn't realize it then, I was in shock. I took his hand, and I regretted I was not holding it when he made the journey out of his body. That haunts me still.

I helped the men from the mortuary wrap Paul's body in a sheet, and together we moved him over to the gurney. I felt it was my last "caregiving" act I could perform for him. I told them to be careful with his left leg, as that was his sore knee. They said they would. They realized I was in shock. Blessings on those who do that kind of work.

I watched in a daze as the burgundy bag was zipped, covering Paul's face, that precious face. I watched the van drive away, bearing my beloved husband of over fifty years and the father of our four children.

I felt slightly nauseated. As the van turned the corner and disappeared, I turned to step back into an empty house. My neighbor made a fresh pot of coffee and sat with me a while. Widowed at 68, I was numb.

I wondered how I could go on. How could I lose the one I'd loved since childhood and continue living? I couldn't think about that yet.

CHAPTER 3

I'M ALONE

I sold our home and bought a smaller house with a large, covered, wooden back deck. I liked the house, but the clincher was when I walked into its kitchen and saw our code word in large letters on a calendar hanging on the pantry door! I felt as if Paul had picked out the house for me. The friendly, convenient Albuquerque neighborhood was just what I needed to help me start my new life.

Late in 2007, almost two years after Paul's death, although I still enjoyed socializing with the neighbors, I had worked through my grief enough to think it might be nice to have a companion. Sometimes the evenings, especially, were lonely.

Because Paul was a wonderful husband, my expectations were high, and I found the dating scene strange and disappointing at my age. Friends set me up with some Albuquerque area men, I went to lunches and dinners, but I found none of the men suitable – or maybe I was not suitable. One told me my Ph.D. intimidated him.

I continued to date, but months passed with no candidates who met my standards. A friend suggested eHarmony.

I said, "Oh, that's for desperate people."

Privately, I was beginning to think I might as well resign myself to remaining single. I'd rather be alone forever than be with the wrong person. I felt I had many good years left, and I hoped to enjoy these years, perhaps with a companion. I tried to imagine life with someone else.

I thought of sex, and while an enhancement, to me it was not the main ingredient for a successful relationship. More important to me were common interests, habits, willingness to compromise where there were differences, and the ability to have fun together and laugh at some problems. I enjoyed sex, but for many years I did not have that outlet, because of Paul's illnesses, and I felt it a small sacrifice, under those circumstances. I did enjoy sharing physical affection, and I thought a long-term relationship should include that.

Curious, one night I clicked on eHarmony's website, and the more I read about eHarmony, the more the idea appealed to me. What would I lose except a few dollars? It might be entertaining.

So, at age 71, I decided to take a chance with eHarmony. I filled out my "profile," and chose geographic parameters of New Mexico and surrounding states – Texas, Arizona, and Colorado. I specified my ideal match, including "social drinker" and "non-smoker."

Most contacts were local coffee or lunch dates, but one nice-looking professional in Colorado drove down and met me for dinner. During dessert he asked, "May I drive down next weekend?" I agreed, thinking I'd keep an open mind. He seemed a perfect gentleman, stayed in a motel, met me for dinner, and never even asked to come to my house.

At our next meeting, I could tell he was already thinking about future plans with me. Feeling honesty was important, especially with the distance involved, I said, "I appreciate the trips you've made, but I will be candid. You're a nice man, but there's no chemistry."

And he *was* a nice man. He said he understood, but he was disappointed. He walked with me to my car, we hugged, and I got into my car and drove home. Fall was approaching, and my faith in eHarmony was fading...

I decided to take a new approach with eHarmony. I reworded my profile and, remembering a past experience, I added a last sentence, "I have a Ph.D. If this intimidates you, we're not a match." I thought that would deter the faint-hearted and narrow my choices.

And it did. There were a few more coffee and lunch dates, but no one appealed to me. I was beginning to think this was not going to work. It was late in 2008, getting close to my 72nd birthday. It was nearing time for me either to discontinue my membership in eHarmony or extend it another three to six months...

PART II

JIM'S ADVENTURES BEFORE ME

CHAPTER 4

JIM'S EARLY YEARS

(WITH TRAITS I FAILED TO NOTICE IN OUR CORRESPONDENCE)

One of Jim's earliest photos sits in a small metal frame now on my desk. He was about four or five years old, wearing what looked like a plaid or tartan bathrobe, little brown lace-up oxfords, and white socks. He is standing in front of a frame house, arms and hands by his sides, feet firmly planted about 18 inches apart, head cocked a bit upward, with an arrogant look and posture. "James G. Hanks, Esq." is inscribed in ink in one corner. He looks as if he is ready to take on the world.

Jim told me little about his childhood before age nine, except he had a Boston bulldog named Mike, and his biological father left the family when Jim was about two or three. My several inquiries of his only sibling who would remember him at an early age went unanswered, so I have been left without much factual data.

It is quite possible an Aspie will have little memory of his early childhood, because of feeling confused about events and avoiding or repressing the memories. Bullying and teasing may cause some incidents to be so painful they are repressed. Stanford tells of a woman whose husband doesn't like to talk about his past. The wife thought he had a bad memory, but now she's realized most of the memories from his childhood were horrible and confusing, and he's buried them (Stanford, 2015, pp. 58, 184). The child can be portrayed as a "brat," because of food preferences, clothing, and sensitivities, and sometimes even family members recognize the child is different and tease and bully him (Carley, 2008, p. 67). Adult Aspies' memories of childhood are often visual and of experiences important to the person – of things, not people (Attwood, 2008, p. 244). Observations of the child's early years by others are helpful in supporting adults' memories of childhood (Attwood, 1998, p. 26). For this reason, diagnosticians like to have input from relatives who knew the child in their very early years. Otherwise, there may not be many memories available.

Because other Aspies' childhoods have been recorded, I can make some reasonable assumptions: Jim may have become frustrated at times and had meltdowns. Meltdowns differ from tantrums, in that Aspie meltdowns in children are *involuntarily* screaming or falling onto the floor or ground, occasionally hitting or biting others, or throwing objects, because of sensory overload; time, and the removal to a quiet place, or providing a calming activity, is required to allow them to decompress. Tantrums, on the other hand, are *voluntary* behaviors designed to get the child's way; the tantrum is resolved easily by giving in to their wishes (Lipsky, 2011, pp. 108, 136; Wylie, 2014, pp. 102-103).

The brains of people with Asperger's are wired differently, and cannot process sensory information in the same way as neurotypicals (Grandin & Barron, 2016, p. 105). A meltdown is caused by too much sensory information, too much input, causing the brain to go off in all different directions, kind of like too many inquiries causing a computer to crash. Aspies may have sensory overload from crowds and noise (Solomon, 2013, p. 222). The triggers may not always make sense to a neurotypical, but they cause emotions to flood an Aspie's brain and inhibit his coping skills. "When working properly and fully protecting the bathtub, the shower curtain prevents water from spilling to the floor. In autism, [the fibers do not prevent the spill] and 'water is all over the floor'" (Casanova, 2006, cited in Bogdashina (2010), p. 58).

By adulthood, many Aspies have developed coping mechanisms that disguise the true severity of sensory problems (Grandin & Panek, 2014, p. 77; Newport, 2001, p. xi). Loud sounds can be aversive, but interestingly, if the Aspie is in control of the volume, louder sound is not a problem (Falk & Schofield, 2018, p. 38). Jim could play a Roy Orbison CD loudly, or watch a movie with the sound up, as long as he controlled the volume. More about meltdowns and specific sensory issues later.

Jim may have been averse to hugging or cuddling (Higashida, 2016, p. 32), had trouble following a list of multiple directions (Attwood, 2008, pp. 203, 222), and might have had repetitive behaviors, which were annoying to others (Higashida, 2016, p. 68; Solomon, 2013, p. 222; Tammet, 2007, p. 49). He may have talked on and on about his favorite topics, interrupting other speakers (Carley, 2008, pp. 15, 17; Tammet, 2007, pp. 74-75). He may or may not have gotten along with other children, but likely he enjoyed playing by himself and had solitary interests (Attwood, 1998, p. 30; Tammet, 2007, pp. 27, 80).

He was probably bullied when he started to school, and maybe all through his school years, because other children may have known he was different, and may have made fun of his idiosyncrasies (Attwood, 2008, pp. 98-99). Many Aspies report having felt different from others when they started school and began to interact with other children (Robison, 2008, p. 20). It is estimated that 90% of Aspies are bullied at school, and sometimes even into adulthood (Aston, 2001, p. 64; Attwood, 2008, p. 98).

They long for friends, to belong, but friendships are not easily made, and often cannot be maintained (Attwood, 2008, p. 89; Tammet, 2007, p. 78). I didn't hear from Jim about any memorable schoolmates – apparently few, if any, lasting friendships were made. Although there are letters to him from shipmates in the Navy, apparently none of these associations developed into lasting friendships, at least after his time in the service.

Persons born with Asperger's do not grow out of it. Many of them learn to hide or modify behaviors as they mature (Carley, 2008, p. 62). Jim may or may not have had all these traits, because all Aspies are different (Grandin & Scariano, 1996, p. 141), but the traits are common among many Aspies.

The behaviors above will be discussed more fully as we go along. If they lessen, it is usually because the person learns to hide or control these behaviors in order to avoid being bullied or teased. They want very much to fit into the rest of the world, but realize they don't. They long to be validated by others (Prince-Hughes, 2004, p. 7). Pretending to be normal is a common survival strategy. "Children try to fit in after the age of eight" (Tony Attwood, interview, 13 November 2013, cited in Wylie, 2014, p. 33). The effort to hide or control their behaviors is called "masking," and you will learn much more about that as Jim and I get acquainted.

I'LL NOW LET JIM TELL YOU ABOUT THE REST OF HIS LIFE, IN HIS OWN WORDS, AS HE WROTE IT TO ME IN MANY EMAILS OVER THE MONTHS WE COURTED:
(THE ITALICIZED PARAGRAPHS ARE MY RETROACTIVE ANALYSES OF JIM'S WORDS AND BEHAVIORS)

My stepfather, a high school graduate and later a commissioned officer in the Navy, corrected me as a youngster when I would say, "So and so is *just* a mechanic, grocer, or other trade."

His outlook was, "He or she *is* a mechanic, grocer, or whatever."

That thinking pattern caught up to me in the service on an initial test, when I answered a multiple-choice question of "What would you rather do...(A), (B), (C), or (D)," and of the choices, none looked too promising to me. I don't remember the other choices, but I picked "garbage collector" as the best of the bunch. That got me in to see the psychiatrist. I am probably a weird kind of guy.

That, in itself, might have made me wonder about Jim, but I thought it was humorous! I still do! In what I consider a strange coincidence, Robison, an Aspie, tells a hilarious story about garbage collecting. At a party of academics, for shock effect, Robison tells them he has a new career, being a garbage collector. They think he is serious. He elaborates and horrifies them with weird details until he tells them he has to leave because of a garbage emergency (Robison (2008), pp. 96-100).

I don't remember much, if anything, about my biological father, also a Naval officer, who left our family when I was two or three, in Long Beach, California. My mother, my older sister, and I stayed with my mother's parents for several years until my mother married another Naval officer.

One day when I was about ten, in our front yard playing ball, a Naval officer in white dress uniform walked up to the house and knocked. Mother answered the door, she and the officer talked for a bit, then he turned and walked back down the sidewalk, passing me. Taught to be polite, especially to friends of my parents, I said, "Hello!" but there was no acknowledgement nor reply. I watched him walk down the sidewalk, and I wondered why he didn't even look at me or speak to me.

Later, Mother told me the officer that came by that day was my father, Earl Hanks. I couldn't understand why my father would not respond to my hello, nor even look at me. That scene still haunts me. I always wondered what that visit was about, and whether it concerned me or my older sister, or both. Mother told me she lost touch with my father soon after that time.

I never had any contact with my father. I have been heavily into genealogy off and on, researching my father and the Hanks lineage. I keep a framed picture of him on the shelf above my computer. Paper copies of my research fill a two-drawer file cabinet and several thick notebooks. I learned my father married twice more, having no children with his second wife, but having two boys with his third wife. The older of those two boys died at a young age, and the younger one lives in another state. I was able to get a phone number of this half-brother, talked to him at least once, and corresponded by mail some. I never have met him, but want to, and plan to someday. I wonder what he looks like – does he look like me? My father is dead by now, of course, but the pictures I have of him show that I look a lot like him.

An interesting fact I dug up in my genealogy is that my maternal grandfather fell from a train and was killed at age 44. He was "riding the rails" on August 13, 1931, to save money, trying to get to his mother's (my great-grandmother's) bedside in San Luis Obispo, California, before she died.

Another surprising piece of genealogical data was that on the 1940 census, a son was listed with our family, John Hanks, one year younger than I, but I never heard of a younger brother named John, and I've never been able to solve that mystery. It may have been an error on the census-taker's part, since it was all hand-written, but I wonder.

In 1941, my biological father was stationed at the Pearl Harbor submarine base at the time of the attack on Pearl Harbor, but was far enough away that he was in no danger. I learned this later in life, through military records. Coincidentally, my stepfather, Arch, was also stationed at Pearl Harbor during the months before the attack, but left a few days before the bombing, as did my mother and baby sister. My older sister and I were staying with our grandparents in California.

Arch was a good father to me and my older sister. He didn't adopt me, but I went by his last name, Morrison, until I graduated from high school. Even though I loved my stepfather, I never got over being abandoned by my biological father.

The seeds of abandonment had been planted in Jim as a toddler when his father left, and again when the visitor failed to acknowledge Jim when Jim spoke to him, and never sought contact after that. Many Aspies have a sense of, and fear of, abandonment, detachment, of having been separate, even if they haven't experienced the loss of a parent, because they feel alien to this world, as if they don't quite fit in (Finch, 2012, p. 56; Goleman, 2007, pp. 112-116,; Robison, 2008, p. 13; Siegel, 2015, p. 353; Wylie, 2014, p. 58). Jim's experience with his father's leaving and apparently not wanting to acknowledge his existence dealt Jim a double-whammy and exacerbated those feelings. More about abandonment issues later.

Arch was sent to training in Virginia and Maryland for a while. In elementary school in the east, all the boys in my class wore knickers, but I wore my regular western clothes, cowboy boots and blue jeans. The kids teased me and made fun of me, but I didn't care. My sister, however, was annoyed. It didn't affect me at all. I don't care what people think.

This is an example of probable bullying, and Jim dealt with it by not caring what people think. Many Aspies say they don't pay attention to, or care, what people think (Falk & Schofield, 2018, p. 67; Hendrickx & Newton, 2007, p. 88; Prince-Hughes, 2004, p. 175). It may be their defense against being hurt. That trait will come up again later.

My family moved back to California, and when I was six, my younger half-sister was born. During this part of my life, I had a Boston bulldog named Mike, which I loved and had fun with.

When I was ten, we lived in a housing development that used to be a prune orchard. The prunes fell to the ground and messed up lawns. The neighborhood kids and I picked up the prunes, after shaking the trees, and charged the homeowner. Then we took the prunes to the evaporator/lye vats and sold them to the processor at 22 cents a 60-lb. lug, or about $5.00/day. Money at both ends. We also cut lawns for a fee. The bulk of that money was saved for school clothes. The next few years I ran a paper route, delivering the Napa Register – 152 papers, $32.00/month.

Soon we cruised to the Philippine Islands, where Arch was assigned. A money-making venture, at age 12, with some friends, was a diaper-washing business. Shipboard with our military parents, we contracted with the wives who were in transit with their young. We'd take the diapers, one dunk in the toilet, then throw them into the showers in our staterooms, turn on the water, and come back in an hour and a half, wring them out, and hang them to dry. After drying, it was back to the owners and payday.

It was heavenly to live in the Philippines. I hopped rides up the coast on Naval transports with the non-commissioned officers, and stayed with other Naval families along the route who had kids. I didn't go to school, and Mother let me be gone for as long as a couple of weeks at a time.

The non-coms were glad to take good care of an officer's kid. We would lie on the beach, eat coconuts and roast pig, spear fish, swim, SCUBA dive, and snorkel. We'd consort with the Filipinos, who would climb up trees, whack down coconuts, and open them for lunch. I ate so much coconut I lost my taste for it for the rest of my life. Sometimes the non-coms took me to a bar with them, sat me down at the bar, and paid the bartender for "as many Cokes as the kid wants," while they went upstairs for a while. I didn't realize until years later what those boys were doing upstairs. I would eventually gravitate back to home base. Mom didn't care. It was the dream existence of a young boy.

A number of Aspies tell about their experiences of living in foreign countries (Carley, 2008, pp. 215-16; Fisher, in Grandin, 2012, pp. 109-11; Wylie, 2014, pp. 140-141). Foreigners don't experience the Aspie behaviors as odd, and Aspies welcome this and do not feel judged.

As the mom of a son myself, I wondered how his mom could let Jim be so free for sometimes as long as a couple of weeks at a time. It may be that he was a handful, and having the sailors and other military families willing to take care of him for a while was a godsend.

By 1947, I was 13, in junior high, and we lived back in the states, in Astoria, Oregon. Between basketball practices and on Saturdays, I worked at turning hay with a pitchfork as it lay in windrows at the County Farm. My grades in elementary and junior high were average.

His sixth-grade report card had mostly "A"s and "B"s. Courtesy, Effort, Dependability, and Neatness are all marked "Satisfactory." By eighth grade, he had all "A"s, with an "A" in Study Habits, and with Certificates of Achievement awarded in Citizenship, Scholarship, and Reading.

In ninth grade, something slipped – perhaps anxiety about an impending move to Japan? Another change for Jim, another location, and Aspies are not keen on change (Baron-Cohen, 2008, p. 40; Dubin, 2009, pp. 48-49; Grossberg, 2015, p. 9). For whatever reason, grades went down to mostly "B"s, with one "A" in Mechanical Drawing, and a "C" in Study Habits.

By high school, he was making an "A" only in Physics. The teen years are difficult for many Aspies, with many changes at school, growth, hormones, and the constant bullying and teasing (Aston, 2001, pp. 58-59; Tammet, 2007, p. 109). How much transitions, moves, and adjusting to hormones and adolescence played a part in Jim's grades, we'll never know, but we'll look at how he did in college later.

Arch was assigned to Narimasu, Japan, and of course, the family followed. I went to high school there, played end in football, and lettered in both football and basketball. I did not work, just had lots of fun.

Interestingly, as I've said, many Aspies do better in a foreign country. The theory is that being different, as a foreigner in another country, is expected, rather than considered strange. Some have said they feel like aliens among their peers in their native country and culture (Lesko, 2011, p. 46; Lipsky, 2011, p. 14; Wylie, 2014, pp. 32, 140-41, 148). "In some ways I am terribly ill-equipped to survive in this world, like an extraterrestrial stranded without an orientation manual" (Sinclair, 1992, p. 302, cited in Bogdashina, 2010, pp. 89-90).

In California, in 1951, I went to South San Francisco High School. While in school, I ushered in a movie theater; worked as a delivery helper for a furniture retail outlet; delivered lumber for a lumber company; and worked as a carpenter's apprentice, building wood-framed houses. As a hobby, I was into mineralogy and collected mineral specimens, usually in crystal form. I cut and polished gem minerals (jade, amethyst, topaz), including faceting the stones, using lapidary equipment.

Interestingly, an individual with autism can turn a crystal "around and around in front of his eyes, catching rainbows," (Williams, 1999c, cited in Bogdashina, 2010, p. 169) as if they are mesmerized. They seem able to appreciate beauty that many neurotypicals miss.

During high school, Mother paid me to do the family baking. I have her coffee cake recipe and her enchilada recipe. I still enjoy cooking.

In 1952, I graduated from high school. About this time, I began to be known by my birth name, James Hanks. It was also the spring my mother gave birth to my Morrison half-brother. When he grew big enough to walk and talk, he often annoyed me, and at times I had to walk away from him, for fear of being physical. He asked question after question, as kids do, but I was a young adult and had no time for such nonsense. I do not like confrontation, and deal with it by walking away from annoying or threatening situations.

Aspies have to work hard to control their emotions. Rage seems to be a constant, because of feeling different, out of place, and misunderstood all the time. They learn to bury it as they mature. Many say they feel if they ever let themselves show the anger, they might not be able to control it (Aston, 2001, pp. 49, 72; Dubin, 2009, p. 106; Falk & Schofield, 2018, p. 158; Grandin & Barron, 2016, p. 398; Wylie, 2014, pp. 105-106).

Jim learned that walking away from things that triggered his anger was the best coping mechanism for him. Whether he was taught that coping skill, or whether he learned it on his own, he often used it in confrontations. He told me he had to walk away from his little stepbrother often, so he wouldn't let go and "pop" him.

I didn't date much, but I did take one pretty Italian girl on a date in high school. I also managed to buy a yellow 1951 Chevy and a rifle. If I needed money, I'd hock the rifle for a while. That Chevy was a neat car, one of my favorite things, and later I wished I still had it. After I got home from the Navy, I decided to go to South San Francisco to look the Italian girl up, but found she was already married. I don't remember any other dates or romances until I met my ex-wife and was ready to have a companion.

"Dating and socializing are . . . major challenges . . ., sometimes compromising our ability to form families and create social networks" and "[Dating] scares the daylights out of most of us. Dating is a game, and many of us do not intuitively understand the rules of the game" (Dubin, 2009, pp. 12, 113).

In the fall of 1952, I enrolled in the Colorado School of Mines in Golden, Colorado, and lived at the Sigma Nu Fraternity house, a service organization. I was majoring in Mining Engineering, but later shifted to Electrical Engineering. The large intro classes were daunting, so I withdrew. I did well in Engineering Drawing and Military Science Tactics, but not well in the other subjects. I was granted a Certificate of Honorable Dismissal.

Transitioning from high school to college is a big challenge to Aspies (Grandin, 2006, p. 18). Jim lived in the frat house, quite possibly was bullied or harassed by frat brothers, and attended large introductory classes filled with strangers, so who knows what effect that had on him as a freshman far away from home. His use of the term "daunting" was revealing. With Asperger's, he needed time between classes and activities to recuperate from the socializing and prevent meltdowns. He was away from home and finding his way as a young adult. He was obviously intelligent, so probably didn't spend enough time in his books. In fact, he told me he rarely read the textbooks, just took notes. I can imagine he found college life confusing, noisy, and overwhelming, causing meltdowns and a need for solitude. Willey found college confusing, and her grades quickly plummeted (Willey, 2015, pp. 50-53). A school that is not very far away from home is a better choice for an Aspie (Newport, 2001, p. 50).

In the spring of 1953, I went to City College of San Francisco, near where my grandmother lived, until the draft called. I was encouraged by my stepfather, the career Naval officer, to join the Navy rather than be drafted. I trained at San Diego, then went to Treasure Island, San Francisco, for electronics school. In June 1954, I was transferred to the USS Tappahannock, AO 43 (a tanker), then received orders to report on arrival to the USS Pasig, AW-3 (a fresh water distilling tanker). We sailed under secret orders to Hai Phong, French Indo China (Vietnam). Hai Phong Harbor was a staging area for people transfer – those who wished to go south or north during the partitioning of the country.

Many persons with Asperger's are rule-oriented. Ambiguity makes it difficult for them to cope – thinking is often black and white, with no gray area (Ariel, 2012, p. 45; Attwood, 2008, p. 118; Hendrickx & Newton, 2007, p. 92). "For those with Asperger syndrome, rules and boundaries must be very clear and precise" (Aston, 2001, p. 74).

Therefore, the military is a choice many make, because everything is prescribed in detail – what you say, what you do, where you go – leaving little to be "wrong" about. "The military was a good fit for me because the rules were very clear. How I was supposed to act and what I was supposed to say were all scripted" (Fisher, in Grandin, 2012, p. 113). The routine of specific orders and duties and ways to address their superiors becomes comfortable, with little to decide. The Navy was surely a more comfortable atmosphere for Jim than the ambiguous academic and social scene at college in Colorado.

In 1956, I was transferred to Tongue Point Naval Air Station near Astoria, Oregon, where I worked a few nights a week stacking frozen tuna in a warehouse at a local cannery. Good money, but working 16 hours a day was tiring. After I was discharged from the Navy in 1957, I kept up with a few of my Navy buddies by mail for a year or so, but those friendships soon dropped off. In a letter from one of them, he asked about my love life, but there was none to tell about. He and I at one time planned a trip to Alaska, but that never materialized.

Apparently, no strong friendships were made in the Navy, and remember, he didn't mention any friends from high school. Aspies usually have few close friends, and many of them prefer it that way (Grossberg, 2015, p. 74). Although deep down they wish they could be a part of the larger group of people, they realize they don't fit in well. They have a better chance of making friends involved with the same special interests, and their closest friends are likely from that group or groups. "A special interest has magical powers. It can help an Aspie find friends among others who enjoy the same interest" (Willey, 2015, p. 133). Later you will learn how that applied to Jim, when we get into the Aspie trait of having special interests.

I moved to Ashland, Oregon, and my stepfather and I did some logging on power line rights-of-way. After that, I did Forest Service contracting in the timber stand improvement project, thinning of trees. When that dried up, I went to California and worked in Compton, in radio repair, using the electronics skills I learned in the Navy. I returned to Ashland to finish college and work in the summer as a gypo logger in the Rogue River National Forest, as a hod carrier for a ceramic tile contractor, and did some construction.

I lived at home with my parents and went to Southern Oregon College in Ashland. I did well in Engineering, Economics, Geology, Biology, Labor Issues, Geometry, Biology, Physics, World Literature, Government, and History. I hardly ever read the assignments, but listened well enough in class and took enough notes to do well. I ended up more educated in upper division Physics. Bottom line, I have the engineering mentality. I graduated with a Bachelor of Science degree, majoring in Math/Science with a minor in Economics.

Living at home afforded Jim with predictability, seclusion when he needed it, and enabled him to concentrate on his studies. Having an engineering mentality is common among Aspies. They like the black-white precision of how things go together and how machines work. Ambiguity does not exist in engineering – things either fit, or they don't. "Sometimes I think I can relate better to a good machine than any kind of person. Machines don't talk back. They are predictable" (Robison, 2008, p. 151).

Aspies find people confusing and difficult to figure out. Because "things" are usually more consistent than people, "'things' are easier to understand than people are for some individuals with Asperger's" (Dubin, 2009, p. 49).

Aspies would like to be comfortable in the larger society, but they aren't, so their focus is shifted to working with things instead of people. "Electronics made sense to me. What I appreciated most about engineering was its plain, yes-no, black-white, up-down, hot-cold logic" (Cooper, in Grandin, 2012, p. 272). Jim's Naval training and working in electronics made a lot of sense.

In May of 1965, I was hired by the General Adjustment Bureau (GAB), in Astoria, Oregon, as an insurance adjuster, and learned various areas of specialized adjusting, from initial training in 1966, to more specialized areas in 1970 and 1972.

I like dealing with figures – measurements, dimensions, replacement values, etc. I am of an old German stoic stock. You know, logical, deliberate, focused, responsible, and I spent my career solving problems – problems relating to insurance matters. This required me to keep an emotional distance from claimants, sticking to the facts in order to get the job done. It seemed to fit my skill set well. I am, by nature, too analytical and not enough of a free spirit. I had my duties, and I enjoyed the job. I eventually learned to use the computer to do research on the files, and became proficient.

Jim unwittingly gave me a list of some of the common traits of Asperger's – analytical, logical, deliberate, focused, responsible. Why didn't I recognize this? Because I wasn't looking for it. My search for a companion superseded my clinical skills.

The statement "required me to keep an emotional distance in order to get the job done" says a lot about Jim's interactions with people. Insurance adjusting requires remaining objective, not emotional, when processing files. Attwood suggests Aspies can choose appropriate careers based on their skills (Attwood, 2008, pp. 295-296). Jim intuitively selected a career appropriately suited to his!

Several years ago, I had an opportunity to speak to Temple Grandin after a talk she gave in Albuquerque. I told her I was writing a book about my husband, who had Asperger's, and her first question was, "What did he do?"

"You mean as a profession?"

"Yes."

"He was an insurance adjuster."

Grandin said, "Perfect. Facts and figures, but detachment from emotions."

(Personal conversation with Temple Grandin, September 1, 2016, quoted with her permission.)

I liked her confirmation of Jim's career choice!

CHAPTER 5

JIM'S MARRIED YEARS
(*WITH TRAITS I FAILED TO NOTICE IN OUR CORRESPONDENCE*)

I married in 1966, in The Dalles, Oregon. I was transferred by GAB to Bend, Oregon, for a short time, then to Pendleton for the first time. In 1970, I was promoted to manager status in Eugene, Oregon, where our son was born.

After several more transfers and trips for training, I ended up in Pendleton again in 1976. I was offered a transfer and promotion to Arizona, but I declined. I did not look forward to a big change, and I love the Northwest.

Transitions, or aversion to change, is a common Aspie trait (Baron-Cohen, 2008, p. 40; Dubin, 2009, p. 48-49; Grandin, 2006, p. 18). Jim's refusing a promotion if it involved a move and change was a clue, if I had been looking for clues.

Our daughter was born while we lived in Pendleton, and when our kids were older, our family enjoyed playing tennis at a nearby city park. In time, my ankles gave out and ended my participation in that activity. I was a fierce competitor with my wife and children. I guess you could say I have a competitive spirit.

A competitive, controlling, or stubborn streak is not uncommon to Aspies, with their high intelligence and drive to strive hard to get along in the world (Carley, 2008, p. 83; Hendrickx & Newton, 2007, p. 107; Stanford, 2015, pp. 66-67, 202, 209). Many of them play to win, and losing, whatever the situation, whether a game or an argument, is difficult for them. You will discover this trait in Jim several times as our story proceeds.

I bought a piece of land on North Hill in Pendleton, and built a house, high on the hill, overlooking the city, which is where I still live. The lawn is large, terraced into four levels. I like doing lawn work, but at times it gets away from me, and, as I get older, it's becoming more of a chore. The gray wooden siding is becoming worn, and the roof needs replacing one of these days. I put the lawn in by myself in the 1970s, little by little, with juniper ground cover in places; trees of various kinds, both deciduous and evergreens, a cherry tree and a star magnolia; and flowering shrubs and flowers, potentilla, roses, rhododendrons, tulips, and daffodils. Takes a good bit of work to keep it mowed and everything trimmed. The house has many windows, with a 180-degree view of the city and the Blue Mountains in the distance.

Was Jim's choosing to build a house high on a hill, overlooking the city, a coincidence? Or was it symbolic of his Aspieness – wanting to elevate his standing in the community, having felt inferior most of his life and as if he didn't fit in. This would not have occurred to me before I got to know him better. His general manner was unassuming, but sometimes choices say a lot.

In 1982, our family took a 30-day vacation to London, France, Germany, and Switzerland. That is the only vacation I took in my 35-year career, although I got 30 days of vacation time per year. I just didn't want those files to get ahead of me at work. I retired as an adjuster in 1992.

Loyalty is a strong trait of Aspies (Ariel, 2012, p. 14; Carley, 2008, pp. 209-210; Grandin, 2015, p. 207; Silberman, 2015, p. 483). Aspies have many skills which are sought by employers, including reliability, accuracy, persistence, attention to detail, enjoyment of routines and procedures, creativity in problem solving, extensive factual and technical knowledge, a strong sense of social justice, a preference for not allowing socializing to be a distraction, a talent for identifying errors for quality control, and a natural ability with cataloguing information and identifying patterns and sequences (Silberman, 2015, p. 465; Wylie, 2014, p. 25). [Employees have a] "tremendous sense of loyalty, dedication, strong knowledge base and solid capabilities" (Willey, 2015, p. 184).

Jim's loyalty and dedication to his employer, and his steadfastness in his work habits, in that he took only one vacation in 35 years, "didn't want those files to get ahead of me at work," was an extreme example. Slipped right by me.

In 2006, family expenses required my working again. I applied for, and was offered a job as a security officer at a law enforcement agency, but when I found out I'd have to carry a gun, I declined it.

Jim again demonstrated his strong sense of loyalty, as well as generosity, by coming out of retirement and taking a part-time job to take care of additional expenses for family members. I believe the unwillingness to take a job requiring his carrying a gun may have stemmed from his fear of not being able to control his emotions. Dubin, an Aspie, mentions a fear of being out of control in general, resulting in being "afraid to confront someone for fear of overreacting" (Dubin, 2009, p. 106).

Walking away from confrontation was Jim's mode of choice. I think it is possible that confrontation while carrying a gun, especially with his fear of losing control, might have made him fearful of a serious result.

I could have freelanced as an insurance adjuster, but the adjusting career got to be problems, problems, problems, all of which needed a solution. Thirty-five years of it sort of wore me out, and that's why I didn't go back to it after I retired from GAB.

I saw an ad for a part-time position with the City of Pendleton, and was hired in the Facilities Department. I work six hours a day, from 6:00 to noon. I do custodial work, mainly at the building that houses the city government offices and the city library. It's routine, everyday stuff, always mostly the same, but I like the people I work with, so I'm happy. It gives me my afternoons free for football in the fall and driving my little red MGB when the weather is nice. While working on my yard, sometimes my mind keeps wandering to that little red car sitting in my garage – doggone, I just have to drop the work and hit the road. I used to be a workaholic, but I'm moving away from it. I start that little car up and get the bugs out, stop by the auto body shop, chit-chat a bit with my body shop buddies, then come home to my easy chair for a bit of watching football. My days of working until I drop are over. Life is too short. I do a lot of relaxing these days, and read Classic Cars magazines, Moss car parts catalogs, and MGB and Sprite repair manuals.

As an adult, I still like to cook. I tend to favor the French style of meals. Chicken tarragon, flank steak and sauce *chasseur*, London broil, etc. I also like Mexican, including enchiladas, tacos, *cerveza*. I make good spaghetti sauce from scratch, fish soup, and pork chops with an apple/onion sauce, good old U.S.A. style hamburgers, mixed greens salads topped with shrimp or pepper chicken, but most of all salmon – fresh salmon (or halibut filet) with rice, fixed a jillion ways, and as I always tell my kids, when times get tough, we eat stewed tomatoes on light bread. On hamburgers, I'm a "mayo" guy! It goes on heavy on both sides of the bun. I like mustard, but use it sparingly, with certain sandwiches like ham and cheese. I'm a master at arranging dishes on the platters and in the bowls. Presentation is everything!

Hamburgers have to be constructed a certain way – exactly the same each time – mayo first, meat patty, Sweet Baby Ray's Barbeque Sauce, sweet pickle relish, tomato slice, lettuce, and more mayo last.

Even in the kitchen, Jim's traits of ritual, rigidity, and perfectionism were in play. The routine of how to construct a hamburger, with no deviations, is not unusual for an Aspie who doesn't care for change and has a habitual ritual (Attwood, 2008, p. 138; Dubin, 2009, p. 47). His presentation was food-magazine perfect.

Jim noted the sunrise and sunset times each day on the wall calendar in the kitchen, another ritual. One day he said he had gained two minutes of daylight per day, and I suggested he now had an opportunity to seek another part-time job of ten minutes a week. He grinned and said he'd rather not.

Eating is another story – I'm a picky eater. I like a few vegetables, but not asparagus, Brussel sprouts, or green peas. If served something that contains green peas, I'll slide them to one side of the plate and ignore them.

I like anything chocolate – anything sweet, period. I have a sugar craving – use at least two, sometimes three, spoonfuls in a cup of coffee. My favorite dessert is cherry pie. I bake fruit cakes to give at Christmas. Fruit cakes are unique, in that people either like them or definitely don't. Sort of like liver and onions, which to me is bad news. I *hate* liver and onions.

My typical breakfast is a bowl of Froot Loops, an apple strudel via the toaster, a cup of coffee, and a banana . . . then out the door to work. When I get home from work, I have more coffee. To me, coffee is good any time of day.

Many persons with Asperger's are picky eaters, having to do with certain odors, flavors, textures, or consistencies. "We taste only four flavors – sweet, sour, salt, and bitter. We don't always eat foods for their taste, but sometimes for their feel" (Ackerman, 1995, pp. 13, 168). Having definite food preferences seems to be a trait common to most Aspies, and fits in with sensitivities to other sensory experiences, which I will discuss later. Many of an Aspie's sensory experiences – olfactory, tasting, hearing, touching, vision – can be affected (Attwood, 2008, pp. 271-272).

Jim exhibited this sensitivity in all senses, except olfactory. He claimed not to have a sense of smell. An autistic person may be "intolerant of high-pitched noises, another of low-pitched noises, one of a fan, another of a washing machine" (Sacks, 1996, p. 273). Jim did not like certain sounds – hand bells, phones or doorbells ringing. He did not like noise in general – he would often mute the sound during football games, saying, "I can tell what's going on. They don't have to tell me."

One commonly mentioned trait is aversion to making eye contact, however, this was not true of Jim. Either he had learned that it was what one does to be successful in life, or that was a trait he never had, because instead of an aversion to eye contact, he tended to give prolonged stares, as if observing a person carefully. Other sensitivities will be mentioned as we go along.

My hobby since the mid-1990s is restoring and driving British sports cars of the 1960s. I own a 1965 Austin Healey Sprite MK3 convertible and a 1966 MGB MK1 convertible roadster. Both have 4-cylinder inline engines, four speed manual gear box, hydraulic clutch and disc front brakes, shoes in the rear. The engines are fed with twin S U carburetors. Fun, fun, fun! By today's engineering standards, they are nothing, but in their years, they were the cutting edge of an inexpensive sports car. Neither is produced anymore. The Sprite is painted

British Racing Green, and the MGB is painted Tartan Red. I get off work at noon, and depending on the weather, I often take the MGB out for a drive. The Sprite is not as dependable, so I don't like to take it very far, but the MGB is my pride and joy. Both of them are black holes for money, but they are special to me. I take the MGB on annual trips with a group of people from the area who also own British sports cars. We go either up into Canada, or to an Oregon destination, depending on the time allotted. Often members take either their spouse or a friend with them.

Giving a great deal of detail and information to someone who is not a British sports car fan is typical of the Aspie trait of talking about their hobbies and special interests in great detail (Attwood, 2008, pp. 197-198; Carley, 2008, pp. 219-220; Falk & Schofield, 2018, p. 67; Grandin & Panek, 2014, p. 15). They assume other people will be as interested in the topic as they are. "Clinical experience of people with Asperger's syndrome has indicated that the degree or dominance of the interest in the person's daily life is proportional to the degree of stress: the greater the stress, the more intense the interest" (Attwood, 2008, p. 184).

I understood little of Jim's description of his cars, but I was awed by such knowledge! He said the cars were black holes for money, but they were special to him. Aspies can be either one extreme or the other financially, from conservative, to spending too much, as on special interests (Aston, 2001, pp. 59-60).

I had a few possessions I prize besides the cars. I told you about my old Chevy, and I wish I still had it. I acquired an Indian blanket, or rug, in Ashland, but it was stolen from a storage shed. I was quite disappointed about that. As an adult, I built a model airplane, a rather large, intricate model with a wide wingspan. A tossed pillow accidentally landed on it and destroyed it. I was disillusioned by that event, and do not engage in any more models. In Japan, when I visited The Temple of the Sleeping Cats, I got a pendant, or medallion, and that is one of the things I still have, and I like to show it off. I have a couple of Japanese painted scrolls that I treasure. My slippers, soft and warm and fuzzy, are among my favorite things.

Aspies are not usually materialistic, but sometimes become attached to "seemingly random objects" (Solomon, 2013, p. 222). Jim was happy to see I owned a Navajo two-gray-hills rug, as if it were a replacement for the one stolen from him, and later, he hung mine in a prominent place on our living room wall.

Aspies can become attached to a predictable outcome, and if the outcome is not as expected, they are miserable, experiencing anxiety (Dubin, 2009, pp. 148-150). When Jim's model plane was destroyed, he had absolutely no interest in that activity again. I saw model airplane kits on a shelf in the garage, unopened.

I find no reference in the literature to generosity being an Asperger's trait, but I know from various clients and their families that it is common, especially when it is spontaneous. Jim could be especially generous, and often gave things away on the spur of the moment, without hesitation, if someone indicated appreciation and enjoyment of the items. I know he gave his archery set to a person who expressed interest in archery, and he gave his table saw to a man in trade for some work on our deck. I expressed delight when he showed me the sleeping cat pendant, and as a result, I wear it on a chain as a necklace. Similarly, he gave the Japanese scrolls away, as you will see later.

My wife and I separated about a year and a half before our divorce, after over 40 years of marriage. The divorce was final in October 2007.

Jim went into great detail about the years before and during the separation and divorce, but said nothing negative about his former wife. Some of the traits of Asperger's are intense loyalty, as I have noted earlier, as well as honesty. "Adults with Asperger's syndrome can be renowned for being honest, having a strong sense of social justice and keeping to the rules. They strongly believe in moral and ethical principles" (Attwood, 2008, p. 118).

Although Jim said his life was an open book, I know that might not be the case with others involved in his story; therefore, I've chosen not to include his details about the separation and divorce. I also know, as a counselor, there are always two points of view in any divorce, and I know only one.

CHAPTER 6

JIM IS ALONE

(*WITH TRAITS I FAILED TO NOTICE IN OUR CORRESPONDENCE*)

I've told you the whole story, or at least my side of it, as honestly as I can present it. The divorce is final, and there is no possibility of reconciliation. After the divorce, I struggled with depression and grief. Two months after the divorce was final, my mother died, so my grief was compounded. I saw several counselors in the area, and sought guidance from my pastor.

Eighty percent of those questioned in one survey of adult Aspies said they do not feel included by society, and think about suicide, and some said they contemplate it daily (Wylie and Heath, 2013, cited in Wylie, 2014, p. 61). One Aspie reports trying it three times, all over failed relationships (Newport, 2001, pp. 255-257).

I do not know whether Jim at any time considered suicide as a means of ridding himself of pain. I didn't ask him, because I do not ask potential companions that clinical question, only clients. If he did, at any time, consider suicide, and someone inspired hope in him, I am thankful. To all who comforted and guided him, I am grateful.

I didn't grow up with any church experience, but was taught good values. I was baptized and joined the First Presbyterian Church of Pendleton late in life, am an Elder, and serve on several committees. I remember one budget meeting at church, and it went on and on. We had previously discussed the same issue at two other meetings. Presbyterians like to jaw and jaw about details, so consensus takes time. This religious stuff is quite complex, when it doesn't need to be. Decision making was always easier in my profession, as the buck stopped with me. Church matters are sometimes frustrating, because the decisions take forever.

Someone who attended some of these meetings later confided to me that Jim showed he was ready for meetings to end by shuffling his papers, laying his writing instruments parallel with the stack of papers or tablet, and continuing to rearrange the items. One Aspie mentions hating long meetings that get off track and could be finished sooner, "or when the gathering drifts off the agenda and runs overtime" (Shore, in Grandin, 2012, p. 46).

One year, I was a representative from the church to our regional meeting to discuss whether the church wanted to allow LGBT participation in the church, and I voted for total inclusion.

This piece of information encouraged me, as that is how I would also have voted on this issue. A strong sense of social justice is a strong trait of Aspies (Grandin, 2015, p. 206).

For years I've been involved with our church's annual Soup Supper, when Dale Wilkins and I make the clam chowder. I've read the Bible, but I'm not formally schooled in it, and I accept the teachings of Christ because they agree with my outlook on life. I have a good relationship with "The Man," but I know little about chapter and verse from the Bible. I believe that faith and belief are not confined to going to church. The world is the church and platform to practice the faith, and it is always present and waiting.

Like many Aspies, logic preempts emotion, even with regard to religion (Grandin, 2006, p. 223). Jim accepted the teachings of Christ because they agreed with his outlook on life, not because of emotion.

I'm a lover of nature. I love watching the sunsets and cloud formations I see from my living and dining rooms; the stars and moon I see from my hot tub on the front deck; and the forested grounds of the church's campground, Westminster Woods, which lies 25 miles east of Pendleton. I helped plan and put the finishing touches on many of the buildings at the campground. I also invest a lot of time with fellow church members, including Dale, my clam chowder buddy, and Bob Downie, keeping the buildings and roads maintained and plowed in the winter, and dead trees felled to prevent fire danger. I think The Man is an artist with nature.

At sundown one evening, I saw a broken strata style cloud cover around 6:15, and the sun peeped through a clear western sky, bouncing off the hills to the south. The rose color of the sun on the hills, with the deepening shadows of the canyons the sun doesn't reflect on, and the white ball of the moon to the east, made a remarkable view, a glimpse of The Man's beauty in creation. The beauty sometimes overwhelms me. It relieves the part of me that tends to be too mechanical. My artwork consists of architectural design and engineering drawing. I would have liked to be an architect. Well-designed and well-built houses and structures fascinate me. No match for nature, but interesting and beautiful to me.

Jim's last few sentences refer to his mechanical bent, a trait common to many Aspies, but essentially, he is describing his pleasure with nature. Aspies are observant and sensitive to details, and can "become transfixed by visual details" (Attwood, 2008, p. 272).

"Sometimes people with autism . . . rescue themselves from overload by escaping to an entertaining, secure and hypnotic level of hypersensation: watching the reflection of every element of light and colour . . ." (Williams, 1999c, cited in Bogdashina, 2010, pp. 168-169).

A number of Aspies mention feeling very connected to nature and having a hard time describing the connection. I have had clients tell me they feel like aliens, and looking at the stars or walking in a forest helps them feel grounded, gives them a feeling of being part of the universe. Others have described it this way: "[Nature] has a calming effect. Contemplating the awe and sweep of the natural world with its rivers, mountains and skies puts things into perspective" (Devnet, in Attwood, Evans, and Lesko, 2014, p. 81).

"Nature calms me down when I'm furious, and laughs with me when I'm happy" (Higashida, 2016, p. 88).

I'll be brief about politics, but I believe that less government is good government, and that is generally looked on by most people as conservative. I'm a registered Republican, but usually vote for the candidate and his or her alleged program espoused while campaigning. I have conservative thinking patterns, but vote my mind and conscience. I am conservative in that I drive a 1997 Buick LeSabre. Still in good shape, so why change? I can go on and on, and am happy to discuss the fine points of politics with anyone who will listen. I'm a Fox News fan, and have it on a majority of the time my TV is on. I like the "talking heads" – Chris Wallace, Bill O'Reilly, and others. I've read several of O'Reilly's books.

I enjoy reading a lot – biographies and books on history, politics, and physics. I read *Faith of My Fathers*, about John McCain, drawn to it by the strong Navy tradition in our family. I read widely about space, stars, black holes, string theory, and the universe. Stephen Hawking is one of my favorite authors. I recently read a book from the library on a subject that always interests me, that being the merging of quantum mechanics and Einstein's theory of relativity as it relates to astrophysics, and specifically, black holes. I know just enough about the subject to find more and more info appealing, but certainly only get the gist of what they are talking about. I find the subject of particle physics or quantum mechanics quite interesting. I took nuclear physics in college, was exposed to the fundamentals, and have since read several books that speak to particle physics and its newer discoveries and relations to Einstein's general theory of relativity. I read a bit about "string theory," but don't put much credence in it. I've never read much about the brain and how it works and the import of all the electrical impulses going on up there, but I am interested. There is a similarity there somewhere with quantum mechanics, in that both deal in energy quanta and interact with an ever-changing active entity. In fact, perhaps my brain is a black hole! I put a lot of words and thinking in, but not much of significance comes out. I need time alone from time to time, to just think or read.

Persons with Asperger's often have above average intelligence (Ariel, 2012, p. 14; Hendrickx & Newton, 2007, p. 124; Wylie, 2014, p. 25). They voraciously seek information on topics of interest to them, retaining a multitude of facts. I could see Jim was an intelligent man!

And humorous! A common myth about Aspies is that they don't have much of a sense of humor. However, many have keen humorous bents (Hendrickx & Newton, 2007, pp. 36, 70, 124-125; Robison, 2008, pp. 40-41), and Jim was no exception, as you will see here, and later. Once Jim set on our lunch table a scrap piece of wood molding from one of his projects, and he had labeled it with a ballpoint pen, "Mr. Moulding." Another day on the lunch table, I found a folded piece of cardboard, set up so it formed an inverted "V" and was labeled "Ant Tent – Do Not Destroy." He knew those things would make me laugh. I got up one morning after he had gone to work, to find a large

Halloween spider with fuzzy legs hanging by a string in the kitchen doorway.

Although everyone needs solitude from time to time, many Aspies need more solitude than a neurotypical (Attwood, 1998, p. 155; Grandin & Panek, 2014, p. 5; Stanford, 2015, p. 92). In his last sentence above, Jim alerted me that he needed time alone, to think or to read. This could have been Jim's way of making sure I understood he needed time by himself, and could have been a tipoff, if I had been looking for one.

I used to tell my kids "Fractured Fairytales," traditional fairy tales modified with insurance adjuster mentality. Remember the three little pigs' houses that were destroyed? Only one pig got payment from the insurance company, because he was wise enough to have a homeowner's policy instead of a fire and extended coverage policy. Did you know that Jack and Jill sued the city for a defective street, resulting in Jack's fall, which prompted him to engage an attorney and pray to the court for relief? I also wrote about a giant tomato that came to life, and a 19-page manual for my kids, called "Real World 101," in which I tell them about jousting with windmills, and other facts of life to watch out for. Someday I'll share that with you.

Many Aspies escape into their imagination and relate to fantasy and fairy tales. "The person may develop a vivid and complex imaginary world" (Attwood, in Murray, Ed., 2006, p. 34).

"Many high-functioning autistic people describe a great fondness for, almost an addiction to, alternative worlds, imaginary worlds such as those of C. S. Lewis and Tolkien, or worlds they imagine themselves" (Sacks, 1996, p. 276).

"From about the time I first started school I developed a great love for and fascination with fairy tales. I just did not seem to fit in anywhere, as though I had been born into the wrong world" (Tammet, 2007, pp. 51, 74).

They also tend to be creative, so they are often very good at creating these new visions of the world (Ariel, 2012, p. 14; Attwood, in Murray, Ed., 2006, p. 34; Grandin & Panek, 2014, pp. 128-133). Several of my Aspie clients were into science fiction, as they felt alien to this world and wondered about all aspects of space and the possibility of life on other planets.

Jim wanted to go to Roswell, New Mexico, where UFOs allegedly landed, and see the International UFO Museum and Research Center. He also wanted to visit the Very Large Array in New Mexico, an arrangement of huge electronic dishes that continually listen for radio signals from outer space. He watched programs on TV about space, UFOs, and aliens, as well as other mysterious other-worldly subjects. He was often glued to the TV series, "The Curse of Oak Island," about an island that was supposedly haunted, where mysterious accidents occurred while people were searching for treasure. The mysteries of space, and events that had no logical explanation, held a fascination for him. Obviously, the correlation of his possibly feeling out of place in this world and his interest in the things I've mentioned, did not occur to me at that time.

In movies, I like chick flicks, westerns of the Randolph Scott variety, a good spy story of adventure or intrigue, and sometimes a wild and crazy film. I think *You, Me, and Dupree* is a very funny, enjoyable film – a true chick flick, with humor that naturally ends well. I have to watch a movie until the credits come on, as I watch for the key grip person, the person who manages and maintains the equipment that supports the cameras. I'm not sure how or why that got started, but after a movie, I won't move without seeing the name of the key grip. I like *You've Got Mail* and *Sleepless in Seattle*, with Meg Ryan. I like movies that are easy to take and require no thinking, yet stir the emotions a bit, something I think is good for me, as I am of an old German stoic stock. You know, logical, deliberate, focused, responsible . . . and have spent my life solving problems, people problems relating to insurance matters, requiring me to keep an emotional distance in order to get the job done. I am by nature too analytical and not enough of a free spirit.

Again, there is his self-reference to the traits common to many Aspies – logical, deliberate, focused, responsible, but with reserved emotions. Low-level emotions are not uncommon for Aspies. "Knowing what my own emotions are has often seemed like a problem, and it may be partly due to my emotional state remaining at a low level most of the time. That seems natural to me" (Christian, in Attwood et al., 2014, p. 183). More about emotions later.

Perhaps the reason Jim watched chick flicks was to learn how to socialize. Some Aspies tend to prefer movies or TV shows with "simpler, more straightforward stories" (Higashida, 2016, p. 75). Many of my Aspie clients say they watch movies and TV shows, some even memorizing lines, trying to learn how to socialize, trying to fit in, another feature of masking.

Rituals and routines are common to Aspies (Aston, 2001, pp. 62-63; Attwood, 2008, p. 138; Silberman, 2015, p. 178), and the key grip ritual could have been a hint to me about Asperger's, if I had been looking to analyze Jim.

Repetitive TV commercials attract some Aspies and become familiar, fun to watch. "They're on again and again and again, after all" (Higashida, 2016, p. 73). Later, Jim's favorites were the Duluth Trading Company commercials for Buck Naked ™ *underwear and the Nutri-System™ commercial, in which men say, "You eat the food, you lose the weight." He could repeat the Nutri-System™ slogan in tones like the guys on the commercial, and he loved doing that, making me laugh. It was another ritual.*

I don't like board games, but I like crossword puzzles and jigsaw puzzles. I have two jigsaw puzzles with vintage car themes. I play Spider Solitaire on my computer a lot, and keep a running score. Playing it is relaxing and calming to me. I play it for hours at a time.

Playing Spider Solitaire sounds as if it is a form of "stimming." Stimming is the term for things many Aspies do as a calming activity, and computer games can be relaxing (Stanford, 2015, p. 163). Other actions, such as spinning, either their bodies or objects; hand-flapping; toe-tapping; or any other repetitive action that serves to release tension and have a calming effect are examples of stimming (Falk & Schofield, 2018, p. 35; Hendrickx & Newton, 2007, p. 35; Higashida, 2016, p. 68; Lesko, 2011, p. 10; Silberman, 2015, p. 196; Stanford, 2015, pp. 144-148). Newport, an Aspie, referred to death as going "to the great stim room in the sky" (Newport, 2001, p. 57). Jigsaw puzzles, because of the shapes of the pieces and how the parts fit together, and crossword puzzles, which combine knowledge and logic, are enjoyed by many Aspies. Other examples of stimming will appear in later chapters.

I like to ballroom dance. I go through the motions and enjoy the activity, but I would not call myself a dancer. We used to go to a Veterans Day dance at the armory here in Pendleton, dancing to a live Glenn Miller-style band. Very enjoyable.

I used to play my guitar a bit and still have it, but don't get it out much anymore. I can play a few things on the piano. Some of my favorite singers are Alison Krauss, Celine Dion, and Judy Collins. I also like Roy Orbison, Alabama, and Johnny Cash. Music stirs the soul, except for some classical pieces, like Ravel's "Bolero." That one drives me dippy – too much repetition of the same note, like the guy's finger got stuck on one key.

The aversion to "Bolero" speaks to Jim's sensitivity to sound, which has been noted earlier.

Growing up in a Navy family, I traveled quite a bit – Philippine Islands, Guam, Japan, Mexico, Canada, much of Europe, and Vietnam (although it was French Indochina when I was there). I've traveled either to or through about half the states. I've lived in Japan, Philippine Islands, California, Oregon, Colorado, Maryland, and a short time in Virginia. I have no desire for further extensive travel.

I began to see my marriage was disintegrating. We separated, and I got word the divorce was imminent, so I began dating several local women, but this did not work out. Too many differences. At age 73, I am lonely and miss female companionship. I decided that since there is no prospect of reconciliation with my wife, I will sign up for eHarmony and see what is out there. I connected with a few women, visited at least a couple of them, one in the Portland area and one in southern Washington, and they visited me. We had interesting times, but the matches proved unsatisfactory.

These dates were just that, taking in events and dinners – nothing further. I have an old-fashioned kind of personality, and while still sexually functional without the help of medicines, I am toned down quite a bit from my younger years. At this time in my life, sex is not the major driving influence in a relationship. Compatibility is what is important to me.

I hold out hope that I'll hit a compatibility bingo with an eHarmony match, even though I've had another birthday and am now 74, and in a few months will be 75 . . .

[Here we leave Jim for a while.]

PART III

WE BEGIN OUR ADVENTURES TOGETHER

CHAPTER 7

I MEET JIM ONLINE
(WITH TRAITS I FAILED TO NOTICE IN OUR COMMUNICATIONS)

The evening of November 13, 2008, I logged onto eHarmony, expecting nothing new, and planning to cancel my membership. To my surprise, I saw a new contact, from a guy named James, age 74, in Oregon.

Oregon? Oregon was not on my list of states. I think eHarmony must have had a software glitch. I didn't know how it happened (and still don't).

Strange how things work out. Much later I learned Jim originally joined eHarmony (or at least investigated it and filled out a personality profile) in June 2007, several months before his divorce was finalized. I specified in my profile that I would not consider someone who was still married, so his profile did not come up for me until he was officially single.

In the photo James posted, he looked kind and gentle, tall and slender, with gray, almost white, hair. His profile said he was looking for his "soulmate," and he did not brag. He said, "I am divorced, my life is an open book, and I have no secrets."

I was immediately awestruck, because in his profile, he mentioned a phrase closely related to the code word Paul and I had agreed on! Do any readers believe in coincidences? It seemed as if James from Oregon was destined to contact Mary from New Mexico. Was Paul confirming this match? So much we don't know about the afterlife . . .

What a refreshing change from some of the profiles that listed accomplishments and myriad attributes intended to impress! James had me hooked with his openness and forthright manner, and I liked his looks – at least I wanted to find out more about him.

I don't remember much more about his profile, except he said he didn't smoke at all and drank only occasionally. I decided I'd answer him. It seemed impractical, because of the distance, but apparently, he had no problem reaching out to someone in New Mexico. I thought it could prove interesting.

At that time, matches could email only through eHarmony. They provided a list of questions, and matches selected questions to send to each other. James sent me a few questions, I answered, and for the next three and a half months we sent emails back and forth at a rapid pace.

I learned from Jim what you've already read about – that he was divorced, stoic, of German heritage, conscientious, a hard worker, well-traveled, educated, disciplined, logical, intelligent, and loyal to commitments at church and at work. He was a picky eater, was lonely, enjoyed his hobbies, and loved nature, but he was not very open emotionally, though he felt things deeply. He liked movies and music, and he liked to read, to cook, and to dance, along with having a deep respect for The Man.

Also, Jim learned what you've already read about – that I was widowed, adventurous, determined, knew how to work, was independent, educated, and had been married over 50 years. I was more emotional than he, and expressed my emotions freely; I was religious, though not currently a church-goer; I liked movies and music; I liked to read; and I liked to dance.

He learned from my profile that I was looking for the right man to date and was not willing to settle – I made it clear I was picky. He said he agreed with my determination to be particular in my choice of another partner "to spend the rest of my life with."

His statement took me aback – *Wait, that's not what I said – the "rest of my life" part – I said "date." He was jumping too far ahead.* I wondered if corresponding with this interesting, but unknown, man in Oregon was such a good idea.

As soon as I had his full name and birthdate, I ran an extensive online background check, to be sure I wasn't wasting my time. I found a years-old parking ticket in California – nothing worse.

Each of us owned our houses (along with mortgage companies), and we commiserated on never-ending house-work and yard maintenance. I let him know I had very little yard maintenance, as I had a xeriscaped yard of decorative rock, but no grass. He wondered how much I had to water the rocks and how fast they grew. I liked his sense of humor – the contrast with his serious religious and nature-loving side. He seemed to be a multifaceted person.

He said he admired my determination in getting a Ph.D., but he was intimidated by it – he quickly assured me he was joking about being intimidated. I could almost feel him winking.

I had questions about the possibility of reconciliation between him and his ex.

"I cannot pursue a potential relationship if I think I will be used as leverage to get her to reconsider. I'm a counselor, remember, so I hear these stories – 'I got another woman, thinking my ex would see what she gave up and reconsider.' I do not want to invest in a friendship or relationship only to have it go south because of your feelings for the ex. The person with whom I develop a relationship will never have to fear competing with the ghost of my husband. I am not looking to replace him. I cannot be your ex, and don't want to be, but also will not expect you to be Paul. I think it's important for us to clear the air and be honest."

He assured me again, "The divorce is final, and there is no possibility of reconciliation."

He still did not denigrate his ex. I liked those character traits of loyalty and kindness.

He added, "By the way, glad you're a counselor. That might come in handy for me."

"Sorry, I don't mix work with pleasure, so I'm not looking at you as a client."

We were on a steep learning curve, and doing it all by email. Since we had not yet met in person, I had no idea how things might progress.

CHAPTER 8

THINGS PROGRESS

One day, I received this from Jim: "We will need to meet at some point. I wouldn't want a 'catalog bride,' and I don't think you would want to be one."

Catalog bride?? That took me by surprise! This was the first reference to my being a bride – of any kind.

I said, "I'm amused about your 'catalog bride' remark – that harkens back to the days of the settlement of the west, when guys and gals corresponded, the woman traveled across the country, and they married, without having met – life was much different then. When I see western movies about the pioneers, I realize what a daring and adventurous life that was."

The friendship was still young.

He said, "I have the philosophy of living in the now. You can bemoan your fate and be a sad victim, or accept life's challenges, disappointments, and joys . . . it's all part of living."

This optimism was another piece of Jim that appealed to me. So far, I had found nothing objectionable about this guy in Oregon – except he lived so far from New Mexico.

Interestingly, living in the now, or wholly in the present, is mentioned as an Aspie trait by several (Hendrickx & Newton, 2007, pp. 36-37; Stanford, 2015, p. 84). Aspies are not likely to hold grudges, because the past is the past to them, and cannot be changed. Much later, Jim's attitude toward a toll ticket will tend to dispute this assertion.

I was becoming more and more aware that our interests were compatible. I began to anticipate his emails as the high points of my days, and we were exchanging multiple emails a day. *Where is this headed?* I wondered.

I told Jim I went to a party, and had a gin and tonic and glass of chardonnay, then my neighbor came home with me, and we had a beer.

He said, "Hmm . . . you must be one tough cookie to handle gin and tonic, wine, and beer in one evening. If you ever visit, I'll take you to the Slickfork Saloon, and we can take bets from the cowboys at the bar. Interesting that you dig gin and tonic, my hard drink of preference, along with dinner wine, of course." I pictured the Slickfork Saloon as either a joint he made up or some side-of-the-road hangout where the low-lifes gathered.

"I nursed my gin and tonic for an hour, then sipped on a glass of chardonnay, which I didn't finish. The beer was 5% alcohol (most beer is too bitter for my taste). I am far from winning any bets with the cowboys, so maybe you'd better cancel our date at the saloon."

The topic led me to ask, "How much do you drink? Are you able to control it, or are you an alcoholic?"

Jim responded, "I am not an alcoholic. I am disciplined and can quit anytime I choose. When I quit cigarette smoking 38 years ago, when our son was born, all it took was 30 lemon drops a day for three weeks, and weekends at home on the weaving loom I built. Needed something to occupy my hands. I do enjoy a glass of wine with dinner and an occasional gin and tonic."

I was interested in Jim's drinking habits, and in our years together I never knew him to drink to excess.

He was an avid Oregon Ducks fan, after living for a while in Eugene near the University of Oregon. He seemed delighted that I not only tolerated football, but actually enjoyed watching it. I told him I yell when watching, even by myself.

He said, "I think finding someone who not only likes watching football and basketball, and yells, but who also drinks wine and gin and tonics is nothing short of a miracle."

This man seemed to have simple pleasures, wholesome hobbies, and a great sense of humor. I continued to be intensely interested.

Close to Christmas, Jim said, "I hope you will be the free-wheeling you, as I am learning more about your independent nature. This is an invitation to you to say anything you want. I don't expect you to walk softly with your words. I am confident you are a pleasant, reliable person. I do well with straightforward communication, even though I haven't always been accustomed to it. You can be you, and I will be me, and maybe together we will end up in a partnership or just good friends."

I said, "Thank you! I teach my clients to use clear and honest communication, and I try to communicate that way. And yes, I am independent and will say what I think and feel. I think that is the only way to have a healthy relationship. I will expect the same from you."

This seemed like a workable arrangement, but as you shall see as our story goes on, the arrangement sounded better on paper than it turned out to be in person months later.

"I love the Pacific Northwest – abundant in beauty, and varied," Jim began. "That may be an issue in a potential relationship, as you have a successful career, friends, and associates in Albuquerque. I tend to favor a simple life. I would like to visit you, perhaps this summer. You are always welcome to visit Oregon. You can stay in my home, but if you have concerns, I know a couple of married females that might take you in. I am my own person and don't fret about what the local wags may say about my conduct. I am at peace with my moral values. I await your thoughts on this invitation, but give yourself time to mull it over. Cogitate and get back to me when you can."

I had not thought far enough ahead to consider a possible relocation for one of us if the friendship deepened. We'd not yet met in person, but Jim was already staking claim to his territory. This was an invitation to visit him – except for setting a date. Without a specific date, it seemed too general to me. In my southern raising, invitations needed to be specific, not "come to see us sometime."

He mentioned his moral values, which, as an Aspie, would likely be firmly set (Ariel, 2012, p. 14), and which would indicate he was probably a nice man. He also mentioned not fretting about what people might think. I've already mentioned that many Aspies don't care what people think. This trait would later become an issue between us.

At almost midnight on New Year's Eve, I wrote, "Lots to think about. You know I'm not afraid to speak my mind. I try to be straightforward, and maybe that will be a quality of mine that over time will annoy you. I think we have much to learn about each other – probably the understatement of the New Year. I hear the firecrackers outside, so I guess it's officially 2009. I hope it's a great year for each of us. I'm cogitating . . . hmm . . . cogitating gives me a headache."

Jim said, "Socrates spent his entire life cogitating."

I replied, "Cogitating is probably the only similarity between Socrates and me."

We were definitely getting more familiar with each other, and the banter was fun. I tried to imagine our meeting. If I met him, my reaction might be, *'What was I thinking – a visit with him?*' Or, maybe he'd feel that way about me. I hoped not, but long-distance communication can be one thing; in person, another. I would have reason later to understand how differently those modes affect a friendship.

I decided to lob the ball from my court and issued an invitation to him to visit me on March 5th. We would have a little over two more months to learn about each other, and if I saw red flags, I would have time to rescind the invitation.

I waited for a response. Instead, I got Monty Python and Austin Powers.

Jim said, "Your epistles are always entertaining and include a silliness factor. You must be a Monty Python fan? One of my favorites, along with Austin Powers. Now, as to your invite for a visit, I'll see if I can get the time off at work. I'll do some checking about March dates. Now it's my turn to cogitate. I'll be 75 years old by then, and we can celebrate! I'll get back to ya. Good night, my dear Mary. I like the way you speak your mind, as I have difficulty reading minds."

This was the first time he called me "my dear Mary," which touched me, and I realized he was growing fond of me, as I was of him.

Jim had unwittingly given me another hint about Asperger's. A common trait of persons with Asperger's is difficulty putting one's self in another's shoes, so to speak, to know how another might feel. It is called "theory of mind," and ties in with empathy, in that it is difficult for Aspies, and for some, impossible, to see from another's perspective and gauge what another person is thinking or what they might be feeling, either by hearing their words or recognizing facial expressions and body language (Ariel, 2012, p. 44; Baron-Cohen, 1997, p. 136; Falk & Schofield, 2018, pp. 49-54; Goleman, 2007, pp. 134-135; Grandin & Barron, 2016, p. 325; Robison, 2008, p. 21; Siegel, 2015, p. 260; Silberman, 2015, p. 259; Wylie, 2014, p. 39). "Some [Aspies] are unable to feel empathy (an 'emotional understanding') for others" (Attwood, in Attwood et al., 2014, p. 276). Ascribing motivation is foreign to them (Bogdashina, 2010, p. 182; Hendrickx & Newton, 2007, pp. 32-33).

Although lack of empathy is well-documented in a number of sources, at least two Aspies disagree with that assessment. In Dubin's opinion, Aspies are capable of empathy (Dubin, 2009, p. 43), and Newport says, "It just takes some of us longer to express [empathy]" (Newport, 2001, p. 283).

When Jim said, "I like the way you speak your mind, as I have difficulty reading minds," he was describing theory of mind, but I didn't pick up on it, because I wasn't looking for it. Many Aspies interpret words literally, so they depend on clear, concrete communication for meaning (Attwood, 2008, pp. 216-217, 224; Baron-Cohen, 1997, p. 142; Carley, 2008, pp. 74, 88; Dubin, 2009, pp. 53-54; Finch, 2012, pp. 39-41; Grandin, 2015, pp. 203-204; Hendrickx & Newton, 2007, p. 91-94; Prince-Hughes, 2004, p. 218; Robison, 2008, pp. 189-194).

He also let me in on his liking of crazy, fun Austin Powers and Monty Python characters. Earlier in this book, I've mentioned Aspies' creativity and enjoyment of "other world" types of entertainment, like fairy tales, science fiction, and the aliens' landing in Roswell, New Mexico.

He was interested in making the trip to meet me. How could our meeting go wrong? Well, there *was* one way . . . I decided to unload more information on him and take a chance on his feelings about it.

CHAPTER 9

THE DIE IS CAST

With a great deal of uneasiness, I wrote, "Maybe this is a good time to tell you I am in debt. When Paul was dying, I got him anything he expressed the slightest wish for, often paying more in express shipping costs than the value of the item, so things he wanted would arrive before he died. I regret none of it – I'd do it again. It is difficult for me to share this information, as it may not mesh with your conservative orientation. I'm excited by your willingness to come down and get acquainted, and I hope this information won't cause you to rethink your trip, but I feel it only fair to let you know."

In a few minutes, I had a response.

"I appreciate your candor. So, you are not a rich widow . . . okay, all bets are off. Ha! Just kidding. I had no vision you were. But have no fear, I intend to take you up on your invite. I am pleased that you provided well for your husband during his last days. At such times, money has no significance. I look forward to the visit. I have checked with the boss, and the dates you picked are a go. I will need such basics as an adequate supply of Bud, a pressed Oregon Ducks flag on the front stoop, and above all, an inspection of the premises to assure there are no liver and onions present. Seriously (but I was serious, oh well . . .), I look forward to meeting you and being chaperoned around New Mexico, with the assurance that no little green men from Roswell will capture me."

My heart danced!

I could hardly believe it! My fears were for nothing. He had shown me a lot more about his character, as well as his feelings for me.

I came home from my neighbors' one evening to find a voicemail on my answering machine. The first call from Jim!

I was excited to hear his voice – it was low, soft, measured, and flat, but not unpleasant. He said he would call again later.

When he called, we talked three and a half hours. There were no lulls in the conversation – it was as if we'd known each other always. He was as funny on the phone as he was in his emails. His dry comments cracked me up.

The low, measured, flat voice could have been a tip-off about Asperger's, if I had been looking for it. Many Aspies have either very loud, strident voices, or low and flat speech with little expression (Attwood, 2008, p. 218; Carley, 2008, p. 93). I have dealt with clients at both extremes. I was so happy to hear from Jim, I wasn't judging his speech pattern at the time.

CHAPTER 10

OBAMA AND POLITICS

I watched Obama's inauguration with tears. I was moved in ways I could not have predicted. I cried because many family members are no longer here to witness this historical development in our country. I cried because of the immense responsibility Barack Obama was assuming. I cried because of the historical and progressive change in direction our country was taking. I was glad for the changes I had witnessed in our country's attitudes in my lifetime. I shared my experience with Jim.

Jim commented, "I'll be brief about politics. Obama's inauguration is a historical development, perhaps showing the maturity of the country as well as the diversity, compared to a century ago. I welcome Mr. Obama to the presidency, and hope he does well. He is intelligent, articulate, charismatic, and has the ability to move people emotionally. He certainly has goals that all can agree on as good and well-intentioned for the citizenry and the world. In addition, he is faced with a host of problems both domestically and in the world community. I pray that he has the tenacity to lead his party to make the sound choices needed to address these problems. Time will tell. Politics is a very rough game. To try and give a diverse and changing population programs that meet all their needs satisfactorily, or more importantly, their expectations, is just impossible. On a lighter note, I think it is always good to shake up the system now and then, and in this case, we have shaken it up mightily. Youth, charisma, intelligence . . . all traits that should prove helpful, so from that standpoint, it is a positive change. I don't worry much about the presidency, but I sure do about Congress, and that goes for both sides of the aisle."

Didn't he start by saying he'd "be brief about politics"? I have condensed his comments. It was a lengthy treatise, and I'm not willing to spend so many pages in this book on politics. Obviously, politics was one of Jim's special interests, and he was interested in sharing his views, at length. Aspies can talk on and on about their special interest topics, seemingly oblivious to their audience's interest (Carley, 2008, p. 17; Tammet, 2007, p. 75).

CHAPTER 11

PREPPING FOR THE VISIT

My daughter, Nancy, called and expressed concern about Jim's visit, a stranger in her mother's home. I assured her that I felt secure, and she or her siblings were welcome to call at any time during the visit. I told her my neighbors were aware he would visit, and they would keep an eye on things.

"I think I told you I am a white-knuckle flyer," Jim said. "My son says I must be quite interested in this lady, to be willing to fly across the country to meet her. I look forward to a fun time. Although you seem nice looking in your photos, looks are not the whole enchilada to seeking a life's partner. I would say it's only 99.5%. Just kidding! Things such as intellect, sense of humor, happiness quotient, and value structure make up the mix. I am likely much more stoic than you. I am still emotional in a deep sense, but more reserved with my emotions."

Jim said he was "emotional in a deep sense, but more reserved with my emotions." By the time high-functioning Aspies are grown, they have usually learned to hide many of their feelings. Some Aspies don't recognize them, and some don't have the vocabulary to express emotions accurately (Attwood, in Attwood et al., 2014, pp. 54, 178). Several of my clients have told me it is mainly because they are not sure of their feelings or do not feel in control of them. Expressing them, letting them show, might be overwhelming (Falk & Schofield, 2018, pp. 34, 158). Aspies also have trouble reading other people's feelings (Attwood, in Attwood et al., 2014, p. 189).

In spite of not having met in person, we were getting to know each other pretty well. Maybe those pioneer women and the men waiting for them got to know each other better than we think, though certainly not as quickly as Jim and I could. In a little over two months of correspondence and phone calls, we had covered a lot of territory. I was beginning to see how one could feel close to someone they'd never met. It was happening to me . . .

Jim said he had a cold that was hanging on. I urged him to see his doctor. He said, "I don't know about this doctor thing. If I go to a doc, I might be told something I don't want to hear, then where would I be?"

A few days later he reported his cold was much better. The stubborn German won.

Many Aspie adults avoid contact with doctors, and have anxiety when having to deal with doctors or dentists, preferring to self-medicate or use home remedies (Attwood, in Attwood et al., 2014, p. 18; Wylie, 2014, p. 154). You will learn much more about Jim's aversion to doctors and the medical field in general.

"I thoroughly enjoyed our phone visit last night. You sound as if you will be fun, Mr. Hanks. We should have excellent weather while you're here next month – in the 70s."

Jim came back with, "What's the 'Mr. Hanks' formality? I thought we were past that. But that's great weather! You must have a direct line to The Man to get that set up."

"The 'Mr. Hanks' was my way of teasing you. I'm a tease and a jokester – I love having fun and laughing. Perhaps during a few days' visit, you'll get more comfortable with it."

He said, "I'm not used to being teased – so I was trying to interpret what you meant. However, I like it – I appreciate the explanation and even more, the tease."

Another oblique signal that he lacked theory of mind – he was not able to interpret my tease and its meaning. Aspies, because they tend to take words literally, have trouble with teasing (Attwood, 2008, pp. 216-218; Carley, 2008, p. 88). Aspies tend to take statements literally (Carley, 2008, p. 74; Cooper, in Grandin, 2012, p. 281; Prince-Hughes, 2004, p. 218; Stanford, 2015, pp. 27, 203-206; Taylor, 2017, p. 65). Obviously, corresponding by email has its drawbacks as a method of getting acquainted, being devoid of tone quality, volume, rhythm, and facial expression. Perhaps he could have noticed my teasing look, if we'd been face-to-face, although, as an Aspie, he might have had trouble interpreting my facial expression (Grandin & Panek, 2014, pp. 72-73; Hane, in Attwood et al., 2014, pp. 184-185; Willey, 2015, p. 145). That revelation was still in our future.

The day before Jim arrived, Nancy emailed me, "Mom, I want to let you know I am thinking about you. Have a nice time (and know, if for any reason it ends up not being what you thought, we're always on your side. Just sayin'...)."

I answered, "I realize this visit is an adventurous thing to do, but you've always known I'm adventurous. I'm optimistic about the visit. You and your siblings are welcome to call at any time while he's here. I'll always have my cell with me."

Jim said, "I'm pleased you're looking forward to my visit, but I'm not without warts. Just remember what happened when the princess kissed the frog, WOW!"

"If I kiss a frog, will I get warts?"

"Perhaps that's the risk you take in exploring life."

"What if I'm not a risk taker?"

Jim said, "Then you miss the opportunity of a lifetime. Maybe I should cancel my ticket, as I am not too refined, having lived here in the outback so long. Oops, special pricing on the airfare, no cancellations or refunds; shucks, I'll just have to hop on the plane and give it a whirl. I watched a program on the History Channel about UFOs and the Roswell incidents. There are strange things down there in New Mexico. I am counting on you to protect me. I'm packed and ready to leave tomorrow! See you soon! This will be Jim and Mary's excellent adventure."

I already knew Jim had a keen sense of humor, and some Aspies don't get humor. Just as I've said, not all Aspies have all of the traits. I so enjoyed his funny conversations. He also again implied an interest in and curiosity of visitors from distant worlds – fantasy (Attwood, 2008, p. 181; Sacks, 1996, p. 276).

Jim added, "There is one thing I failed to specify in my eHarmony profile, and that is, a suitable companion must be able to overhaul a 4-speed synchro tranny in Brit cars with eyes closed."

I had no idea what a 4-speed synchro tranny was. I wondered how it would be to spend a few days with this Brit car enthusiast. I slept some that night, but my brain whirled. What was I about to get myself into? Little did I know . . .

CHAPTER 12

WE MEET IN PERSON

A large Ducks flag from eBay was draped over my front door. One neighbor caught me before I left for the airport, and said, "I hope you locked up your jewelry and silver."

I laughed, but she said, "You don't really know this man."

I admit she set me thinking. No, I really didn't know this man. I thought I did, but my mind conjured all the newspaper and magazine stories about the hazards of online dating, that no matter how good someone might seem from a distance, they could say anything to get women interested. Sometimes the result was not pretty. Would I be sorry to have him visit, be in my home? Would I be vulnerable to someone with bad intentions? I was adventurous, but was I taking a chance? But it was too late for that line of thinking.

Thursday, March 5th, driving south on I-25, I looked at my watch every few minutes, hoping the traffic to the airport would keep moving along. I parked in plenty of time, and rode up the escalator. My hands were sweaty. What would Jim be like in person? Would I recognize him? How would we get along? While I waited, I picked the cuticle on my thumb to the quick.

As passengers began to come through the security gates, I held up a poster I'd made, of Donald Duck on a green and yellow background, the Oregon Ducks colors. Jim appeared, saw me, grinned at the poster, and walked over to me, pulling his small rollaboard. I expected a hug, and was primed for it, but he was formal. He shook my hand, and instead of "hello," his first words to me were, "You're short."

Awkward.

"Shorter than you thought?"

"Yes, I'm used to taller women."

I felt I was a disappointment. I knew both of us were a little on edge, so I attributed it to nerves.

Jim's greeting was a classic example of the Aspie trait of failure to have a filter before opening one's mouth (Aston, 2001, p. 65; Grandin, 2006, p. 156; Grandin & Barron, 2016, p. 327; Hendrickx & Newton, 2007, pp. 24, 97; Robison, 2008, p. 194; Solomon, 2013, p. 281; Wylie, 2014, p. 31)!

I didn't see it as that at the time, but as our story unfolds, you will begin to see other instances of his traits of bluntness and honesty.

He was tall and slender, and immaculate, in a navy sports coat, shirt with tiny pink and navy stripes, open at the neck, and khaki Dockers. His white hair and rugged good looks blended with the kind face I recognized from his photos. A noticeable fleshy mole on his left cheek, about the size of a pencil eraser, not apparent in his photos, was not a distraction, but a unique feature of his appearance.

I was disappointed when he didn't hug me. So, this was the stoic German I had been emailing. Not too romantic. *The next five days might be long...*

We engaged in nervous small talk, got his luggage, and drove to Olive Garden for a pasta dinner and wine. While we enjoyed our meal, he seemed to loosen up. When we got to my house, he saw the Ducks flag, broke into a grin, and said, "You really did it!"

"I pay attention and aim to please."

I showed him his room and bathroom. We sat and talked into the evening, but he was tired from traveling. We finally said goodnight (still with no hug) and went to our respective rooms.

I woke up early. I put on my jeans and a blue-flowered top, and was in the kitchen making coffee, trying to be quiet and not wake him. His door was closed. Soon he appeared, dressed for the day in jeans and a blue striped shirt. He struck a pose – big smile, one leg to the side, and his arms spread wide, one higher than the other, in a 'ta-da' pose, which made me laugh. His night of rest had done him good. Certainly, the ice was broken for the day!

We sat in the living room, drinking coffee and talking, me in my easy chair, Jim on the couch, wearing his slippers. He said his feet often hurt, because a car ran over his right foot when he was young, and it had given him trouble ever since. He wears his slippers when he can, because the fuzzy, soft lining cushions his feet.

It may be true that his foot was injured when he was a child, and I have no reason to doubt that, but another explanation for his affection for his slippers might have been because Aspies have sensory issues with tight or scratchy things next to their skin, and the slippers were lined with soft lamb's wool and were loose enough to be comfortable. That would never have occurred to me at the time. One Aspie says "…I hated having my feet bound up in the stiff canvas of tennis shoes, or the slippery leather of dress shoes. To beat that feeling, I wore house slippers to school" (Willey, 2015, p. 46).

I was glad Jim felt at ease. Later I would learn of his preferences in clothing – soft fabrics, nothing scratchy or starched, and most comfortable in the same type of shirt every day (Grandin & Panek, 2014, p. 93).

The phone on the table by my chair rang.

"How are things, Mom?" Nancy's voice.

"Things are fine, Jim arrived on schedule, and we're sitting here drinking coffee and visiting, planning what we want to do today. Jim seems like a very nice man. I don't think he's an axe murderer."

Jim and I were grinning. Nancy was quiet. I regretted the tease. I thought it was sweet of her to be concerned and call to check on me, and my eyes got watery.

"Bad joke," I said. "I appreciate your checking on me. I'm confident I'm in no danger. We're going to have a nice day sight-seeing, temps in the 70s. You can call anytime."

Froot Loops were on hand for breakfast. I was trying to impress the guy. After breakfast and more coffee, we decided to go to Old Town, the original downtown area of Albuquerque. We browsed around the gazebo in the plaza and walked into the old church, established in the 1700s. I handed a passerby my phone and he took our photo in the picturesque courtyard – our first photo together!

We ate lunch at La Placita, across from the plaza, in the room with the tree growing in it. I think the red chile enchiladas were too hot for Jim, but he got through them. He said, "Bend, Oregon, has a restaurant with a tree growing in it, and sometime I'll take you there." He was assuming all would go well on this visit – that he'd want me to visit, and that I'd want to go to Oregon.

We went home after lunch, to rest and plan our afternoon. I handed him a printout of possibilities for him to peruse, all touristy sites.

"So what looks interesting to do this afternoon?"

"Didn't I see a Lowe's on the main street that goes into town?"

I smiled, thinking he was joking. "Yes."

"Can we go there?"

"Are you serious?"

"Yes, it will be fun to check it out."

I laughed. "I've never thought of Lowe's as a tourist attraction, but if that's what you want to do, of course we can."

At Lowe's we walked up and down every aisle, he demonstrated Monty Python's silly walk, we laughed a lot, looked at every bracket, board, and bolt, and walked out after three and a half hours. He was as happy as my grandkids after shopping in a Lego store. And so was I.

Another Aspie tip-off might have been that he wanted to spend an afternoon in a big home repair store, looking at everything. Many might have been more interested in seeing unusual sights around Albuquerque, but he had eyed the Lowe's and was eager to see all the tools and construction items. Remember he said he'd have liked to be an architect. Also remember he told me he has the engineering mentality, a typical trait of Aspies.

After we got home, we had sandwiches and talked. He had noticed the file cabinet in the spare bedroom he occupied, labeled "Genealogy."

"I see you are into genealogy," he said. "I have spent many hours online and in libraries, filling out my family tree. Once I lost it all online, and became discouraged. I now prefer to use paper copies, which fill a number of large binders. I've been to the Family History Library in Salt Lake City, and learned a lot there."

He went on, "I've read a bit on DNA, and specifically, mitochondrial DNA. An interesting book is *Adam's Curse* by a guy named Skye. The thesis is the genetic corruption of the male sex component of DNA to the point that in some 25,000 years hence, it will be so modified that it won't work as intended anymore, and absent evolution into a unisex mammal, the human race will be no more. He also wrote a book titled *The Seven Daughters of Eve*, which deals with female mitochondrial DNA genetics and traces humankind back to its origin, hence the seven daughters concept. Very interesting."

Jim was on a roll, and I heard that his interest in genealogy had in part to do with researching information on his biological father. He said he had a hole in his heart that had never healed from having his father abandon him – a yearning to connect in some way. He talked for over an hour on his research.

This was a lot of detailed information to give me in a late afternoon on our first visit, but I was interested. I could tell his interest bordered on obsession. If I had been looking for clues, I might have realized this was one of his special interests. A typical Aspie trait is to have either one or multiple interests they love to explore and talk about at length (Aston, 2001, p. 30; Attwood, 1998, p. 168; Falk & Schofield, 2018, p. 67; Frith, 1991, p. 14; Grandin & Panek, 2014, p. 15; Grossberg, 2015, p. 9). Since I was also interested in genealogy, it did not seem odd to me at the time.

My next-door neighbors, near our ages, had us over for chocolate cake and ice cream that night. They were impressed with Jim from Oregon. Neighbor Jim, an intellectual, welcomed discussion with a peer. As we were leaving, he winked and whispered to me in private, "A quality man."

Later that night, Jim and I hot tubbed, drank Merlot, and looked at the stars. He stretched his arms wide, leaned back against the tub walls, and laid his hands on the top edges.

"You have good hands," I said. They looked sturdy, somewhat leathered and worn, as if they had done a lot of work.

As we discussed many topics, Jim said, "Do you think one's dreams and goals change as life progresses and as life takes us in different directions?"

"Yes, I do. Why?"

"I agree with that, but I can't say I had a dream other than marriage, family, kids, good job, retirement, and live happily ever after. My attentions shifted to different hobby interests, but there was never a specific dream of 'must have' that was centered in my soul. You said earlier you have a dream of publishing a book. Fill me in on your dream."

I was surprised by his interest.

"Since I have published articles, I see a book as a natural progression. I think my experience managing senior housing communities, plus my grief counseling, have meshed to give me insights into elder caregiving. I want my book to be a resource for families and caregivers, so they understand how older people grieve their losses. I will eventually get it written."

Some Aspies float along in life without a clear-cut plan for goals and dreams for the future. Marshack tells of an Aspie husband who says he realizes his wife has dreams, and he doesn't know why he doesn't (2009, p. 13). A common trait of Aspies is living in the present and putting the past behind (Hendrickx & Newton, 2007, p. 36-37). They tend to live in the now. It may be that Aspies are too busy constantly trying to fit into the puzzle of society to plan far ahead. The dream Jim had earlier was one that didn't work out for him, and he was open about not having a backup plan, but I was pleased about his interest in my goal, and I didn't read anything into his statement except disappointment. He had given a subtle Aspie clue, but not enough to alert me.

Knowing Jim's interest in vintage cars, I had scouted out the J&R Auto Museum in Rio Rancho, just across the Rio Grande. Saturday, we arrived as they opened. We both enjoyed it and spent several hours looking at over seventy vintage cars. After we left, Jim began telling me more and more about his British cars.

Jim said, "I need to do some work on the MGB's 4-speed tranny when I get home, because as we Brit sports car owners say, 'It still needs a bit of sorting out.' A tweak here, adjustment there, and tune up to proper speed and torque."

I could see he had much more than a passing interest in vintage British cars. Again, a special, perhaps obsessive, interest I failed to recognize as an Aspie trait. I simply thought of it as a nice, wholesome hobby.

We had lunch at Burger King, at Jim's suggestion, then we were off to Trader Joe's to get snacks for a get-together with neighbors that night. In Trader Joe's, he pushed the basket and silly walked, and I laughed. He said he was glad I thought it was funny and was not embarrassed. I loved his down-to-earth, unselfconscious approach to life.

He obviously didn't care what people thought, but again, I didn't pick up on that. Because Aspies don't care what people think, some enjoy provoking reactions in people for humorous effect (Hendrickx & Newton, 2007, p. 36).

When I invited him to visit me, I asked him if it was okay to have some neighbors in to meet him, and he said it would be okay, but to have name tags. When my neighbors first heard Jim was coming to town, and they were going to get to meet him, they talked about making a poster for the front door with labeled grids, so each person could vote on various qualities as they left the party. They teased me about my eHarmony man, but were very protective of me and wanted a good look at him. The poster did not materialize, thank goodness.

We got ready for company and heated some appetizers. We furnished the wine, and everyone brought a dinner dish. I distributed name tags. Jim was social; he smiled a lot, conversed a lot, laughed a lot, and the party was all I could ask for. He fit in well with the neighbors. One even gave me a silent thumbs-up. The last of the neighbors left after three and a half hours. Afterward, Jim and I had wine and hot tubbed. He, especially, was exhausted. It *had* been a busy day.

At that time, I had no idea what I had put Jim through. A gathering of people he didn't know, knowing he was on display for hours and hours. It takes a lot of energy and determination for someone with Asperger's to endure such an evening, and to do it in style. "Masking" is the term for their behavior under such circumstances (Carley, 2008, p. 62; Prince-Hughes, 2004, p. 28; Wylie, 2014, p. 33). A rash of exhaustion and some meltdown time afterward is common. The intellectual and emotional exhaustion from masking can be enormous (Attwood, in Attwood et al., 2014, p. 52). In Jim's favor were the hot tub and wine after the guests left, and both of us being "talked out," enabling him to relax and head for bed soon afterward.

Jim settled onto the couch Sunday morning, drinking coffee, and said he was glad we had nothing planned until evening. We had kept a pretty energetic schedule since his arrival, so after breakfast, we read the paper. He wanted the classifieds, to check and see if he saw a vintage Brit car for sale at a good price. In the afternoon, I suggested we walk the few blocks down to the Juan Tabo flood-control dam and climb to the top, as it provided a nice view of the city.

That evening, we rode the tram to the top of Sandia Crest, the over 10,000-foot mountain bordering the east side of Albuquerque, and had dinner at High Finance Restaurant. As the tram smoothly took us to the top, the day was sunny, with little wind, and we had a spectacular view of the mountain.

Jim said, "I've ridden the tram at Wallowa Lake, in eastern Oregon, but the scale of it doesn't compare with this one."

Our table at High Finance was by the west window, overlooking the city, per my reservation. We both ordered salmon, and Jim was impressed with it.

"This is the best salmon and the best wine I've ever had."

I was surprised he thought salmon in Albuquerque was better than salmon in the Northwest, but maybe the atmosphere had a lot to do with his enjoyment. The sunset was incredible, as we finished our dinner with crème brulé and coffee. The tram ride down was magical, the city lights twinkling. Hot tubbing and wine at home ended the evening. He was a gentleman, and we were becoming good friends, but so far, I had no indication it would be more than that.

Monday, I took him to my counseling office and introduced him to the other people who worked there. He wanted to see the houses I had lived in over the years, and where my kids went to school, so we drove around Albuquerque, stopping at Applebee's for lunch. We both ordered Oriental chicken salad, both said we rarely have anything else there, and we laughed about the coincidence of our liking the same thing.

This may be a good time to note that Jim had a few chain restaurants he liked, and especially when traveling, he chose Burger King or Applebee's. Rigidity in habits, and dislike of change, especially for a picky eater, is a common trait of Asperger's (Grandin & Barron, 2016, p. 143; Grandin & Panek, 2014, pp. 74, 94-95; Solomon, 2013, p. 222). If you remember, I said we had lunch at Burger King on Saturday, at Jim's suggestion. He liked fine restaurants, too, but for quick, stop-in meals, Applebee's or Burger King were tops with him. He knew a Whopper at Burger King or Oriental chicken salad at Applebee's would be consistent.

In the afternoon we decided to stay at home and visit. We still had a lot of getting acquainted to do, and our discussions covered a variety of topics. Some we agreed on, like movies, and our not especially wanting or needing further travel; some we didn't, like politics, and liver and onions, but we agreed to disagree.

We went to dinner at one of my favorite Mexican restaurants, El Pinto, one my family had patronized since the mid-70s. The weather was pleasant, and the patio delightful. We finished out the evening in my hot tub.

Afterward, as I was getting ready for bed, I stopped for a moment and realized we were finally interacting in person, and we were having fun!

For Jim's last full day, I planned an outing to Acoma Pueblo, an hour's drive west of Albuquerque. Even though nothing serious had been discussed, I could tell we were becoming close. Before we left, I felt the need to confront him with my debt issue in person, to be sure he understood. I still felt uneasy about it, and I didn't want to hide or minimize details that could have an effect on our friendship.

Jim stood in the door to my bedroom while I finished fixing my hair for the trip. I turned to face him, and bolstered my courage.

"Jim, I need to confess something to you that might make a difference in how you feel about me. I told you I'm in debt from Paul's illness, but I didn't tell you the extent of it. I want to be honest with you. I know you are fiscally conservative, and I need to know what you think of me for carrying a load of debt."

Jim looked at me, expressionless, and was silent.

My heart sank. *Will our trip to Acoma be fun, or will there be a pall over it?*

After a silence of about ten seconds, but which seemed longer, Jim, still looking at me with a blank expression, said, "How much in debt?"

When I told him the figure, which to me was significant, he was again quiet, brows slightly furrowed. Although I budgeted carefully and was gradually whittling the amount, I knew it might affect his opinion of me. I waited for his reaction, every ounce of me tense.

He broke the silence.

"Well, we can handle that. I thought from what you said, that you were much deeper in debt than that. What are you worried about?"

My leg muscles went limp, and I sat down on the edge of the bed.

Jim still stood in the doorway, smiling.

He used the term "*we* can handle that," implying we could handle it together. I felt as if light had entered my body and released any tension. I knew our day's trip would be fun.

He said, "C'mon, let's go see the city on the mountain!"

We talked freely on our drive to Acoma. A barrier had been lifted. We arrived at the Acoma Visitor's Center and waited outside for the van that would take us to the Native American settlement called Sky City, on top of the mesa. It has been continuously inhabited since it was built to ward off marauders, in 1150 A.D. While we waited, it was evident Jim was at least as, or more, interested in the architecture and construction of the Visitor's Center than he might be in the village we were going to see. He wandered around the building, pointing, and commenting to me on the mix of wood and rock, and the way it was designed and put together. He admired the large, long wooden beams across the tops of the portals, and the wooden pillars that supported the roof, territorial style. I remembered his saying he would have liked to be an architect.

The intensity of his examination of the building and comments about how it was constructed could have been a clue about Asperger's. A trait of many Aspies is that they like making sense of how things are put together (Attwood, 2008, p. 286; Prince-Hughes, 2004, pp. 24-25). Willey, an Aspie, describes her fascination with architecture and drafting. "To this day, architectural design remains one of my most favored subjects and now that I am older I indulge my interest, giving in to the joy it brings me. When I feel tangled and tense, I get out my history of architecture and design books and set my eyes on the kinds of spaces and arenas that make sense to me; the linear, the straight lined and the level buildings that paint pictures of strong balance" (Willey,2015, p. 61).

However, Jim had worked in construction as a young man, so these details could conceivably have meant more to him than to the average visitor, even without the Asperger's aspect, so I was interested in his obvious enjoyment of the design of the building, not reading more into it.

The van arrived, and the guide told us the history of the pueblo on the way up the mesa. As we reached the top and were shown around the village, Jim was fascinated by the way the old church and homes were built of adobe, stucco, and mud. We bought a few pieces of pottery from residents who shared tables of their wares. Bowls of soup at the café in the Visitor Center before heading home tasted good.

After hot tubbing that night, we put on our robes, and I sat at my computer to show Jim some pictures of my family, at his request. He stood behind me, and after a few minutes, he said, "I think I've seen enough pictures. Let's do some huggin' and chalkin'."

What?

I was shocked, because nothing romantic had been talked about, nor acted upon, during the entire visit – we had talked a lot, had fun, and become better acquainted, but not so much as a hug had taken place. I knew what he meant, because "Huggin' and Chalkin'" was a song popular in our pre-adolescent years in the late 40s, made famous by Hoagy Carmichael.

Jim took my hand. "Let's go sit on the couch."

We did, and he took me in his arms and kissed me for the first time. I had not been kissed like that in a long time. It was magical. I had feelings I thought were long gone, but as he hugged me, I grasped the collars of his terry cloth robe and pulled him closer. I felt like a teenager.

He said, "I think we should link up our lives."

I thought I was hearing things.

"I'll move to Albuquerque to be with you." Another kiss, a tighter embrace.

I pulled back, feeling things were going pretty fast.

"My house is too small and my garage is too small for all our cars. The extra ones won't even fit in my driveway."

He said, "I'll sell the two little sports cars."

I was stunned, because I knew they were his treasures. I thought in the heat of the moment he didn't realize what he was saying. The wine in the hot tub earlier might have played a part. What he was saying sounded out of character for the conservative Republican I thought I knew, who needed time to process information – at least about debt – but apparently, other things moved through his mind at a quicker pace.

I tried to put on the brakes. "You need to think about that statement. We will talk later about that."

"After the great time I've had visiting you," he said, "I can't do without you."

I was still reeling from his ardor and his talk of what sounded like marriage. After spending a fun few days together, we were definitely becoming bonded. We kissed again, and he pulled me to a standing position, took my arm, and said, "Let's go where it's more comfortable."

That night, for the first time, we shared a bed.

CHAPTER 13

DAZED

The next morning, we lingered over breakfast and coffee. Jim's flight was at noon. We talked more about the prospect of joining our lives. We realized we were in love, but I said we had to go slowly. We had to figure out the financial picture, figure out many other things, and get to know each other better. We had gotten to know each other through emails and phone calls during the past four months, and had finally met in person and spent only a little over five days together. That two people could communicate, meet once, fall in love, and already be talking about possible marriage seemed unbelievable. There seemed to be no "red flags." However, moving so fast made me nervous. This time it was I who needed time to process information.

Jim said, "I want you to come to Pendleton in April." I said I would. A month seemed so far away.

If I had been alert to his Asperger's traits, this would have been another one. Aspies looking for a companion often move quickly, from dating to talk of marriage (Attwood, 2008, pp. 304-306). They are on a mission toward a goal to finding a suitable companion, and when they feel they have met the right person, they think their mission is accomplished, and move on quickly toward either marriage or living together.

We kissed goodbye at the airport. He said, "I love you, my Dudette," and held me close.

"I love you, too."

I teared up, because I knew I would miss this fun, handsome, kind, understanding man. I waved to him as he went through security, and as long as we could see each other.

I left the airport in a daze. His Dudette? Was this real? Did he really love me? And was I in love with someone for the first time since Paul's death?

My reactions and emotions surprised me. I knew I was falling for Jim. He seemed to be all I wanted in a companion. He was willing to move to Albuquerque. Was I willing to move to Oregon? I felt I might be, if that was what would work best. Even that surprised me, because Albuquerque was my home, and I owned a business here. Lots of things to think about and discuss and decide.

I had a hard time going to sleep that night. I kept thinking about the huggin' and chalkin' session the night before, and what the future might hold.

CHAPTER 14

SEEKING ANOTHER OPINION

After Jim's visit and before mine, I sought out another appraisal, which may seem strange to those who know me, but do not know everything about me. I saw an ad for a local psychic, and I wondered what she might have to say.

Adventurous, I made an appointment. I didn't know her, and she didn't know me. She had no way of knowing what was going on in my life.

As I sat across from her at her dining table, a cat jumped into my lap. The woman began to deal Tarot cards and interpret them. I'd never seen that done. As she spoke, her voice became sing-song. I listened carefully. She said I'd been through a life change, had lost someone important. I gave no sign of recognition. One card indicated I had met someone, someone who had been in the Navy, and she said I would live in another state with him and he would be the source of great happiness. She said his personality was not like the person I had lost, but he was honest and open, and had good qualities. She saw a future of learning for both of us.

My time was up, I paid her, and walked out to the car wondering how she could know all that. Would I have felt differently if she had said I was mixed up with an unsavory character and should flee? I'm not sure. All I knew was that there was enough in the mix to make me believe she really did see things I couldn't. And she saw no red flags.

I told Jim about my meeting with her, and suggested we have our horoscopes drawn. He agreed, and we did. It seemed the stars agreed with our future together. To me, it was an entertaining thing to do, but I still felt we had to be cautious as we continued the steps of getting to know each other.

CHAPTER 15

PREPPING FOR MY VISIT

After Jim got to Pendleton, each of his emails ended with professions of love. Our emails were much less formal, more intimate, and he continued to keep me laughing.

Relatives and friends asked for details about the visit. They got some details, not all.

I sent a letter to my children. I wrote, "Jim and I had such a good time together. It was a lovely visit, all I'd hoped for, and more. Jim is eager for me to visit him in April. I will fly into Portland, and we will sight-see across the northern part of Oregon, on the way to Pendleton."

Jim told his family, "She likes watching football on TV, pro and college, and presented me with a Ducks flag she bought on eBay. She has a guitar, cooks pretty well, has a hot tub and loves tubbing . . . so we have similar tastes. She is a shorty, but sometimes good things come in little packages. Has three children and some grandkids, and is what you would expect of a long-married 72-year-old. Also likes gin and tonic. WOW!"

A few days after Jim left, I received a greeting card from him. The front was a picture of a little girl and a little boy kissing, and inside it said, "I needed ya. I got ya. I'm keeping ya. Love ya, Jim." It is framed and sitting on my bookcase shelf today. If I were a teenager, it is one of those things I'd put into my treasure box and keep forever. As I say, when joking about my future, "That's one of the things I'm taking to the nursing home with me!"

I kept telling Jim marriage was not inevitable. "I think we need to take it slowly and think this through." Rushing into things seemed premature and unwise. I told him I was buying a ticket to Portland for April 16th.

His response, "Yabba-dabba-do!"

During that visit, I wanted to see him in his own environment and find out all I could about him. I was still looking for differences that would indicate our relationship might be problematic. The connection seemed too good to be true.

I questioned Jim some before my visit to Pendleton, "Have you thought about all that's at stake – your privacy, finances, blending of lifestyles and families? No need spending time, energy, and money flying back and forth, if you have doubts. I consider my visit another opportunity to get acquainted, and nothing is to be assumed about the future. My goal is to find the best, most compatible companion, and I think I've made that clear. However, each of us has to feel the same about a potential step into a different life."

Perhaps evading my query, giving him time to process, Jim sent me this response: "I was going to get out the lawnmower and terrorize the lawn, while soaking in the sunny weather. But oops, it's raining and cloudy . . . so, now what to do? How about some music from the CD shelf? I found some empty cases. That led me to search for the CDs, and I found old catalogs, phone books, and general debris. So, I am in cleanup mode, requiring a trip to the recycle center. I am living in the now. It's too late to start another project, so after I finish this email, it's time for a bit of cherry brandy while I play a few games of Spider Solitaire, which I do most nights. It has a calming influence on me – sometimes frustrating, but mostly calming."

I smiled at the visual image he had constructed to lighten the atmosphere, and I found the whole paragraph amusing, as well as a transparent attempt to get off the "where-to-live" and "what am I doing?" subjects.

Something I still did not pick up on was his nightly Spider Solitaire games, which he said had a "calming influence." Certain behaviors, almost ritual-like, called "stimming," serve as regulators, to calm overwhelming emotions. Hand-flapping, foot-tapping, video games, or simple repetitive behaviors such as crinkling pop or beer cans, rattling ice in glasses of drinks, or playing the same game over and over are examples of stimming (Falk & Schofield, 2018, pp. 35, 40-41; Hendrickx & Newton, 2007, pp. 35-36; Higashida, 2016, p. 68; Silberman, 2015, p. 195; Solomon, 2013, p. 222).

If I had been looking for Asperger's traits (which I obviously wasn't), I might have seen a connection between my questioning and an indication that Jim was experiencing emotional discomfort. He stated he played Spider Solitaire "most nights," which also might indicate he often felt overwhelmed by emotions – sadness, loneliness, depression, indecision, fear, abandonment. Even his choice of a part-time job, janitorial work, to help with family finances, could have been a form of stimming (sweeping and mopping, dusting, cleaning toilets – all repetitive tasks), helping him discharge pent-up emotions over the relatively recent marital separation and divorce (Lipsky, 2011, pp. 76-78).

A few days before I was to leave for Portland, I got a greeting card in the mail, saying how much he was looking forward to my visit, with this note: "This card is a softening-up technique used by all axe murderers, and I didn't want to get out of profile."

The night before I left, Jim called. "I invite you to my hot tub party, which begins at 8:00 p.m. tomorrow. That's after the pizza and wine. I have an Oregon Ducks ball cap for you, so we can tour in the red machine one day and wave to the town's Oregon State Beaver fans! I should get to the airport about 1:00, depending on traffic, and will try to be at the arrival area. If you get in before I get there, we can meet on the concrete bridge that connects the terminal with the parking garage. Tonight I've watched *The Quiet Man,* with John Wayne and Maureen O'Hara . . . fantastic movie, perhaps one of Wayne's best. It was a great day in the late afternoon, sunny and temps in the mid-50s, big clouds causing light shadows on the hills. Very peaceful and great to be alive. Get a good night's sleep and have a good trip."

Sounded like a good meeting plan, but . . .

CHAPTER 16

A ROCKY ARRIVAL

I walked through security and expected to see Jim. I didn't see him. I went to baggage claim. Still no sign of Jim. I saw a sign, "Parking Garage," with an arrow. Revolving doors led me to the concrete bridge, and I felt he would be waiting there. He wasn't.

I leaned against the decorative wrought-iron bridge railing and waited for what seemed like a long time, maybe 20 minutes. I wondered what had happened – had we gotten our wires crossed about the time, or the day, or had Jim had car trouble or an accident on his way to Portland? It was a little over 200 miles from Pendleton, and a lot could happen during a three-and-a-half-hour drive. I ached to get in touch with him, but he didn't have a cell phone.

Who doesn't have a cell phone these days? Frustration mounted, but all I could do was wait.

I longed for something or someone familiar, so I called Nancy and said, "I'm here at the airport in Portland, but Jim isn't. I feel like Meg Ryan in *Sleepless in Seattle*."

What if Jim had decided he didn't want me to visit? What if he had changed his mind? What if he wasn't who I thought he was? Meg's thoughts. Nancy said she was sure he'd be there soon. I was comforted, hearing her voice, then . . .

Jim burst out of the revolving doors.

A quick, "He's here!" to Nancy, and a quick click off.

Jim came up to me, hugged and kissed me.

"I forgot there are two concrete bridges. I always go in on the other one, and I've been waiting there. After a while it dawned on me that you might be here."

I looked across an open expanse, to the other end of the terminal far in the distance, and there was, indeed, another concrete bridge on the other end of the building that also connected to the parking garage.

"Sorry I wasn't on time to meet you at baggage claim, but glad you're here."

We got into his comfortable, gray, 1997 Buick LeSabre and drove to an Applebee's for lunch before heading to Pendleton. Our cheerful banter over our Oriental chicken salads made up for the mix-up in our meeting. The day was sunny and bright, as were our spirits. We were together again.

We got onto I-84 heading east, and soon came to Multnomah Falls. A magnificent sight! A passerby took our picture by the sign. We were running later getting back to Pendleton than he'd expected, because of the mishap at the airport, so some of the sites he wanted to show me, he pointed out as we passed, and said, "We'll see them close-up another time."

We drove east along the gorge, beside the wide Columbia River. Except for the Mississippi, this was the widest expanse of river I'd ever seen. Dozens of huge wind turbines marched along the wide banks of the gorge. We soon headed southeast from the river, passing vast wheat and hops fields to our left, and copses of young trees in rows to the right.

Late in the afternoon, Jim said, "Now look, when we top this hill – the center of western civilization! Ta-da!"

We rounded a curve, and in the valley, between hills and wheat fields to the north and the Blue Mountains to the south, lay a small settlement, Pendleton. My eyes were wide, and my heart fluttered. *This may be my home someday.*

Jim said the population is normally about 17,000. Even though I thought of Pendleton as a small town, that is about ten times the size of the little Texas town where I grew up, even counting the years of the oil boom. He added that in September, when the annual Round-Up takes place, the town holds five to six times the normal number. I wondered how the little valley, long, but narrow, could accommodate that many people.

On the way into town, he pointed out the prison, the junior college, the courthouse, the church, the post office, and Main Street. I tried to absorb what he was showing and telling me – the courthouse building, where he worked, which also housed the library; the church, where we would go on Sunday. He drove up Main Street, to show me the downtown area – a Penney's, several restaurants, and a few small stores. We stopped at Papa Murphy's to pick up our pizza for dinner. I had the warm box in my lap the rest of the way to his house.

I was eager to see where he lived. I'd seen pictures, but not the real thing, and not inside the house. On Main Street, we drove north this time, and over a bridge. "The Umatilla River," he said. "It runs through town."

We approached a steep hill, still on Main Street, but now a residential area. Main Street dead ended at the top of the hill, and Jim turned west, onto Johns Lane. The houses were newer than most of the ones we'd passed.

"Get ready," Jim said; then, "Here we are."

He drove down into the steep driveway and parked. It was dusk, and from where I sat, all I could see was the front yard. Jim got my suitcase out of the trunk, and we walked down many steps beside the garage, ending up on a wooden deck. I saw the hot tub to my left, and the front door directly in front of me. Jim opened it and ushered me into the foyer.

I was stunned by the beauty of the house, even before Jim turned on some lights. A lovely tiled foyer, with a high window overhead, facing into the living room below. Jim took me first down a long hall to our right and dropped off my suitcase into the guest room near the end. He said it used to be his daughter's room, and I saw a quaint, cozy, window seat facing the front yard, the kind almost anyone would like to curl up in and read. He showed me the master bedroom at the very end of the hall, a larger room. One wall was all windows, with a door that opened onto a small wooden deck overlooking the town below. I was in a different world. *Is this where I might live?* The master bath, a full bath, opened onto the room. Back down the hall, the guest bathroom was across from the guest bedroom. Jim pointed out a linen closet, and another bedroom on our left, used as an office, where he had his desk and computer. I saw where his many emails to me had been composed, and where he played Spider Solitaire. The laundry room, across the hall from the office, had decidedly dated 1970s macramé patterned wallpaper, the only wallpaper I'd seen.

We were again at the foyer. To our right, five steps led down to the large living room, with more windows than I'd ever seen in one room. Windows dominated the west and south walls, except for the brick fireplace. Jim told me he built the fireplace and hearth. The south wall of windows showed the back yard, and the lights were coming on, far down in the downtown area where we'd just been. I stood in awe. A dark green leather couch and easy chair faced the fireplace, plus a few small tables, one holding an older television. The room dwarfed its furnishings. The west wall of this room had windows, too, plus French doors that led onto a large wooden deck with window seats all around. From the south edge of the deck, we could see 180 degrees – far to the west, south, and east. The panorama was mesmerizing. I'd never seen anything like this house!

We went back up the five steps to the foyer again, and on our immediate right was the dining room, with windows all across the south and east walls. Jim pointed to a beautiful rosewood dining table, with obvious pride. The door to the kitchen was on the north wall of the dining room, or the kitchen could be accessed directly from the foyer. It had 70s linoleum, a brown block pattern, with hints of green and yellow, and unusual cupboards, with doors, or coverings, that Jim told me were cantilevered and rolled up and down, like the covering on a roll-top desk. He demonstrated how one worked. The drawer fronts were 70s avocado. A window over the sink, on the east wall, overlooked the next-door neighbor's lawn. There was a slender window at the end of the cabinets on the north wall, and beneath it was a built-in table and bench, forming a dinette area. Opposite the bench was a matching chair. The narrow window looked out on the front deck and hot tub.

It was dinner time and we were hungry. I sat on the padded bench and watched Jim put the pizza into the oven. Jim poured each of us a glass of Riesling. We were both so glad to be together again. I told him how amazing his house was, and he told me it needed a woman's touch. I didn't comment that parts of it seemed devoid of color and warmth. I imagined the fireplace, when lighted, would add ambience and warmth. After pizza and wine, we put on our swimsuits and got into his hot tub, larger than mine, and a bit hotter.

We relaxed into the bubbling jets and warmth, held hands, and looked up at the stars. Below, we could see the city lights, but the stars and moon above us were our focus. We were where we belonged – together.

Jim got off work at noon the next day. He told me he had a daily habit of enjoying a lengthy tub bath after getting off work, both for cleanliness and for relaxation. Today he skipped the relaxation part, and just freshened up. We met

Jim's friends, Judy and Dale Wilkins, for lunch at the Red Lion Inn. When the discussion turned to football, I blurted out something about "all twelve men on the field." Of course, being a football fan, I knew better, but I was nervous, meeting these special friends, and I was embarrassed. Judy and Dale were gracious and made little of it. I was glad to meet Judy, and to put a face with Dale's name, since Jim had told me about his and Dale's clam-chowder-making partnership for the church's annual Soup Supper.

After we got back into the car to go home, I said, "I'm sorry I said 'twelve men on the field.' I think I was nervous. Did that embarrass you?"

Jim turned to me, took my hand in his, looked me in the eyes, and said, "Nothing you could ever do would embarrass me." I felt trusted and loved.

Since trust will play a part later in this book, now is a good time to say it is something that is difficult for many Aspies, because of having been bullied throughout life, and the lack of theory of mind. If a person has been abandoned or mistreated, it is not surprising that trust does not come easily (van der Kolk, 2014, p. 158). If they can't know what someone else is thinking, they are unable to gauge their intent, and they have difficulty knowing who to trust (Wylie, 2014, p. 39). However, over time, they can develop trust and feel secure with someone who is honest (Finch, 2012, pp. 219-220; Hendrickx & Newton, 2007, pp. 123-125; Stanford, 2015, pp. 128, 204-205).

I was glad for a chance to see the layout of his home and yard in the bright afternoon light. He showed me the oversized garage, where he kept his two little cars, one red and one green. I got a close-up view of them and was promised some rides. I spied an axe with a long handle in one corner of the garage. I took Jim's picture holding it, and the mock portrayal of an "axe murderer" amused us.

We went to the church office one afternoon, where I met the church secretary and the pastor. We attended church Sunday, and I met a number of Jim's fellow church-goers. Jim introduced me to one stocky, gray-haired woman, and she raised her eyebrows when Jim said I was from New Mexico. Most people were friendly to me that morning, but I intuitively felt coolness from some. Apparently, few people knew about the southwestern woman in Jim's life. He was not one to broadcast his private life unless there was a reason for it. He was aware that news traveled quickly in that church, something I would learn later.

As we drove home, Jim said, "I hope you're not a bell-ringer. We have a handbell choir that plays sometimes, and the sound is an assault to my system."

Bogdashina cites Blakemore et al. (2006), suggesting that "autistic brains are 'tuned' to higher frequencies," and Bogdashina adds, "This 'higher-vibration' capacity of the senses goes parallel with the acute, often overwhelming sensitivities to sensory stimuli, when certain stimuli (which are different for different people) are very disturbing to individuals with autism" (2010, p. 167). This sensory aversion to high-pitched handbells could have been a clue to Asperger's, but I didn't catch that.

We packed sandwiches and ate while driving over to Wallowa Lake, a scenic area two hours east of town. On the way, Jim said, "I have a concern that you may have to give up too many things – friends, work, town – should we find we are right for each other, even if we split our time in each state. It surely would not be my intent to find you unhappy up here in the North."

I said, "Yes, I've thought of that. It does seem to be going well with us, and I ponder the future. I can be happy anywhere with the right person – it's not the environment, it's the person. We've talked about splitting the time – keeping my house and spending some time there and some time here, which might work out. I think it's unlikely you would ever want to move to Albuquerque permanently, as I know you love Oregon. I'm not ruling out spending all the time in Pendleton, because I think I can be content if we decide to marry and live here. I like things about every place Paul and I ever lived. I always look for the positives. I am resilient, and I feel a life companion of the right kind is much more important than the location."

Soon I could see granite cliffs towering above a lake among Ponderosa pines. Jim showed me the tram that took riders high up on the cliffs, a much smaller version of the tram in Albuquerque. We walked arm-in-arm to the lake's shore, where we stopped to look up and admire the cliffs. I was caught up in the beauty of the scene, like a photo from a travel magazine. Jim turned to me, took me into his arms, kissed me, and told me he loved me.

He said, "You add a new dimension to this place."

A delightful Sunday in Oregon!

One afternoon we drove out to snowy Westminster Woods, and he showed me the campground buildings he helped design and build. He designed the tall cathedral windows that took advantage of the magnificent pine trees outside the dining room/kitchen building.

We were the only ones around, so as we gazed at this inspiring setting, I said, "Jim, are you serious? Do you really love me and want to marry me?"

"Is there any doubt? I don't make commitments lightly, especially when it comes to a lifetime companion for the adventures of the world."

I said, "I am serious about commitments, too – to say I will love someone, honor them, care for them no matter what, for the rest of my life. I meant it at age 18 the first time, and if that's what we decide to do, I will mean it in my 70s for the second time. No difference."

We walked up to the camp chapel, which had walls of glass to connect people inside with the nature outside. I could see why Jim enjoyed working on the buildings and grounds of this place, in tune with The Man's handiwork.

During the week, we took walks around the neighborhood; we shopped at Safeway, where he did the silly walk again, while pushing the shopping cart, sending me into giggles; we ate spaghetti with Jim's special sauce and garlic-buttered French bread; we had ice cream cones at Dave's, a mainly teen hangout; we drove up Airport Road in the MGB and took the curves fast, a thrill like I'd never experienced; and we enjoyed a steak dinner at Hamley's Restaurant, after which he took me around the corner and showed me the Slickfork Saloon, to prove it really existed. Evenings were spent in the hot tub, gazing at the stars.

One evening in the hot tub, he said, "You may be a Democrat, but you are not a political liberal. You hold onto some basic truths about political standards of conduct and directions that continue the philosophies of our founding fathers. Based on your attitude and lifestyle, I think you are one who embraces generally conservative values."

I just listened, not wanting to get him started on a long discourse about politics. I knew he was interested in politics, and I would later learn that sometimes he exhibited that interest in a good way, but sometimes a way not so good.

Jim remembered I had mentioned I liked to play penny slots, and one afternoon he surprised me by driving to the Wildhorse Casino at the edge of town, without telling me where we were going. When he parked, he handed me a $20 bill. He didn't play, but sat on a stool beside mine, amidst the colorful, lighted slot machines with their clangy, rhythmic jingle. I asked if he wanted to play, and he said, "No, I get my thrills from watching you have fun."

After the $20 was gone, which didn't take long, he got up from his stool, took my hand, stood me up, held me close, and we danced between the aisles to whatever song was playing. We got some strange looks, but we didn't care. I was mesmerized by this man, as we danced out of the building into the sunlight, and drove to Burger King for a Whopper.

Soon it was time for the fairy tale to end. Neither of us was ready for the visit to be over. At the Portland airport, we had a goodbye kiss, I boarded, and was off to Albuquerque and ordinary life again. I felt as if I'd walked out of a dream.

The next night, Jim called and said, "Had a blast with you. Miss you already – just think of all the conversation we could have had in the hot tub tonight. As I sit here in my robe and reflect on my tub time tonight, with no wind and all the stars out ... would have been much better with you here with me. Look forward to making that arrangement permanent."

He said goodbye, then he started singing "I'm Just a Country Boy." He hung up, still singing...

CHAPTER 17

SOME FAMILY PLANS

I decided to print the application for Oregon counseling licensure to see what it would entail. Applying for reciprocity looked like a lot of work. If I ended up moving to Pendleton, I wanted another private practice, and obtaining an Oregon license was the beginning of a saga I could not then imagine.

Jim said, "How about another visit in early June? I can pick you up in Portland again, then head south from there to visit relatives. I even have a salmon dinner lined up at my sister's. How about that?"

That sounded great. I was glad I would meet his relatives. I had made it clear that I wanted him and my kids to meet, before any final plans were made. I told him I wanted to meet both his children, too, if we decided to blend families.

My girls had a family reunion planned for Fourth of July week, on the shore of Lake Michigan, I debated inviting Jim, but decided not to. I knew my kids were still grieving their dad, and maybe this reunion was to be a means of group closure. I felt putting Jim into the mix this early in our relationship would be a mistake. He seemed to understand.

Nancy called with details about the reunion. I told her Jim and I were getting more and more serious. She took it matter-of-factly – I expected her to be surprised, but my kids are smart, and they had to know all these cross-country visits were not just for something to do. I think they were all digesting what might happen, and were getting used to the idea of my finding happiness with another man. I told her I was not planning to invite Jim to the reunion, that I wanted it to be our family only.

The next night I had a call from Julie. "Whatever will make you happy, Mom, is fine with me, and I'm sure Jim is a nice guy or you wouldn't be interested in him."

I called Jim and shared all this, told him the girls said we were welcome to visit them when it was convenient, that they were looking forward to meeting him.

Jim said, "Pleased to hear your daughters apparently are comfortable with the direction you wish to go in your life. I sense these kinds of things are important to you."

"Yes, they are. While I'm independent and will ultimately do whatever I want to do, it's comforting to know my kids support me in major decisions."

Jim said, "Obviously, we both have to live our own dreams and hope all in both families receive our friendship as a positive. I'm sure all your kids miss their dad, and that's natural. However, life has to move on while encompassing those memories and weaving them into the present. I will look at coming to Albuquerque later in July, when you get back from your reunion. I can meet your son, Paul, at that time, or at a later time, if that's better. I am open to try to fit any workable schedule."

We tossed around whether he would meet Paul in July or wait until later. I mentioned it several times. No decision was made. Jim said he needed time to think about it.

If I had been thinking about Asperger's, even in the back areas of my mind, I might have recognized the trait of needing processing time, since Jim needed time "to think about it." Processing time, thinking time, is required for most Aspies before they commit to a decision (Hendrickx & Newton, 2007, p. 107-109; Higashida, 2016, pp. 12, 18). "Making quick changes looks like a non-autistic way of thinking; we are deep thinkers and need processing time to make changes" (Maguire, in Attwood et al., 2014, p. 66).

"It seems a long time until your visit in June . . . about 25 days . . . hard to wait, so looks like we will have to get down to brass tacks and solve the problem permanently," Jim said on the phone. "Mary Muffin, I wish you were here to watch a movie with me. Work today was the usual scenario, standing for six hours with two ten-minute sit-down breaks. My legs and feet don't tolerate that well, and as a consequence I have leg and foot pain constantly. I enjoy my long, soaking tub baths after work. They help relax my muscles. Sometimes muscle cramps wake me in the night, and I have to get up and walk them off."

"Sorry about your muscle cramps. I was awakened last night by a noise outside. I got up to check on things, found nothing out of the ordinary, went to the bathroom (which I normally do at least once in the middle of the night – you need to know that), then got back into bed and went to sleep."

Jim's muscle cramps and my nocturnal trips to the bathroom will be worth remembering. I had no idea at that time, the part they'd play.

Jim worked it out to be able to meet Paul in July.

"I learned from our phone session the importance you place on this meeting. When I realized how important it was, then I was sold, and all I had to do was make the arrangements. I told you I am weird. An idea is floated, I mull it around in my head, take a position that fits *my* thoughts . . . discover that perhaps it has a higher priority to a soulmate or friend . . . then change my position. If I didn't want to do it, I can assure you I am stubborn enough not to do it. I don't do anything I don't want to do."

I said, "Your willingness to come meet my son says a lot about you and your love for me. I hope you know I appreciate your gesture of kindness and love."

As I've said, people with Asperger's generally do not process ideas as quickly as neurotypicals. Slower processing means slower responses. I could have realized that if I had been looking for Asperger's, but I didn't, because I wasn't. I was in love.

I got an email from Jim, "Haha! I wrote more emails today than you! I beat you!"

I wrote back, "Is this a competition or a collaborative effort? Mull that one over, my friend!"

This would not be the first time Jim exhibited a competitive spirit during our friendship. Because of being the victims of bullying and teasing, Aspies often compensate by wanting to be in control, to win, and I failed to pick up on that trait (Stanford, 2015, pp. 202, 209). Playing as a team, or going along with a committee, isn't usually one of their strong points. This is one reason many Aspies have trouble in an employment setting when group projects are required (Grossberg, 2015, pp. 34-35). They prefer to compete on their own. An example of disagreeing with a committee will show up later.

Jim had humorous forms of competitive behavior. Sometimes at lunch, he finished his sandwich before I did, and said, "Ha-ha, I finished before you did!" If he looked out the window and saw our next-door neighbor mowing his lawn, Jim would say, "Can't let him get ahead of me." Soon I would hear the whirr of our lawnmower. I knew Jim was outside in competitive mode.

Toward time for my second visit to Oregon, Jim said, "Soon I get to go to Portland and pick up this babe, then whisk her away to Oregon's southland. I miss you hourly. I seek you as a partner in my life in every way, and I love you more day by day. Have a great day tomorrow, move into it gently, and thank The Man for it."

I said, "See you before long. I'm excited!"

CHAPTER 18

A BETTER AIRPORT RECEPTION

My second arrival at Portland's airport was better than the first – Jim was there, leaning against a pillar and grinning, as I came out of security. We fell into each other's arms, so glad to be together again.

On that bright June day, we drove down I-5, through Eugene, stopping at Applebee's for our Oriental chicken salads, then talked while driving farther south to meet some of Jim's family. Jim said it didn't look as if it would work out to meet his daughter anytime soon.

I said, "I will do whatever you think best about meeting your daughter – it would be nice to drive up to her place in Washington and see that part of the country. I think if you and I are thinking about sharing the rest of our lives, it's important to meet each other's kids, and for them to meet us. I don't look at it as seeking their approval, just as being courteous and getting acquainted."

"I must comment about meeting my kids," Jim said. "It's interesting that my kids have not expressed an interest in meeting a potential partner to their parent as have yours. Now we can guess as to the reasons for this, and perhaps, due to your career field, you will have some answers. Could it be that you and Paul bonded better with your kids than my spouse and I did? Or one reason I hope is not the case, 'Is my personality somewhat intimidating to my kids so they won't express what they think in this area?' My philosophy is kind of heavy toward individuality, and perhaps that doesn't bode too well for family bonding. Who knows? Perhaps I intellectualize too much. I appreciate your candor and honesty in this and in a general sense – a trait I am not used to from some of the people closest to me in my life. Anyway, none of this discussion is a problem to me, and your way is likely the way to proceed. Your analysis gave me a bit more insight as to where you were coming from, when you said it was not for their approval, but as a courtesy."

Emotional bonding may be more difficult for some persons with Asperger's, since many say they enjoy more alone time and enjoy solitary pursuits. Aspies often have trouble even identifying their emotions, and expressing them is difficult. Also, emotional bonding is often difficult for persons who have experienced betrayal and/or abandonment by persons close to them, especially early in life (Finch, 2012, p. 56; Goleman, 2007, pp. 112-116, 177; Karen, 1998, pp.397-398; Robison, 2008, p. 13; Siegel, 2015, p. 353; Wylie, 2014, p. 58). Carley, an Aspie, lists a common feeling expressed by Aspies in his experience, "The realization that there has always been a gulf between you and your loved ones" (Carley, 2008, p. 45).

Bennett-Goldman comments on qualities of clients she's had who have a strong fear of abandonment. "Underneath the desperate attempt to be rescued that many people feel who have this emotional pattern runs a panic so severe that it feels like a fight for life, a fear of being extinguished" (Bennett-Goldman, 2001, p. 85). Any, or all, of these factors could have played a part in Jim's "philosophy of individuality."

We stayed with his older sister, a gracious hostess. As Jim and I stood chatting in her kitchen the next morning, side by side, with our arms around each other, I laughingly made a wisecrack answer to Jim, saying he couldn't control what I do. His sister commented that it seemed Jim had met his match.

Later in the day, Jim and I went to visit his younger sister and her husband. I was greeted with open arms and felt very welcome. His sister served us delicious huckleberry pie – something I'd never had. I confessed I didn't know huckleberries were real – I always thought "Huckleberry Hound" was just a made-up alliterative reference to a cartoon character. Everyone laughed at my naiveté.

That afternoon, Jim and I went across town to visit his son and family. I got a warm welcome with hugs as soon as I stepped out of the car. I felt everyone approved of me and was glad Jim had found someone with whom he was comfortable.

Jim took me to the town's cemetery, at my request, so I could "meet" his mother and stepfather. We wandered around the picturesque cemetery and found their graves. I felt honored to be on hallowed ground there. I'm sure I would have loved those people who raised Jim.

On the way back to Pendleton, Jim took the scenic route to Crater Lake National Park, Oregon's only national park. At the visitor center, I bought a book about pioneer women and their trials. Afterward, a grumpy passerby took our picture, though it was windy and we looked cold. When we tried to drive around the lake, the road was closed because of snow and ice. This was unusual to a woman from the southwest – snow on the roads in June? We went a different way, to Diamond Lake, and over to Bend. We had lunch at Pine Tavern, the restaurant with two large ponderosa pines growing inside the dining room, and picturesque views of the river along the back lawn of the building.

As we drove on to Pendleton, with our hands laced together, we talked about marriage in concrete terms for the first time. I silently admired Jim's strong, sturdy hands. I told him I would not change my name, since I used it professionally. He had no problem with that. Marriage was no longer a fantasy, but a real plan. Jim was tired of living apart, and so was I. We decided October would be the wedding month, since son Paul would be in the states then. I wanted all our children to be at the wedding. I did not want to be the cause of Jim's missing a Ducks football game, so I made a private note to myself to check to see if the Ducks had an off weekend in October. Details began to take shape.

We arrived in Pendleton late Saturday, and went to church on Sunday and the annual June Cruisin' car show downtown in the afternoon. I met many of Jim's car enthusiast friends and enjoyed visiting and looking at all the cars on display. Salmon dinner at Raphael's restaurant topped off the evening. Later, we watched the full moon and city lights from Jim's hot tub. Love was in full bloom.

Monday and Tuesday were spent sleeping late, eating leisurely breakfasts, and having unending discussions. Jim took his beloved long tub baths to prepare his muscles for the days of activity – silly walking in Safeway, making his spaghetti sauce, baking his coffee cake, zooming around in the little cars, and talking more about wedding plans.

I said, "I might start preparing to get my Oregon counseling license." I was licensed in New Mexico at the highest level, and had been licensed a number of years, so I was not concerned about becoming licensed in Oregon as well. Jim said it should be no problem, as he got his insurance adjuster's license in neighboring Washington without a hitch. How could applying for licensing become a big issue?

Jim said, "I think I said something about our developing chemistry. I was wrrrooonnng. I think that's how you say that last word. It's so seldom applicable to, or used by me, that it is difficult to say. I now see that the term 'developing chemistry' does not apply, as we already *have* the chemistry. We arc on a journey of discovery, with new adventures around every corner. By the way, I dropped eHarmony some time ago. Mission accomplished."

While Jim said "wrong" was a difficult word for him, I took his explanation as humor, but I was to learn that it was extremely rare for him to admit he was wrong – about anything. The trait of perfectionism makes it difficult for Aspies to admit they are wrong. Attwood explains over-compensation for feelings of incompetence in social situations brings forth an arrogant manner. "[The person with Asperger's] goes into what I describe as 'God mode,' an omnipotent person who never makes a mistake, cannot be wrong" (Attwood, 2008, p. 26). Their brains are wired for them to think they are right about everything, and many of them rarely apologize for anything. They cannot be wrong, never make mistakes, use intimidation and arrogance and inflexible attitude to achieve authority and control (Hendrickx & Newton, 2007, p. 107). In an attempt to cover up their feelings of inferiority, they attempt superiority (Dubin, 2009, p. 21). Some are perceived as arrogant, and, in fact, much later, one of my friends said she saw Jim as arrogant before she got to know him.

Jim said his "mission was accomplished." To him, this meant he had managed to be attentive and mask his Aspieness long enough to win me (Attwood, in Murray, Ed., 2006, pp. 45-46). Attwood quoted one woman, who said of her partner, "He had won the prize and didn't have to pretend any more" (Attwood, 2008, p. 306). I had no idea of the import of those words at that time. Aspies can be successful at controlling their traits for periods of time in order to reach a goal.

Jim invited me, as his Dudette, to visit again in September for Round-Up, the annual Pendleton event of rodeos, parades, dances, and western dramas. At the airport, the goodbyes were tortuous – they got harder with every visit. I boarded the plane with tears, although I knew I'd see him again in a month, when he came to meet Paul.

When I got home, Jim's email was waiting for me. "I'm back from Portland, pizza is in the oven and beer in hand. WANT YA, MISS YA, LOVE YA! I'll call later. Lonely Jim"

I told my kids, "I know it will be hard on you in many ways to meet Jim, but I think you will like him. There is no intention of his being a substitute for your dad, but a companion for me. My relationship with your dad was a totally different part of my life. I think life has different eras, and I see a new one beginning, which I believe will be a good one, too."

And thus I moved on to a new era.

CHAPTER 19

ALWAYS ON MY MIND

I finished reading the book I bought at Crater Lake, about women in wagon trains, and found it fascinating. I thought of my great-grandmother, who came from Texas to New Mexico in a covered wagon with her husband and three children, one of whom was my grandmother. I'm sure that was a harder trip than I can even imagine.

Jim said, "We have two interpretive centers relating to the Oregon Trail, less than a hundred miles from Pendleton. We can go there when you visit in September. I am a bit lonely tonight. I'll look forward to sharing dinners and movies with you after we're married."

I said, "Companionship means having home be a refuge and a haven for both – a place to look forward to, after a day's work, knowing someone will care how you feel and be supportive. At least, that's how I've always felt about married life."

Jim said, "Yes, home is where the heart is. It is also the place, as you say, to communicate and commiserate with the main one in your life . . . takes the edge off things and makes you realize you have it made. I think having a spouse be one's 'very best friend' encompasses all of the traits you mentioned."

I said, "Being best friends describes it all – the one you want to confide in, share with, care for, and be close to. When

I was a little girl, my dentist had a wooden plaque on the wall in front of the chair with a picture of a little child (androgynous, dressed in blue overalls with long golden curls) standing beside a big collie, and the words, 'A friend is someone who knows all about you and loves you just the same.' That memory, both visual and verbal, has stayed with me all these years. That is my definition of the perfect companion. I look forward to seeing you after I arrive home from the family reunion. Paul will get here the next day. I'll have time to get the liver and onions on to cook so they'll be ready for you. Oh, never fear – Paul doesn't like them either, so you're doubly safe. Hope you have a nice Father's Day!"

My telling Jim that "having home be a refuge and a haven" probably was appealing to him, as Aspies like to have a place where they can be themselves (Castleman, in Attwood et al., 2014, p. 195). "In order for a person with [Asperger's] to lead a happy life, he must have a soft place to fall, a home, a refuge, and a comfort zone where his [Aspieness] is respected" (Stanford, 2015, p. 56).

One day I told Jim a tenant in my office building had her tiny baby, with the sweet name, Bristol, there, and I asked if I could hold her. I attended a friend's funeral in the afternoon.

Jim amazed me with his perspective, "I am interested in your report on your day. Holding a friend's baby (new life) and afterward going to a friend's funeral (passing life). The transition periods of life from start to finish. Interesting – the continuum of life." How perceptive and philosophical of him to connect those events. His insights ran deep!

Jim asked me to verify the August dates lined up for the trip east to meet my girls and their families, as he needed to get the dates locked down on the calendar at work. I sent them, and Jim wrote, "Thanks for the info – now one more game of Spider Solitaire for this white-knuckle flyer before bed."

Was he needing to play Spider Solitaire as a stimming activity to alleviate his anxiety about flying? I didn't know it then, but I'm sure for a white-knuckle flyer, traveling to Albuquerque, Illinois, Michigan, back to Albuquerque, and then back to Oregon was a daunting and anxiety-producing prospect for him. By using "Spider Solitaire" and "white-knuckle flyer" in the same sentence, he even unwittingly connected the stim and the flights for me!

I said, "I talked to a preacher, whom I've known for years, and he said he will be honored to marry us on October 18th. He wanted to know all about you, so I told him you are an axe murderer, but I love you anyway and am willing to take my chances."

"So, you think October 18th is the bingo date?" Jim said. "But what if the Ducks are playing? Will you have a big screen TV there? Oh yeah, I forgot, need a kegger, too."

I said, "The Ducks are open that week – I already checked. Really! Do you think I'd plan our wedding and make you miss a Ducks game? You underestimate me. Come to think of it, you've never actually *asked* me to marry you . . . kind of like you're assuming I'd say 'yes.'"

Jim is astonished. "You're serious? You mean you checked the Ducks schedule for the 18th? Even if it were a Ducks game weekend, do you really think that would matter? I am a fan, but some things are worth more than a game. I love you, and yes, we will marry. Have a good day on the airship tomorrow, heading for Michigan to your family reunion. You probably will, 'cause you aren't a chicken like me. I spent some time this afternoon hitting the song videos on the computer. I miss you – you are, to me, just like the song Willie Nelson sings, 'Always on My Mind.'"

CHAPTER 20

FAMILY TIMES, PLANS, AND MEMORIES

My three children, their spouses, my grandchildren, and I stayed in a large beach house, on the eastern shore of Lake Michigan, with abundant sleeping rooms for everyone, as well as several large rooms for gathering and visiting. The girls had chosen a beautiful site for the family reunion, just steps from the beach.

I wasn't sure how things would go. Husband Paul had been gone three and a half years, and I didn't know whether to talk about Jim or not. I knew my children were still in various stages of grieving and might resent my injecting conversation about Jim into the event. We played both indoor and outdoor games, worked jigsaw puzzles, talked, walked down the road to the ice cream shop, went to the beach, and fought mosquitos. We assigned meal prep and cleanup duties.

I called Jim and said I was nervous about the whole get-together. Only one person had mentioned Jim privately, and after I answered a question, nothing more was said. It was the best example of the "elephant in the room" phenomenon I'd ever experienced.

Jim said, "We will create a new family and social ties, unique to us. It will be a different relationship from the past with your family and also with mine – not better or worse, just different. I look forward to that, and I think you do, too."

I said, "You put it so eloquently and sweetly. Yes, we will create a new family dynamic and interact in different ways with your family and mine, but you and I will be our own family."

Jim said, "Life is a series of passages or transitions. I intend to continue the passages, live in the now, and enjoy each day."

I said, "You are good for me in so many ways – I love you, Jim Hanks. I went to an outlet mall with the girls today, and I found the perfect dress for our wedding. It's exactly what I had in mind."

"Glad you found the ultimate dress for the big event. Sometimes things just fall into place. I have confirmed with my boss about the August dates to visit your daughters and families. I will just have to clamp my teeth and go on a few of those infamous flying machines."

I said, "Speaking of teeth, you said you were going to the dentist. How was that?"

Jim said, "It was okay, but at some time in the not-too-distant future I will have to have the remaining teeth pulled, as the enamel is giving way. I am also a chicken at the dentist."

Being a chicken at the dentist could have indicated anxiety associated with anything medical, a trait of some Aspies, as I've discussed earlier.

All in all, the reunion turned out to be a special time of interacting with each family member there, making treasured memories. It was our last time together as a large Johnson family, before Jim officially became a part of it.

After I got home from the reunion, I picked Jim up at the airport early that evening. Paul got to Albuquerque the next day. Jim and Paul met cordially and got acquainted, we went out for Mexican dinner, and they seemed to enjoy each other right away. Both had similar senses of humor, and they acted as if they were old friends. Jim left the next morning, and Paul left the next day. I so appreciated Jim's respect of my wanting them to meet, and his effort to make it happen, and I told him so.

Our trip to Chicago and Detroit to visit the girls and their families was arranged. Conservative Jim said, "When you reserve a rental vehicle in Illinois, check the price on a motorcycle and a sidecar . . . I can borrow an old motorcycle jacket!"

"I'm ignoring the motorcycle request, although I give you points for being hilarious. On to more practical things. I'll make an appointment with the preacher for a meeting with him when you're here, before we leave for Illinois.

Jim said, "I've asked my son to be my best man."

I responded, "I'm so glad – that will be perfect."

I mentioned, "I got the box of husband Paul's clothes ready to ship to a friend in Tucson, who will make quilts from them for my kids. Going through the clothes was emotionally draining."

Jim said, "Yes, sorting things brings back memories. This helps to put life and the transitions into a better perspective. It is the design of The Man. You are special to me, special enough to marry and spend the rest of my life with. My love for you might be expressed differently than you are used to. I am not as well versed in expressing that in words as you are, but I am working on it."

Another reference by Jim to his feeling inadequate about expressing his emotions in words. As I've said, Aspies often have trouble even recognizing their emotions, and it is sometimes difficult for them to put their feelings into words.

Jim said, "I see our wedding as an enjoyable gathering celebrating a new beginning. I count you as my very best friend and lover. I miss you. My laid-back approach to life can take you off the squirrel cage and allow you to kick back and smell the roses. Our pairing is complementary, as you can motivate me not to be a bump on a log. Now I need to hit the sack. The 4:30 alarm comes pretty early, especially when I wake up every time the air conditioner cycles."

"You must be a *very* light sleeper."

"Yes, I am. Hugs and kisses for the Muffin. I love you."

In one study, as many as 70% of Aspies reported sleep problems (Wylie, 2014, p. 48). Many Aspies have issues involving falling asleep, and staying asleep (Grossberg, 2015, pp. 84-85).

Jim's being a light sleeper would eventually cause a problem.

CHAPTER 21

VISITING THE GIRLS

Three days before he was to fly to Albuquerque to start our trip to the Midwest, Jim said, "My long hours at work, plus working on this hillside lawn for four hours, did a trip on my knee yesterday afternoon. When I quit and came in for lunch, the knee hurt, and it was difficult to put weight on it. I thought hydrotherapy would help, so I hit the bathtub and hot water. Afterward I hit it with an ice pack. Helps the pain and also the mobility. I plan to stay off it all day."

"Maybe you should get in with your doc and see what he/she thinks."

"Well, Ms. Muffin, I don't have a doc. Up here in the north we rely on home remedies. Besides, if you go to a doc, he or she might tell you something you don't want to hear. Besides, the knee is just a natural universal joint so all you do when it wears down is apply gear grease. I definitely need to be in shape for the great trek to Albuquerque, Chicago, and Detroit."

"You might consider a cane for the airport."

"I might. Canes allow you to look like an older, distinguished gentleman of stature and wealth – and might attract a babe or two."

I overlooked the comment about attracting babes, Jim's knee improved, and he assured me he'd be on schedule for our trip.

This may be as good a place as any to talk about water, and its effect on the senses, since Jim mentioned hydrotherapy. I've already said that Jim liked tub baths – long, relaxing tub baths – but not showers. I mentioned his preference once, and he said he didn't like water hitting him from above, especially on his face (Attwood, 2008, p. 281). A couple of other Aspies mention water. One says he has a fascination with water, as if it's a primeval connection. "In the water it's so quiet and I'm so free and happy there. . . it's as if we've got all the time in the world. . . when we're in the water we can really be at one with the pulse of time" (Higashida, 2016, p. 71).

"I loved the sensation that came from floating with the water. The water was solid and strong" and "Water continued to enchant and calm me" (Willey, 2015, pp. 28, 35).

Another says water hurts, is painful when it hits his body. "For someone not on the spectrum, sensory issues are something that cannot be imagined or truly understood" (Tolleson, in Attwood et al., 2014, p. 124).

Like these other Aspies, Jim didn't like water hitting him, especially in the face, but loved spending time in his hot tub and in mine.

Jim arrived in Albuquerque, and we stopped at Burger King for Whoppers on the way home from the airport. We met with the preacher, and afterward went to a local jeweler, where Jim bought my engagement ring, and we bought wedding bands.

The next day, we flew to Chicago. Jim clutched my hand as we took off. When the wheels came up, or we heard some new noise, he tensed up. I patted his leg and said, "That's normal. No worries." Made me aware of what he went through on his multiple trips to Albuquerque.

In Chicago, in August, we got our rental car, and started to Nancy's house. We came to a self-pay, automatic toll booth and neither of us had change, so Jim tossed a dollar bill into the basket. We breezed right on through.

During the two-day visit, Jim met Nancy's husband, Wes, and their four children, who were teenagers and in their early 20s. We all went to a car show in downtown Wheaton, and Jim was in his element. The next day we visited the Cantigny Gardens. So many colorful flowers and relaxing water elements – and we happened to see an outdoor wedding in progress on the meticulously landscaped grounds. Back at the house, we played indoor and outdoor games with the kids. Everyone seemed to like Jim. One leg of our get-acquainted visit was successfully completed!

Jim and I drove through Indiana to Detroit, and on to Grosse Pointe, Michigan. We arrived at Julie's house, where the kids ran out to greet us, followed by Julie, and husband, John. As we visited in their living room, eight-year-old Chloe got up on the couch with Jim and studied the mole on his left cheek.

"What is that on your face?"

"It's a mole. I've had it a long time." He seemed amused at her curiosity.

I showed them my engagement ring, and Chloe frowned. She looked at the ring, then back to Julie. Julie told her Jim and I were going to get married. Still perplexed, Chloe said, "But she's married to Grandad."

I smiled and said, "When your husband is no longer living, it's okay to marry again." She looked satisfied with my answer.

The afternoon saw Jim and me playing board and card games with the kids. I knew Jim didn't enjoy playing these kinds of games, but he entered into them enthusiastically. The next day John was at work, so the rest of us took a picnic lunch to a large recreational area by Lake St. Clair, where we watched yachts sailing as we ate our sandwiches and fruit. The kids and I swam in the pool, while Jim and Julie visited poolside. When John came home, a lovely dinner from the grill topped off the day. Another successful get-acquainted visit.

Jim and I headed for the airport. It was pouring rain so hard the wipers were swamped, but Jim navigated the wet, heavily-trafficked freeways through Detroit like a champ. This time I was the one who was white-knuckled!

Jim flew back to Oregon a few hours after we arrived in Albuquerque. Before going to bed that night, I wrote, "I had a blast with you on our trip. Thanks for getting us through Detroit traffic and the rain without a casualty. And thanks for all you did and just for being *you*. My girls and families were impressed."

Jim responded, "I enjoyed the trip, but it was good to get home to my own bed. Love you."

I'm sure after all that masking, Jim was glad for the solitude and comfort of his house and hot tub!

Jim said he was tired and wasn't sleeping well. I said, "Are you nervous about the wedding? It will be a big change for both of us, but I feel confident it will be a good change. I hope that's not worrying you. Level with me, okay?"

"Yes, I am thinking about the wedding. It is, as you say, a big change in both our lives. It will be the beginning of an adventure, a new life, which will require adjustments for both of us. I think about the wedding and the years that follow. It will provide needed companionship and be a lasting special friendship. I think what wears me down is work; not the job, just the physical drain it puts on an old body. The old feet and legs sure do get tired; I notice the pain every day. I've had that since I was about fifty, but not as painful as lately. I used to be in a job that had four to five hours a day of sitting. I'm tired out when I get home these days, and want to sit. But hey, I'm 75 and still kicking, and football season is just around the corner, so things are A-OK. I've spent 75 years observing priorities, both mine and those of others, so I enjoy the time to take in the day and what it may bring. When I'm gone, The Man won't worry if I didn't vacuum the floor or clean the toilet today."

"I know you work hard and are tired. I just want to be sure you aren't feeling apprehensive about the festivities. I look forward to a future with you. I will always love you. As I've said, I, like you, don't take commitment lightly. When I visit in September, I want us to laugh and have fun and let the rest of the world go by. I know I need to lighten up, and maybe you do, too."

I accepted all Jim said. However, we had made a whirlwind trip across the country in a short time, meeting and interacting with a variety of people who were new to him, and he was the center of attention, so I knew those events contributed to his fatigue and restlessness, just as the March party with all my neighbors wore him out. Again, he engaged in masking for a time, and was exhausted, needing time to recoup. It takes an emotional toll. I did not recognize his behavior as masking at the time.

CHAPTER 22

ROUND-UP FUN

Jim said, "I have our Pendleton Round-Up tickets – the rodeo, the Happy Canyon play, and a barbeque and dance, with live music, dancing girls, booze, and likely uncouth behavior. We can go to the cowboy breakfast on Thursday or Friday, take in the Main Street events at night, and the parade on Saturday morning. I received an invitation to our wedding and thought I'd best RSVP, as I do plan to attend. I have a room at the church reserved for our Pendleton reception. Looking forward to your visit. I will not work on church things while you are here. That is to be *our* time. A friend wants me to go to a car show with him on Saturday, but I advised I was picking you up and couldn't. His reply? 'Well, you need to get your priorities in order, as car shows come first.'"

"Wow! I rate higher than a car show? That's encouraging."

Jim said, "Tonight I got hooked again on *Sleepless in Seattle*."

I said, "I love that movie. I told you that's how I felt the first time I visited, when I stood on that concrete bridge at the airport waiting for you. I kept thinking, 'What if he doesn't show, and I have to go back in and fly home?' Fortunately, we found each other, just as they did, and we assume they lived happily ever after, just as we will. I look forward to seeing you soon. Bringing my boots and jeans. I'll be a cowgirl on the arm of a cowboy."

Jim picked me up at the Boise airport this time, and as v
drove to Pendleton, the terrain on the far east side of Oreg(
reminded me of New Mexico, not at all like the forested, w
venue around Portland and the coast. By now, Jim's hou
(soon to be *my* house, too) was familiar and comfortable fi
me, and we settled in.

We spent one afternoon and evening at various Round-l
activities in our boots and cowpoke gear. The rodeo w
exciting, and the play at Happy Canyon was a history of tl
region, with local actors. At night, we went to the dance. ,
we danced, I was euphoric. Someday this would be my tow
It was teeming with people in western wear and trailers fi
of horses. I loved the excitement, and I loved being with Ji
once again!

Jim asked a good friend to be in charge of our Pendletc
reception. As we finalized plans, she said she was planning
fly to Albuquerque for the wedding. She remarked to Jim th
maybe he would want new clothes for the wedding, tl
people would think him handsome in a new suit.

Pragmatic Jim responded, "I don't think so. My slacks ε
navy sport coat will be fine. I don't care what people think

*Another hint of Asperger's I missed – Jim's not caring w
people think.*

During the week, we attended more Round-Up activi
Saturday the Ducks won their game, and Sunday after chι
we zipped over to a nearby town, Pilot Rock, in the red toγ
just to enjoy the beautiful day. I loved it when Jim revve
convertible up around the curves. Life was good!

The days passed quickly, and I could hardly believe i
time to head back home. Another tearful parting, but a
accomplish before the wedding next month.

I found this email when I got home: "Hey, I enjoyed the visit very much, and you are a sweetie pie. My daughter said she will be at the wedding. My sisters and brother-in-law will not be there, but will hit the Pendleton reception. See ya, love ya, miss ya."

I said, "I've reserved a private dining room for the Saturday night before the wedding, at a Mexican restaurant near my house. Please let your family members know. Judy Wilkins called today, and she and Dale are flying in Sunday morning and planning to be at the wedding. I am thrilled about that, and I'm sure you are, as well."

CHAPTER 23

A TICKET AND
"ARE YOU SURE?"

Early in October, Jim told me he received an Illinois toll ticket for over $60.00, for tossing a dollar bill into the coin bin at the toll booth on our August trip. He was furious and wanted to challenge it in court, saying, "A dollar bill is legal tender in the U.S.," and he shouldn't be penalized because he didn't have change. That would involve a trip to Chicago, so he stewed over it for a while. He finally went to the bank and got a cashier's check to pay the Illinois Toll Authority. Although he ended up reluctantly paying the fine, he never let it go, as you will see later.

Jim had trouble following unwritten societal rules, or not paying attention to them, as demonstrated by his not caring what his peers thought about his wearing cowboy boots and jeans at school in Maryland, his funny walking in stores, and not caring what people thought about his wearing his old sports coat at our wedding. But, seeing in a black-and-white way, he thought basic hierarchical rules should be firm (Ariel, 2012, p. 45).

"Many people are frustrated by rules. For the most part, however, rules have been a source of comfort to me" and "changes in rules – or simply seeing these ignored – were a

source of major distress to me" (Permer, in Attwood et al., 2014, p. 68).

"I had to do things my way and I always questioned illogical rules" (Wylie, 2014, p. 20).

"For an autistic person it is very difficult to blindly accept any rule or law when there is no justification for it, especially when we see areas where failure is likely" (Lipsky, 2011, p. 67).

Jim railed against his Illinois fine, saying, "A dollar bill is legal tender in the U.S." and should be accepted as payment in any state. Law was his thing. He would have made a good attorney. When I was struggling with getting licensed in Oregon, he mentioned to our attorney that he thought the federal "interfering with interstate commerce" rule should settle the issue, no matter what the state counseling board ruled. Rules of law had a hierarchy – societal rules were sometimes foreign to him. These traits of Asperger's should have been clear to me, but I was in love with this lovely man.

Rules came up after we were married. I got home from the beauty shop one day and when he made no comment, I said, "Did you notice my new hairdo?"

"I don't comment on women's hair."

"Why?"

"Well, once I said to a woman, 'What happened to your hair?' and I learned that was not a good thing to say, so I just don't comment on women's hair."

This made me laugh, but I did not see it as an Asperger's trait at the time. Finch, an Aspie, in his hilarious book, refers to learning social rules (Finch, 2012, pp. 18-19). Fisher, another Aspie, became very good at memorizing and following rules, once they were made clear (Fisher, in Grandin, 2012, pp. 106-107).

This brings me to grocery shopping. Going to the store without Jim was an ordeal for me, since the bags had to be carried down 24 steps to our front door. Seeing Jim sitting in *the living room watching TV was irritating to me as I made trip after trip from the house to the car and back. Sometimes establishing a rule clearly imprinted it on his mind, something I learned later (Stanford, 2015, p. 205). One day I said, "I need help carrying in the groceries when I go to the store by myself." That became a rule Jim could understand, clearly stated, non-emotional, and never again did I have to ask him to help me.*

Nancy called one afternoon. "Mom, are you sure? Are you sure you want to do this?"

We had a lengthy conversation, and I could understand her wanting to make sure I was doing the right thing – at my age, and with all my connections to Albuquerque. I assured her I loved Jim, and had no reservations about my decision. There was not a shred of me that felt what I was about to do was strange or risky. My adventurous spirit was in action.

I was getting antsy about selling my house. Jim said, "Don't sweat the house sale. Have some patience. Sounds as if you're having fun with the wedding preparations. It would drive me crazy. If I planned it, it would be with the Justice of the Peace at the local courthouse. By the way, I learned my daughter won't be able to make it to the wedding."

I said, "I'm sorry she won't be able to make it. I know you are disappointed, as am I. And by the way, I can't imagine trading this wedding preparation chaos for a simple Justice of the Peace wedding. We will have a blast at the actual event. Everything should go smoothly. Ours will be a simple – repeat – simple ceremony. No complexities, no excess formality, and we will end up husband and wife. Just think – in a week we'll be in Taos, in northern New Mexico, and all the preps will be a memory."

Jim said, "I must say you've done a magnificent job this past month getting all the details of the wedding together, packing, arranging for moving, listing the house, cleanup of the house, and closing your business. I could not have done that in a short time. I'm looking forward to the wedding, then our hideaway in Taos for a few days. Good night, my sweet, enjoy the new day, and I will be at your doorstep in two days for our excellent adventure."

CHAPTER 24

HUSBAND AND WIFE

Jim arrived on Friday before our Sunday wedding, and so did the rest of my family members, with flights staggered from early afternoon until evening. The family and out-of-town guests joined us for dinner Saturday evening, feasting on Mexican food, amidst introductions, getting-acquainted conversation, and laughter. One of my friends from out of town was a Mustang collector, so Jim had someone to talk with about cars. No before-wedding jitters for the bride and groom, as Jim and I were confident we were making the right decision and were ready to start our lifetime adventure!

On Sunday, the New Mexico sun shone as if it were celebrating us. In my small back yard, family and a few special friends began to gather for the ceremony. The piano had been moved onto the deck. Good friends, Mary and Cindy, who were coordinating the wedding, had decorated with cobalt blue and white, and kept the afternoon moving smoothly. It was a sentimental setting for me – the altar was an antique trestle table belonging to my first in-laws, and the white cloth with blue cross-stitched design that covered the table was embroidered by my mother years ago. A large wreath with blue and white flowers and heart-shaped ornaments hung from the tree behind the altar. The pastor had officiated at my first husband's funeral three and a half years before. As guests gathered, a classical guitarist filled the air with love songs, as he had done for family events over the years.

Granddaughter Chloe served as flower girl, and grandson Jack was the ring bearer. My teenage granddaughter, Claire, attended me as junior bridesmaid. Jim's son was his best man. Soon, Jim and I were cued and came out onto the deck, smiling, arm-in-arm, Jim looking handsome in his navy-blue sports coat and gray slacks, and me in my blue dress that matched my eyes. We couldn't have been happier!

Melissa Manchester's "Through the Eyes of Love" filled the air, as a friend played the piano and sang. When the pastor asked, "Who gives this woman to be married to this man?" my three children stood and answered in unison, "We do," symbolically "giving me away." There were moist eyes, mine included. My heart was bursting with joy! My children were giving their blessing to my union with this good man.

Jim repeated the vows we had written: "Mary, I take you to be my wife. I commit myself to encourage you to reach your highest aspirations and potential as an individual, and your continued usefulness in God's kingdom. I promise to love, honor, and nurture you in sickness and in health, in adversity and in prosperity. I promise to be true and loyal to you only, according to the design of God, until death shall part us."

I then repeated the same vows to Jim, with a surprise ending, "And I promise never to serve you liver and onions." There were snickers, and Jim grinned. The rings were given, and a benediction followed.

It was the most glorious day I could remember in a long, long time. Relatives and friends from seven states honored us with their presence. More love than that deck had ever seen, I was sure. Jim and I kissed, and the pastor shook Jim's hand and hugged me. We signed the marriage license, and our sons signed it as witnesses. It was official!

We received many more guests at the reception, including the psychic who had foreseen this event, held in the large back yard of my next-door neighbors. The cheesecakes with various toppings, made by a friend, stood on a tiered stand, with a topper of Donald Duck and Daisy, symbolic of the Oregon Ducks. Mary, our wedding coordinator, had painted and decorated all the champagne bottles in our wedding colors. All our guests greeted us with smiles and laughter in a long receiving line, giving Jim and me congratulatory hugs. After champagne had been poured for all, our sons each gave a toast.

After photos, mingling, and goodbyes, Jim and I left the reception and went to a motel in Albuquerque for the night. He said he had never been hugged so much in his life, especially by strangers, and although he was glad everyone was friendly, it made him uncomfortable at times. I assumed hugs were probably a southern tradition, and perhaps wedding receptions in Pendleton were conducted more formally. I wondered how I would fit in, since I was a hugger.

We took slices of cheesecake and a bottle of champagne to the motel, and we ceremoniously enjoyed them and relaxed before going to bed as husband and wife.

Again, the masking must have been exhausting for Jim – a long, eventful day, many people, most of them strangers to him, and we were the center of attention. Not only all the excitement, but in addition, the physical touching – many persons with Asperger's don't want to be touched a lot, and social hugging is often difficult for them (Grandin & Panek, 2014, p. 8; Higashida, 2016, p. 32).

We spent our honeymoon in Taos. My son gave us two complimentary nights in their adobe casita, a lovely little hideaway, very close to the town square. We were joined in life, and we were in love – with each other, life, and future adventures. In the mountains, it is always cool after the sun goes down, so after dinner we built a fire in the kiva fireplace, watched the calming blaze as the logs crackled, then snuggled into the night . . .

After two luxurious days and nights in Taos, Jim and I were off to Pendleton. We bought a mug as a honeymoon memento, at the café where we ate breakfast, The Olde Tymers Café, in Red River. Yes, we were old timers, two old timers in love.

After a couple of long driving days, coming into Pendleton felt good. When we arrived at 220 NW Johns Lane, Jim opened the front door, and with a wide-armed flourish and a big smile, ushered his bride over the threshold into his home, now *our* home. I would be living with this magnificent man in this beautiful, multi-windowed house on the North Hill, with the immaculately kept multi-level lawn! Fall was gorgeous in the northeast part of Oregon. I was at home and at peace.

However, I had no idea what lay ahead.

PART IV

OUR INITIAL ADVENTURES AS WIFE AND HUSBAND

CHAPTER 25

ANOTHER RECEPTION AND A FIRST CHRISTMAS

Early in November, Dale and Jim worked all day at the church, making clam chowder for the annual Soup Supper. I was eager to enter into this part of Jim's life.

The night of the supper, Jim and Dale were behind the scenes stirring the clam chowder, while people gathered and were served. Jim came out of the kitchen to where I was helping Judy with the crafts sales, and told me his daughter was there, and he was going to take a break to eat with us. Surrounded by a room full of people, I met my stepdaughter for the first time. I recognized her from pictures Jim had sent. I saw a tall, stately young woman, who carried herself with grace. Jim introduced us, and she was pleasant to her dad's new wife, as we sat across the table from each other, ate our bowls of soup and slices of homemade pie, and engaged in small talk. I imagined it a strange experience for her to see her dad with the new woman in his life.

Our Pendleton wedding reception was the day after the Soup Supper. Our large wedding portrait hung behind the refreshment table, along with the blue and white wreath from the wedding. The serving table, with a blue cloth, held a chocolate cake with white frosting, a thin blue border around the edges, and pink roses with green leaves, inscribed "Congratulations Jim and Mary, October 18, 2009." Donald Duck and Daisy topped the cake. A potted plant of pink tea roses, a bowl of fruit punch, and assorted blue and white wedding-related décor graced the table. Pictures from our wedding and reception were displayed around the room. Jim's daughter stayed over for the party, and his sister and brother-in-law came from southwestern Oregon. My nephew and family came from Spokane. Many of Jim's friends came from a wide area to check out his new bride and wish us well. The room filled, and conversation and laughter echoed as people greeted us. Jim gave a short welcome speech and kissed me before we cut our cake. As I suspected, from Jim's comments about the hugging at our Albuquerque reception, this was a more formal group, and not a lot of hugging went on. However, I felt enveloped with love by family and friends. I was now a Pendleton wife – Jim's wife, a role I welcomed.

In the days to follow, I unpacked and gradually found places for everything. Jim was helpful and encouraging that soon things would be arranged and life would settle down. He assured me I could do anything to the house I wanted, to make it seem more like mine.

"This house is now your house," he said.

I decided to focus on putting everything away and getting ready for the holidays before I made any changes. I joined Jim's Presbyterian Church early in December. Everything in which I could become involved would make this new town seem more like mine.

It seemed early for snow on December 12th, but living in the Pacific Northwest, I was to find out a lot about snow that was new to me. Even though I had lived in Illinois and Michigan, where snow was dealt with efficiently, snow in Pendleton would prove to be a different story.

Jim and I drove to Westminster Woods, where there were acres of beautiful trees. We waded through the snow, and after a great deal of comparisons, chose a large, well-shaped tree to cut. When we got home, Jim worked and worked, getting the tree affixed to the stand and perfectly aligned. We combined decorations from both families and had fun decorating our first Christmas tree as a couple. I was happy to see Jim enjoying the decorating process as much as I did. Preparing for Christmas that year was like a fantasy – new husband, new home, new environment – I felt blessed.

Jim's wanting the tree to be perfectly straight – and I mean perfectly – could have been indicative of his penchant for perfectionism, sometimes a trait of Asperger's (Dubin, 2009, p. 47; Tammet, 2007, p. 50). The lawn had to be mowed and edged perfectly, the shrubs trimmed perfectly, the spices arranged perfectly in the cabinet, and now the tree had to be perfectly set up.

For now, I just saw the tree's positioning taking much longer than I thought necessary (though I didn't say so). I sat on the stairs, drinking hot apple cider, and let him do his thing.

Jim's daughter spent our first Christmas with us. After dinner on Christmas Eve, I attended to the kitchen, and as I walked down the few carpeted steps from the kitchen into the living room, I could hear Jim and his daughter talking. When I appeared, I was met with sudden silence. I realized I had surprised them and interrupted a conversation.

"So why did the room get silent when I walked in? Were you talking about me?" I said with a smile, not thinking they were.

Jim said, "You're welcome to be in on the conversation. I asked my daughter about her mother."

I felt awkward in that moment. Trying to assimilate into this new family and expecting the conversation to resume, I said, "Well, you can go ahead," although I hadn't expected to be part of a discussion about Jim's ex on our first Christmas Eve.

Silence.

Without a word, Jim got up, facial muscles taut, grabbed a log from the basket, threw it on the fire, and stalked out of the room. I had never seen him act that way. I didn't follow him, because I felt it would be rude to leave our guest alone. A CD of Christmas music filled the silence.

I stared out the wall of windows, looked past the lights on our first Christmas tree to the lights of the town below, and found myself wondering aloud if I'd made a mistake leaving everything I knew, marrying Jim, and moving to a new town. I regretted his daughter's witnessing our first conflict and my voicing my dark thoughts in her presence.

I was in shock. It was Christmas Eve, Jim and I were newlyweds, we had company, and Jim had left the room in a huff.

After a while he came back down to the living room and joined us, and all seemed outwardly normal again, though to me there were many unanswered questions. As I recall, nothing was mentioned about the earlier conversation, and we talked and laughed the rest of the evening and had dessert.

I was confused, because in our early emails Jim told me I didn't have to be careful with my words, yet I felt sure I had touched a nerve. Was he nervous because his daughter was visiting? Did they want to talk more about his ex? Did he have regrets about my presence? The holiday was not starting out to be the first Christmas together I had imagined and looked forward to.

Although I usually used the guest bathroom as my own, since we had company, Jim and I were forced to get ready for bed in the same bathroom. I searched Jim's face for a look of regret or compassion, but saw no evidence of either. I put on my warm, red plaid, flannel gown, washed my face, and brushed my teeth. We went to bed in silence.

Jim said nothing, but kissed me, reached for my hand, and held it close to his chest until we both fell asleep. I didn't press him for an explanation, because I didn't want his daughter in the next room to overhear. To be honest, I probably also had some fear of abandonment, from my toddler experience, and Cathy's, my parents', and Paul's deaths, so I didn't confront Jim. I wanted this relationship to last. Soft, quiet tears ran onto my pillow, and I spent a restless night.

Christmas morning, the atmosphere was brighter. Jim made a coffee cake for breakfast, before we opened our gifts. I don't remember the gifts, or what we had for dinner, or when his daughter left to go back home. I've tried to remember, but I think the Christmas Eve events permanently erased, or at least dimmed, memories of that first Christmas. Most of it is a blank. I remember taking pictures in front of the Christmas tree after we opened our gifts, perhaps only because I've seen those pictures. I'm sure we had phone calls from our other children.

I hoped I had misjudged Jim's actions, but no mention of the Christmas Eve scene was ever made, and I decided not to stir up trouble. His kiss and reaching for my hand that night was the closest thing I got to an explanation or apology.

Now, looking back, I can only imagine the emotions that Jim was trying to control – here he was with the daughter by his first wife, spending Christmas with his new wife, and probably struggling with memories and present reality. I believe his leaving in a huff was to be alone long enough to calm himself and prevent losing control of emotions he couldn't seem to handle. I had taken it personally, but now I don't believe it was directed at me personally.

I had experienced a side of Jim I didn't know existed. I approached the new year with a sense of foreboding. I began to wonder whether I had made a huge mistake . . . marrying . . . moving . . .

CHAPTER 26

LIFE GOES ON

Toward the end of January, Julie called, saying she and John had a healthy baby boy, Henry, giving us another grandchild, and son Paul visited for the first time, on his way home from a business trip. I was excited to have a new grandson, and to have Paul with us. My unpleasant memories of Christmas Eve were fading, and I felt life was on an even keel again. Julie sent pictures of baby Henry, and Paul and Jim had a good time together. Their mutual sense of humor was fun to be around. They reminded me of times my dad and my uncle got together and told jokes when I was growing up.

In February, after Paul left, and before my birthday, after lunch one day Jim said, "Let's drive to Tri-Cities. I want to buy you something for your birthday."

I was surprised, but thrilled. Tri-Cities, Washington, a combination of three adjacent towns, Kennewick, Pasco, and Richland, was a little over an hour's drive north of Pendleton, and a popular shopping destination. On the way, we passed a sign, "Coffin Road."

"That's a morbid name for a road," I commented.

Jim said, "I don't want a coffin. I want to be cremated."

"Really?"

"Yeah."

"Well, that's not a fitting subject for my birthday." I laughed, but tucked that piece of information into my memory.

In Kennewick, at Columbia Mall, he guided me into Coldwater Creek, where we browsed the racks. Jim roamed the store and handed me several items to try. He brought a book along, and the clerks watched him, as he picked clothing for his wife to try on and sat and read while he waited. One of them asked him what he was reading.

"Oh, it's about physics and black holes," Jim said with a charming grin. And it was.

"You read that stuff for fun?" she asked, eyes wide.

"It's fascinating," Jim replied.

I came out of the dressing room wearing one ensemble after another. Jim looked up. "I like that one, too. I think you should get all three outfits."

"Really? That many? One is enough."

"Yes, you look good in all of them. Happy birthday!"

When we got home, he gave me a sweet card and an orchid plant. What a birthday!

I was surely mistaken about his earlier behavior. At least I wanted to be. I did not want the fantasy of Camelot to be flawed. The next incidents came without warning.

CHAPTER 27

WHEAT RANCHING AND A HOUSE CHANGE

I was not familiar with wheat country, having been raised in Texas with sheep ranches. On a drive through the countryside one day, Jim told me about the practice of "set-asides," in which a field lies fallow, and the government pays the farmer a subsidy for not planting during that time. At least that's how I understood his explanation. Jim, being a conservative Republican, said he did not agree with farmers being paid for "doing nothing" on some of their land.

I was making an effort to get to know some of the women in Pendleton, and one morning I invited a woman for coffee who owned a wheat farm, or as some call it, a wheat ranch. Where I came from, farms grew plants, ranches raised animals, but when in Rome . . .

She stayed for lunch, and Jim came home and joined us at the table. Conversation came around to farming, and Jim made a derogatory remark about set-asides. I could tell by her face and body language the woman was annoyed, but Jim continued talking, apparently not caring that he was insulting the area's tradition of either current or former farming practices. She politely did not try to engage in the conversation nor give a rebuttal. I wanted to crawl into a hole.

After she left, I said, "I could tell she was insulted by your remarks about set-asides, Jim."

"I was just giving my opinion."

"Well, you told her your opinion, but it opposed her opinion, and possibly practices, and she was my invited guest. She was nice enough not to engage in an argument."

He didn't seem to realize she could take his remarks personally, but I was embarrassed, and I hoped it would not interfere with my friendship with the woman. Fortunately, she was able to parse Jim's behavior from mine, and she remained friendly to me.

Most Aspies lack a filter to alert them when something they want to say is not appropriate and would seem rude to the recipient. They speak honestly, and often can seem thoughtless or rude. If they have an opinion, they voice it. It is a social problem that can alienate people. The trait of not caring what other people think, blended with their lack of theory of mind, prevents Aspies from monitoring their own conversation and interpreting facial expressions and body language. "Infants observe from an early age the body movements and, a few months later, facial expressions of their caregiver and others. With autism, this early mirroring is compromised" (Hane, in Attwood et al., 2014, p. 185). This lack of mirroring inhibits the developing of facial expression or body language recognition (Grandin & Barron, 2016, pp. 326, 335-341; Hendrickx & Newton, 2007, pp. 111-112).

The next day, while Jim was at work, I was still upset by the above incident, so I decided to make my first change in the house. I began ripping the wallpaper off of the walls in the laundry room with vigor. Several edges came loose, and I slid my fingers under one and vented my pent-up frustration. *I'll get that stuff off – whatever is under it can't be worse.* The wallpaper, printed with a macramé pattern, tore off in huge pieces, leaving bare, unpainted wallboard. I filled a large trash bag with crumpled wallpaper, and the laundry room walls were bare. To me, that was an instant improvement. Someday I would paint it.

I felt better. When Jim got home, I told him and showed him what I'd done. His comment, "Well, it was old wallpaper, probably as old as the house. It needed to come down."

CHAPTER 28

LEARNING NEW RULES

In late February, I began to work on obtaining my Oregon counseling license. The person I spoke to at the board's office in Salem assured me I could get my license by reciprocity, and that it would take about ten days from the time they received the form. I was relieved it would be that easy. I mailed the form, and on the way home from the post office, I went by the library and got a library card. One more connection with the Pendleton community.

Jim came home from work, and I was bubbling with excitement. He didn't say much when he walked in, maybe "Hello," so I followed him over to the kitchen sink, where he was washing his hands and looking out the window. I leaned on the top of the cabinet, propped myself with my elbows, and began to reel off the information about the apparent ease of getting my license, my trip to the library, getting my library card, and the fact that now I could check out books.

Without turning to look at me, changing his expression, or showing any acknowledgement of, or interest in, what I was saying, he said, "You talk too much." A matter-of-fact statement, spoken in a conversational tone.

I was startled, and my excitement was gone. We sat down to lunch, and I was subdued. I told him he hurt my feelings. No response, no apology. We ate in silence, except he said, "I need to mow the lawn today." I wasn't sure what to think about this newest strange behavior.

Lacking the ability to know how remarks can affect others, Aspies make remarks others consider rude (Solomon, 2013, p. 281). Sometimes, with great effort, they can mask, saying only tried and true comments they have used successfully in the past or copied from being observant of other conversations, but it takes great energy for them to do that for any length of time.

Jim had been at work for six hours, making an effort to blend in, but now he was home, his safe place, and he could be himself. I did not recognize that then – I was too busy thinking of myself and being hurt! If I had recognized the Asperger's trait, I would have known to allow him to recover from his work morning before sharing my news (Weston, 2010, p. 79). Later I would understand, but later wasn't that moment, and the sting or hurt or disappointment lingered.

Jim decided to repair the concrete block retaining wall near the front deck. A large tree, now removed, had caused some pieces of the wall to buckle. Repairing it consisted of removing the broken pieces and sawing the rebars apart, in order to place the new blocks correctly. It was warm outside, and Jim was working hard on that wall. As a little girl, I'd often take my dad a glass of cold water or lemonade when he was working on an outdoor project. I went out on the deck, holding out a glass of lemonade. "Here."

He didn't even turn to look at me.

I was surprised and hurt when he said, "No, don't interrupt me. I'm into this."

He was setting his rules. Would I ever learn them?

Aspies, when working on a project or special interest, can get into a flow, into the zone, and don't want to be interrupted (Attwood, in Attwood et al., 2014, pp. 34-35; Dubin, 2009, pp. 110-11).

I would learn more about that tendency, as, at times, it also pertained to working on cars, working on genealogy, and watching football. Jim was never again abrupt about it, but I learned not to interrupt him at certain times. Later I was to learn many rules new to me.

CHAPTER 29

SPRING IS ON ITS WAY

In March, the day after Jim's 76th birthday, he planted tomato seeds into small pots and placed them on trays in the dining room by the windows, to take advantage of the sunlight. He said he did that every year. I'd never known anyone who grew tomato plants from seed, so I was eager to see how that would work. We watched them daily for signs of sprouting. It was a ritual. Soon we noticed a few tiny green tips, and we celebrated wildly, like kids, dancing around the dining room!

Spring weather brought optimism about the outdoors and life, and motivated us to go to Walmart. After we spent time in the automotive department looking at radios for the MGB (something we did at any store that had automotive equipment), we ended up at the garden center and bought a pink rose bush for the front bed. Eventually we stopped by the TV display, where Jim liked to see what was new. Rows and rows of big-screen TVs. Jim said, "I want a new TV, but I'll wait another year or so for a new HDTV. After all, you are surely more of a prize than an HDTV, and I already have you!" With his arm around me, we migrated out of the store, and after unloading the rose bush at home, we went to Great Pacific for turkey sandwiches and wine.

Everything seemed to be going smoothly again. Spring had brought a series of fun and interesting activities, Jim was in his humorous mode, and I was happy. I usually had a positive attitude and outlook, so I tried to move past the occasional weird things Jim said and did. I felt a new marriage required adjustments; things would eventually work out.

Or at least, I hoped they would.

PART V

A MIX OF ADVENTURES

CHAPTER 30

CRITICISMS

Jim and I were having dinner, enjoying the view from our abundance of windows overlooking the city and the Blue Mountains in the distance. I mentioned some family news, just everyday stuff I learned from a family email that day.

Jim commented, "You talk about family a lot. I thought we'd be discussing history, or physics, or politics at our dinners."

I looked to see if he was joking. He wasn't.

"Yes, family is important to me. I can talk about other things, but I thought you'd enjoy hearing that piece of information."

I hung my head. I felt he was disappointed in me . . . and maybe in his choice of a new wife. I wasn't accustomed to being a disappointment to anyone.

Aspies love talking about the things that interest them, but not always listening to things that are peripheral to their interests (Grandin & Panek, 2014, p. 15; Lipsky, 2011, p. 198; Solomon, 2013, p. 222). Lesko, an Aspie, says, "I pretty much only want to talk about what I want to talk about!" and "It has nothing to do with being selfish; it's just the way our brain functions," and "This is very classic of someone with Asperger's syndrome" (Lesko, 2011, pp. 177-178).

I failed to pick up on that, and the effect again was hurt feelings. I felt I had failed to be the wife he expected. His idea of interesting dinner conversation was to talk about things he found interesting, like history, black holes, or the current political situation. Or cars – I guess he failed to mention that as another acceptable topic.

The state of my desk in our shared home office was a minor thorn. Jim's was always neat, uncluttered, everything in its place. Even his pen and pencil were perpendicular to the edge of his desk, almost measured. My desk was always cluttered, piles of paper on every square inch, no seeming organization to anyone except me. I did keep my pens and pencils in a coffee cup. Jim mentioned, more than a few times, that he'd like my desk to be more orderly, but I didn't see it as a problem. It was *my* desk, and I didn't attempt to keep it better.

One day he asked me for a weeks-old paper, something to do with something he'd ordered and handed me the receipt at the time. I wondered why he wanted it, and really felt it was a test, to see if I could find it. Within ten-second searches of two separate piles, I had it, and handed it to him. If it was a test, hoping to make me admit my desk was in chaos, it didn't work. He finally gave up commenting about it.

Aspies can be either chaotically disorganized, or organized and excessively neat (Ariel, 2012, p. 28; Attwood, in Attwood et al., 2014, p. 155). Obviously, Jim fell into the latter classification. How he kept his desk was of no consequence to me. He was also neat in the kitchen, with everything in its place and the counters kept uncluttered.

I had lived by myself a few years and was accustomed to doing things as I pleased. I was mildly annoyed when he made it plain he'd rather I be neater. Thinking he was trying to control me, it did not occur to me to see this trait of Jim's as indicative of Aspieness.

I have a habit of getting up at least once at night for a bathroom break, no matter how much or how little the fluid intake. It disturbed Jim, the light sleeper, even though I closed the bathroom door before turning on the light, tried to be quiet, and was quickly back in bed.

"You wake me up every night," he growled, as I got back into bed.

How could he complain about an essential act? It got so tiresome I again began to wonder if I had made a mistake marrying him. The charming man who courted me was changing, now that we were married. It was not at all like him, or at least not like he was before marriage, to be so inconsiderate and irritable, and that was puzzling to me. Before marriage, I mentioned I usually got up at least once during the night. Had he forgotten?

Some mornings when I lay in bed in the dark after Jim had gone to work, I wondered aloud, *"What have I done? What . . . have . . . I . . . done?"* It became a mental mantra to me, as I tried to figure out what was causing the change and what the future held. If this adventure was a mistake, it was a huge one. I had left everything familiar to me to be with this man I loved, but often felt I was a disappointment. His behavior was definitely a disappointment to me.

I didn't complain about his getting up some nights and walking around to relieve his leg cramps, although that interrupted *my* sleep. I was tired enough of his erratic behavior changes that divorce flitted through my mind. The thought of enduring his frequent criticism and hurtful behaviors the rest of my life did not appeal to me. I was serene and peaceful before I married him – lonely at times, but my life had no hurtful elements. I wanted the guy who won my heart, the one I thought I knew. I couldn't imagine living like this forever, but I had counseled couples and their children during a divorce, and I knew how traumatic it could be, even for adult children. So, although the term occurred to me, I could not imagine doing it . . . I would not give up. I was determined to figure things out.

In the wee hours one morning, Jim again made a remark about my bothering his sleep. I had had it.

I threw back the covers and said, "I'll go sleep in the other room, since it bothers you for me to get up. I told you about this habit before we married. What about your leg cramps that get you up sometimes? I don't complain about that." By now I was out of bed, and grabbing for my pillow.

When Jim spoke, I heard a pleading, childlike quality in his voice that surprised me. "No, I don't want you to sleep in the other room."

By now I was crying. I shouted, "Then don't make such a big deal about my getting up. If I could help it, I would. I don't do it to irritate you. I'm so tired of this! I don't want to live my life this way."

I expected him to brush off my complaint, as he usually did. This time he reached over, took hold of my hand that held the pillow, and drew me down close. By now fully awake and alert, he softly said, "I don't want you to be unhappy. Please don't leave me."

My eyes opened wide, and I felt my eyebrows rise. I had never mentioned leaving – not to him, nor to anyone. I was taught that spouses were never to speak unkindly about each other to anyone, so I had never shared my frustrations with anyone, even my family. Even my Facebook posts were always positive about our relationship.

I was touched by his softened voice, a plea, and I said, "I will not leave you. But we have some things to work out."

I was not going to leave this bio-fatherless guy over an issue like this, only to feed his insecurity about abandonment. I was willing to wait and see how the pieces of this strange puzzle fit together. There had to be a reason he was changing.

I already realized Jim had deep-seated abandonment issues over his biological father's leaving the family when Jim was young. I felt this was why he spent time on genealogy, tracing his father's family. Even though he grew up with a stepfather he loved, he admitted to me that he missed the tie to his biological father. He said he couldn't imagine why his father had abandoned him at an early age, ignored him the one time he saw him, and never communicated again.

"Undiagnosed autistic adults have a much higher chance of being rejected or abandoned by their parents and relatives than do diagnosed children" (Wylie, 2014, p. 58).

"Yes, [her client] does have feelings of worry over being rejected and alone," and "Those deep feelings surface only when [he] is truly threatened" (Hollands, 1985, p. 26).

"...an individual who has been humiliated repeatedly as a child may find rejection as an adolescent or adult extremely disorganizing" (Seigel, 2015, p. 353).

I believed Jim deeply feared being abandoned again by people close to him. Years later, I found confirmation in a diary in which he had written, "I fear loneliness. I fear being alone and abandoned."

CHAPTER 31

FINDING MY PLACE

Everyday activities filled our lives. We ushered at church; I went to a sewing group at the downtown quilt shop, where I worked on a cross-stitch Christmas stocking for my grandson; I attended a writer's group at the art center building, and met a few other people interested in writing. I was making an effort to find my place in this community I had chosen.

Most people were warm and welcoming; some were not. As the second wife in the house on North Hill, I learned to endure or overlook the occasional unpleasant experiences, sometimes confronting. I was Jim Hanks' new wife, and people had to adjust.

One woman said, "You know, Jim's other wife speaks several languages and taught at the college. We all thought you'd be intimidated by her." I wasn't sure who the "we all" were, but the clear implication was that I had been discussed. I smiled. I'm not easily intimidated.

One person told me she regularly kept in touch with Jim's ex, so, "You might not want to be my friend."

"I'm sure Jim's ex-wife is a lovely woman, or Jim would not have married her, so your friendship with her doesn't affect my friendship with you, as far as I'm concerned."

A few people at church spoke to me with the effect of a cool blast. Polite, but with an air of "we don't really care for you – we liked Jim's ex better." I let it roll off. The social cliques of some were already well-set.

The nearest I got to folding was when two church people, at different times, called me by the ex's name. One had never met me, but associated the ex's name with Jim. That could be overlooked, but it stung. The other, who was a friend of Jim's and the ex's, called me by the ex's name when I answered our phone, the day after we had had a lengthy get-acquainted chat at church. That one I confronted, because to me it did not seem accidental.

It was not always easy to be the second wife, but I had anticipated some of that.

The days were filled. I worked at unpacking boxes in the garage and found books I had looked for; our new pink rose bush had quite a few new shoots on it, inspiring me to keep an eye out for buds; I had calls from Albuquerque friends; Jim made his spaghetti, filling the house with spicy aroma; and we watched movies. We enjoyed Cherry Garcia® ice cream at bedtime, and afterward, a cherry cordial.

The purple orchid Jim gave me for my birthday had a new bloom on it. I'd never had an orchid plant, so this was exciting. Nine blooms now, and another bud to go.

After dinner one evening, I walked down the hall and heard Jim down in the living room, strumming his guitar. When I got down, he played and sang, and I was entertained. As he sang "Pretty Woman," one of the Roy Orbison favorites, he cut his eyes at me, with eyelids floating up and down, and grinned in his flirtatious way. I focused on enjoying the good times, and I loved this man. Things between us seemed to be improving, until . . .

CHAPTER 32

VISITORS

Jim answered the phone in the kitchen and talked, then hung up. I was down in the living room, so although I could hear him talking, I couldn't understand any of his conversation. He called to me, "How would you like company?"

"When?"

"Right now. They're in front of the house."

"Who is it?"

The doorbell rang, and, without answering me, Jim opened the door. I heard the couple come in, and I could tell by Jim's friendly greeting he knew them well. I got up and walked toward the entry to meet them. By the time I took a few steps, they were into the living room. Jim introduced them to me as "old friends."

It was a strained visit, because I knew nothing about this friendship. They talked about recently seeing a child of theirs. To make further conversation, I said, "Do you have other children?" thinking that a fairly safe topic.

Both their faces blanched, and I could see I had put them on the spot. They both looked at Jim, the wife turned to her husband, then to me, and told a story that seemed to give her pain as she talked. I felt tension in the room.

I was peeved at Jim for not briefly filling me in on that important information before he answered the door. After they left, I said, "They could have waited a few minutes before you opened the door, while you at least told me their names and a sentence or two of history of the friendship. I am uncomfortable being surprised by long-time friends of yours I don't know anything about."

"Why?"

"I wouldn't have asked about their children if I had known the story."

Jim said he couldn't imagine why that would make me uncomfortable.

I felt blindsided. That couple never visited us again.

Jim's lack of theory of mind made him unable to understand my discomfort at making the guests uncomfortable. His social skills were lacking. He could not see the visit from my perspective. At the risk of belaboring the point of theory of mind, empathy, and social skills, many sources discuss these traits at length (Ariel, 2012, p. 44; Baron-Cohen, 1997, p. 136; Falk & Schofield, 2018, pp. 49-50; Grandin, 2006, p. 114; Grandin & Barron, 2016, p. 325; Grandin & Panek, 2014, pp. 72-73; Grossberg, 2015, p. 9; Hendrickx & Newton, 2007, pp. 111-112; Robison, 2008, p. 21; Siegel, 2015, p. 260; Solomon, 2013, p. 281).

From Jim's perspective, I had learned the facts from the woman, and that should have been okay with me. He seemed not to notice the woman's difficulty in telling me about their child. To Jim, the story was factual, not emotional. To me, it was heart-rending, and I could sense the guests' pain.

CHAPTER 33

HALCYON DAYS

Better days followed. I passed the first lesson in "Jim Hanks' informal Brit car driving course." He took me and the Sprite out to the empty parking lot at the Community Building. I sat with a square block of foam behind me in the driver's seat, so I could reach the pedals. Jim sat beside me. I learned the gear positions, and although the car lurched forward the first couple of times, I soon had the hang of it. Zoom! What fun!

The next day the weather was again beautiful, so we took the MGB for a lesson this time, but only after working the newspaper's crossword puzzle at the lunch table. We did that most days, and between us, we could get almost all the words. Jim was acting as he did during our courting days, full of fun and adventure; he was teaching me to drive his toys. I felt like Jim's queen.

One sunny afternoon, a couple of Jim's friends from out of town called to say they were parked in the RV lot at the Wildhorse Campground, out on the reservation, and hoped we could get together.

Jim said, "Sure, why don't you come for dinner tonight?" I felt by his automatic invitation they were people he knew well.

The dinner invitation was fine with me, though I'd never met these people. I kept the house neat, so I always felt comfortable having people over. To prevent a repeat of the earlier experience with friends of his, I asked Jim for some background, and he gave me a few details – he and the guy used to work together, and his wife had a background similar to mine.

"Are there any topics I should avoid?"

"Not that I know of."

"Stop and think about it a minute. Are you sure?"

A pause.

"Not that I can think of. You'll like them."

I felt forewarned. Having this information was helpful.

The couple arrived, and there was immediate rapport, with hugs all around. The dinner was a success, with good conversation, laughter, and a feeling of camaraderie. Jim served London broil, one of his specialties. I found the wife and I had a lot in common. Jim and the husband talked about old work memories. A very enjoyable evening.

After that, we saw them frequently when they were in town, and our visits were always fun. I was glad to have their friendship.

By prompting Jim beforehand, he had a chance to think about these people and try to think what I might want to know, making sure the evening would be enjoyable for me. I think he was proud of himself for being able to reassure me. I told him how much I appreciated the difference between this visit and the earlier one with the other couple.

Jim belonged to a group of British car owners, and every year, they planned a several-day trip in caravan. The first trip I went on was to Hood River, Oregon. The MGB was carefully prepped for this outing, buffed and shining, and I heard Jim revving the engine, checking for any sounds he might not like. Jim was relaxed and at ease among his friends who shared his obsession and love of the little cars. The group conversations sounded like a foreign tongue to me, and they talked as if the cars were alive, anthropomorphizing them – "She uses some oil," or "She can take the curves without swaying." Jim was in another world, one he loved. I was surprised to hear them talking about finding turds and orange peel on a car after a paint job, but I learned, to my relief, they were referring to imperfections in the final drying of the paint, probably barely noticeable to the average person, but anathema to car enthusiasts.

I found it exhilarating to ride long distances in a convertible, seeing the majestic cliffs in the morning sunshine, consistently taking the curves at high speeds. I was learning to be the wife of a British sports car enthusiast, and I liked the role.

Although many Aspies have trouble making friends, they do well with friends who have the same interests, and that contact boosts their self-esteem (Grandin, 2006, pp. 162-163; Attwood, in Attwood et al., 2014, p. 53; Maguire, in Attwood et al., 2014, p. 132-133). Jim had a number of friends through his interest in cars, church activities, and people where he worked. Although he counted them as friends, I'm not sure how close they were, or how much of himself he revealed to any of them. Interactions were based on proximity and common interests. Jim was a valued part of the vintage car scene, and put out a monthly newsletter to other owners for several years.

Taylor, an Aspie, speaks of being baffled by conversations at gatherings, and when I read that, I thought of myself, looking at his statement from my perspective, and how baffled I was at this gathering of vintage car enthusiasts and their conversations (Taylor, 2017, p. 63)! Baron-Cohen, I believe, gives a good explanation of conversations between Aspies this way: "Technical language, is, in a sense, more factual than 'social language,' which is riddled with figurative phrases that require one to compute the speaker's unspoken meaning or intention" (Baron-Cohen, 1997, p. 142), and which can be persistently difficult for Aspies. The car owners called a turd a turd!

On a Saturday, Jim won a second-place plaque with the Sprite at the "June Cruisin'" Pendleton car show. The afternoon was filled with introducing me to, and visiting with, his local car friends. He enjoyed telling interested passers-by about his little cars he had displayed. A few days later Jim took me for some more MGB and Sprite driving practice. Lots of laughter and fun, and I was getting better at driving the cute little cars.

In June, my cousins from Texas were to visit us. We couldn't wait to show them around Pendleton. The weather was beautiful, so Jim and I did yard work, sprucing up for the visit. On the lowest level, the cherry tree and the vinca minor were in bloom. Lavender edged the eastern rim of the lot, and the neighbors' lilacs provided both color and fragrance as they crept up the hill, ending in a bed by our front deck and blending with the orange calendulas. Pink rhododendrons graced the front of the bedroom windows, and on the upper level there were daffodils, tulips, roses of yellow and red, potentilla, purple sage, and a star magnolia bush. We got bags of bark for the flower beds. We got pretty pink, deep purple, and lavender petunias, the wave variety, to fill the planters on the deck, and the flowers would eventually cascade down the sides. Our new rosebush, with quite a few buds already, would have light pink blooms in a few days. Thanks to Jim, the lawn was in perfect shape, as usual. The sprinklers spewed rainbows above the grass.

Our cousins arrived for a whirlwind visit. We drove to Westminster Woods and showed them around – they were impressed. In town, we showed them where Jim worked, our church, and we celebrated Father's Day with brunch at the Red Lion. Lots of talking, lots of laughter during their visit. Jim cooked a farewell dinner their last night, and all was smooth the whole visit. Having family with us was special, and I began to miss them as soon as they drove away. I was relieved Jim exhibited no unusual behaviors for them to witness.

The last few weeks had been fun, and my cousins' visit, delightful. We were settling into a comfortable routine, and my worries about Jim's behavior were pushed to the back of my mind.

The church group in charge of the campground hosted a cookout at the Pendleton aquatic center, on the west edge of town, where there were grills and covered picnic areas by the pool. Teens from another town worked on a project at the Woods, and this was their farewell event. It was a jolly group. Jim's friend and helper at the Woods, Bob Downie, was there, and I met his wife, Jackie, who was also a therapist. Jackie and I found we had a lot in common, and she was to become one of my closest friends.

The teens had finished their project, and that June night, snow fell at the Woods. Jim said it wouldn't last long. I had never known it to snow in June, but I still had a lot to learn about weather in the Northwest. Though I had lived in the Midwest, where snow was abundant in the winter, it didn't snow in June, at least not where I had been.

Jim came home at noon one bright and beautiful day, and put out both fists. I chose the left one, and he opened it. It was a colorful cartoon sticker that said, "Wild Thing, You Make My Heart Sing!" I put on a happy face and jumped around like a wild thing. Jim laughed and grabbed me, held me close to his chest, and said, "Do you hear my heart singing?"

I stuck the sticker on my shirt, and we drove over to the Oregon Trail Interpretive Center, five miles east of Baker City. The ruts where the wagons rolled west were visible – I was in awe of the pioneer spirit. The wagons could travel about two miles per hour as long as there were no mishaps. Life in the early settlement of the west would have been hard. I was reminded of the conversations Jim and I had exchanged about my being a catalog bride. That seemed so long ago. I wondered if the catalog brides of those settlement days also had surprises when they began living with their new husbands. I felt sure that was true.

One beautiful June morning, we checked the garden. The string bean plants were beginning to climb the frame Jim built, and the tomato plants he grew from seed were blooming. We went to Safeway to pick up some fresh salmon for dinner, and chicken fried rice and sweet and sour chicken from the deli for lunch, and Jim did the silly walk, pushing the cart, while I laughed at him. He said he liked it when I laughed and appreciated his funny antics, even in public. We lingered at lunch, since Jim had to be sure he had all the green peas in his fried rice pushed to the edge of his plate. That night, he cooked our salmon, in the way only he could. It was the end of a most enjoyable day.

On the Fourth of July, we sat in our darkened living room, with the loveseat turned to face the big windows, far above the city lights. With glasses of wine, we watched the community Fourth of July fireworks across town, and I sang "Happy Birthday to the USA," to the delight of Jim (or was that a look of disbelief?). At any rate, he laughed – may have been the wine. We were adapting from sharing a bed, to sharing a house, a community, and a life.

The next week Paul visited again. We enjoyed sunshiny weather, great companionship, an afternoon tour in the fun toy cars, Jim's great spaghetti for dinner, a walk on the gravel road through the wheat fields late in the evening – a near perfect day.

Visits from my son were high points in my life – when he was here, Jim was always jovial and enjoyed talking and joking with Paul. They seemed to have a strong bond. I didn't think Paul suspected I was going through hard times emotionally over Jim's odd and hurtful behaviors – or maybe that's one reason Paul always managed to arrange business trips that included visits to Pendleton. He may have been more perceptive than I realized.

No strange behaviors had occurred recently, and maybe they were over. *All marriages have adjustment periods.*

CHAPTER 34

THE LICENSURE ISSUE

In July, I was eager to open my counseling office, and looked at several offices in town, but none appealed to me. I heard Jim's footsteps on the long wooden staircase beside the garage – those sounds still made my heart race with pleasure, the event of the day, when Jim came home! He arrived home that day with a flyer he'd picked up at the library, about an office for rent at 202 SE Dorion Avenue. I called about it, and we went to see it. Three ground-floor rooms in a downtown brick building: a waiting room, an office, and a large room for classes. I liked it right away, but I thought the rent was steep.

Jim said, "It's worth it for what you get – a nice office in a great location. We can manage the rent."

With great pleasure, I rented it, and I looked forward to opening my practice. Surely my license would be forthcoming before long.

But . . . the licensure process was dragging on and on. It turned out that reciprocity was not going to be as easy as I had been led to believe. Jim didn't understand why a counseling license was different from an insurance adjuster's license, which he had easily obtained in a couple of states. I groused at lunch, as I was still waiting for a response to the most recent information the board had asked for, and I got nothing in the mail from them that day.

Jim finished his sandwich and said, "You're so negative. I'm tired of listening to it. You're making a mountain out of a molehill. You're still the same person, with or without a license. You don't even need to work – you're 73 years old!" and he left the room, taking his coffee with him, in the honeymoon mug.

I followed him, "But I *want* to work! Counseling is what I do. It's an integral part of who I am!"

He didn't respond, and didn't seem to realize how the process of becoming licensed in Oregon was taking a tremendous toll on me.

His attitude and criticism hurt, and I was angry. Without saying anything to him, I got my car keys and purse and took an hour's drive by myself, to cool off. I circled around and around the town, on rural roads, fuming aloud about the slow licensure process and Jim's failure to understand how it was affecting me. When I returned, Jim was watching TV, didn't ask where I'd been, and seemed oblivious that I had been gone. No sympathy and no apology were offered.

A neurotypical would have had no trouble interpreting my demeanor, but, as I've said, most Aspies are unable to interpret other's expressions or sympathize (Robison, 2008, p. 21). Lipsky, an Aspie, says, "Many autistic individuals don't care about someone else's feelings, so listening intently or compassionately to someone 'vent' their emotions to them is as exciting as watching grass grow" (Lipsky, 2011, p. 199).

"Rather than experience various emotional blends, they may just get irritated by another who is being somewhat emotionally negative" (Kimball, 2005, p. 19, cited in Bogda-shina, 2010, p. 146).

One day in late July, I came down from getting the mail, and while we were at lunch, I opened a letter from the Oregon board with anticipation of good news. I ripped into it – only to read aloud in disbelief, "Your request for licensure is denied."

No request for more information, no explanation. Instantly, my world crumbled. I could feel the shatters falling inside me as my heart broke. I could not believe it. I dissolved into a sobbing jag that lasted several minutes.

I expected some reaction from Jim, but not what I got. He again chastised me about my negativity.

"You act like it's the end of the world," he said.

Of course, it *was* the end of a big part of my world, but he did not get it. It had to do with my identity, which Jim could not understand. He got up from the table, walked down into the living room, and was strangely distant and cool all afternoon and evening.

Nothing more was said about licensure, but the next day, when he came home from work, he brought me the second volume in *The Girl with the Dragon Tattoo* trilogy, *The Girl Who Played with Fire*, which he knew I wanted. He rarely brought me gifts for no special occasion, so I interpreted his offering as an attempt to make up. Still no apology, but I thanked him, accepted the book, and was glad to have it.

"Some people with Asperger's/HFA [High Functioning Asperger's] are unable to feel empathy (an 'emotional understanding') for others" (Attwood, in Attwood et al., 2014, p. 276).

"Usually we don't even know if somebody is being affected by a situation if they aren't telling us verbally or shouting it out" (Suglia, in Attwood et al., 2014, p. 277).

"While people with an ASD [Autism Spectrum Disorder] may have emotional empathy for experiences that they themselves have been familiar with, they may have difficulty being empathic with emotional experiences they have not personally known" (Attwood, in Attwood et al., 2014, p. 288).

Jim's failure to feel my disappointment about the letter denying Oregon licensure, and failure to sympathize, indicated he lacked theory of mind, which should have been evident to me. However, my love for this man, and my not wanting to judge him, blocked my recognition of that trait. His failure to apologize, not realizing he had hurt me deeply, was another trait common to Asperger's.

At the end of the month, at Jim's suggestion, we consulted an attorney about the licensure issue. I learned that, according to the state statute, I could legally open my counseling practice, as long as I was "pursuing Oregon licensure," so I forged ahead with my plans to move into the office. Meanwhile, I composed, and mailed, another letter to the Oregon board at Salem. I knew, or thought I knew, there had to be a way to be licensed in Oregon.

In retrospect, I wonder whether Jim's suggestion to see an attorney was to keep me quiet, or because of his sense of social justice, an Aspie trait that has been mentioned earlier. At the time, I felt he was supportive of my desire to open my practice, and I choose to believe that was his motive.

CHAPTER 35

THE PICNIC

One day, Jim suggested a picnic at a little park he knew, several miles south of Pendleton, called Bear Wallow Creek campground, near the small town of Ukiah. It was misting lightly when we got there. Not ideal picnic weather. We found a clean table, unpacked our lunch, and opened our cans of drink. Squirrels scurried around us, and insects buzzed and landed on the table, along with drops of rain. It was cool, wet, and the creatures acted as if we were competing with them for lunch. I didn't enjoy the weather nor the environment, and I was constantly shooing animals and bugs. We ate our sandwiches, chips, and bananas, and left the rustic picnic area. I wasn't conscious of complaining, other than trying to keep the critters away, but as we drove away, Jim said, "You ruined the picnic by complaining."

"I wasn't complaining, just keeping the table and area free of unwanted guests."

We drove home a roundabout way on a narrow highway, going to Heppner, a small town that was new to me. The picnic experience had dampened the atmosphere and me. I was cold in the car, even with the heater, and asked Jim to stop and let me get my heavier sweater out of the trunk. He pulled over to the narrow shoulder and stopped. As I got out, Jim said, "Be careful. Don't go out into the road."

Already in a foul mood because of being accused of ruining our picnic, I snapped, "I wasn't planning to. I'm not a child." Jim popped open the trunk, I grabbed my sweater, put it on, and slammed down the trunk lid.

The thick sweater felt good. When I got back in, I continued, "I don't know why you felt you needed to tell me not to go into the road. I was getting my sweater out of the trunk. Why would I go into the road?"

"I wanted to make sure. This is a narrow shoulder."

"Sometimes the things you say are patronizing. You act as if you're dealing with a child."

We drove a few miles in silence before we got to Heppner. Rolling into town, Jim said, "Let's get some coffee." We sat in the cozy café and held the hot coffee in our cold hands, and we shared a slice of cherry pie.

Jim started swooping his forkful of pie like it was an airplane, and making motor noises, "chir-rug, chir-rug," and "bombs away," just before it went into his mouth. I began to laugh. So did the two people at the next table. I loved his silliness, and it was hard to stay angry with him when he acted silly. Nothing about the picnic was mentioned, but the ice was broken. The coffee warmed us, Jim was funny, and once again I realized why I married this sometimes-goofy, entertaining man.

Because Aspies feel they are smarter than anyone, and always right, they can seem patronizing at times, pointing out the obvious. I am independent, and being told what to do (in this case, what not to do) does not set well with me, so I took his comment "not to go out into the road" personally, not realizing it was his Aspieness in action.

CHAPTER 36

GOOD TIMES

Daily life jogged along – early morning walks between the wheat fields, reading, and having our traditional Saturday night hamburgers made by Jim. Only he could prepare them properly – exactly the same each time – mayo on the bottom half of the bun, meat patty, Sweet Baby Ray's Barbeque Sauce, sweet pickle relish, tomato slice, lettuce, and mayo, before plopping the other half of the bun on top of everything. I was never allowed to make the burgers, because he grinned and said, "You don't know how to build them right." This was the same man who also had to peel tomatoes before using them for anything, cut the cores out of strawberries, and slice cheese paper thin. "Thin to win!" he'd say. These were his rules, and he was sticking to them! He modified my burger by putting on a slice of cheese, at my request.

Routine is important to Aspies – whether it's the daily routine, or something as simple as constructing a hamburger in exactly the same way, or preparing other foods. Routine makes the world predictable to those who are uncomfortable with change. I noticed Jim expected things to be put back in their place after use, and he was emphatic about it. I considered Jim a bit obsessive/compulsive, but did not connect the dots. Attwood estimates that 25% of Aspies exhibit obsessive/compulsive traits, but since it is a common Aspie trait, it is often not diagnosed separately (Attwood, 2006 [sic], cited in Dubin, 2009, p. 59).

While eating our burgers, we watched movies, enjoying life together. The tomatoes were ripening, the beans were growing, the roses were blooming, and my tubs of petunias by the front door were glorious bursts of color, beginning to cascade down the sides of the containers. I was optimistic, and happy to be opening my practice. Maybe things were settling down – or at least I hoped so.

CHAPTER 37

INTERRUPTING
AND BLUEGRASS

In August, I learned friends from Albuquerque would pass through Pendleton on their way to Seattle, so Jim and I agreed to ask them to have dinner and spend the night. Dinner started out fine, but the conversation somehow turned to politics. I was uncomfortable, because I knew getting Jim started on politics would be a mistake. He had strong opinions, and didn't hesitate to state them to whomever would listen. I tried to change the subject, to no avail. Jim was hooked on one of his favorite topics.

Our guests were Democrats, and while I was also a Democrat, mine and Jim's political views were never an issue between us. However, he could easily make it an issue in conversations with others, and tell them why the country was in trouble because of Obama. One of our guests tried to make a positive point about Obama, when Jim cut in and began to tell him why Obama's plan would never work. The poor guest never had a chance. It was an awkward situation, marring the lovely London broil Jim had presented on the platter with perfection. My appetite was gone, but I continued to pick at my food until our guests finished. I served dessert, and soon afterward the travelers said they were tired and were going to bed early, which saved the rest of the evening.

In our bedroom and out of earshot of our guests, I said, "Jim, you have an annoying habit of interrupting and overriding people when they are talking. Why do you do that?"

"I didn't know that's what I was doing."

"Well, you do. Sometimes when you interrupt me, I stop you and tell you to let me finish. Other people also feel that way, but are too polite to tell you. A word of apology to our company might be in order before they leave."

No response to my words, and no apology was given the next day.

Aspies often interrupt when someone is speaking, and continue to talk, overriding the interrupted person, especially when the topic is a favorite one of the Aspie (Attwood, 2008, p. 209; Grandin & Panek, 2014, p. 7). The Aspie considers his/her opinion to be the correct one, and is not aware of the "it is rude to interrupt a speaker" societal rule. When corrected, an Aspie has trouble apologizing, as has been noted.

We had a near-perfect day a few days later – an early morning walk, chillin' out most of the day, and some light yard work. Jim abruptly interrupted our lawn work by saying, "Let's head down to Great Pacific and get a bite to eat."

I was surprised at his suggestion, as I'd heard him say it catered to highbrows, and he didn't enjoy being there.

"I thought you didn't like to go there."

"It's better with you," he said.

We put up the yard tools and drove downtown to enjoy wine, chips, salsa, and sandwiches, listening to the local bluegrass players. At home later, we had shrimp salads and watched a John Wayne movie – a great day and evening.

However, things could turn sour quickly.

CHAPTER 38

PHONE BOOK AND DEPRESSION

The current issue of the local telephone book lay on the kitchen counter. Jim's ex-wife's name was still listed, with his. I asked him to call and have the listing changed, so he did. I heard him make the call.

The new issue arrived and still had her name listed with his, at our number. I guessed his call had been too close to the printing deadline. I occasionally got calls for her.

"The new phone book came today, with your ex's name still in it. Please call again and make sure they will change it in the next issue. I'd do it, but since the phone is in your name, they probably won't talk to me about it. Sometimes when I answer, people ask for her."

Jim stopped eating his sandwich long enough to raise his head, looked me in the eye, and made his point clear. "It's no big deal. I will, when I get to it." That ended the phone book discussion, for the time being.

His dismissive comment hurt my feelings. It *was* a big deal to me. I had another year of answering calls for his ex, and I wanted it changed before another year's issue.

For the rest of the day and the next day, I did not initiate conversation, and gave one- or two-word answers to his questions. We didn't have our usual fun times, laughing and joking. I soon tired of it. Jim did not seem to notice.

On the third day, I said, "Jim, do you notice I'm not talking much to you? Do you notice I'm giving you short answers to your questions?"

Jim was riffling through the day's mail with his head lowered. I wondered whether he was paying attention.

Without raising his head, he said, "Yes, but I thought you were preoccupied or in a mood. I didn't think anything about it. I know sometimes women have moods."

I said, "I was giving you the silent treatment, because I was angry. You said you'd call the phone company when you got to it, implying it was not an important request. I felt you were not being sensitive to my feelings. I feel unimportant when you say some of the things you say, the way you say them."

No comment from him, and he continued looking through the mail. I had wasted two days of our lives, and he had not noticed, had thought I was preoccupied or "in a mood." I learned giving him the silent treatment was an exercise in futility, and I had stated my case about my feelings, so I let life return to normal.

That night he said, "Let's go have a salmon dinner at Raphael's." No more was said about the phone book listing.

Days later, however, he told me he'd called the phone company, and they said his earlier call had missed the deadline, so the name would be changed in the next issue. Again, no apology for talking sharply to me earlier.

Remember, Aspies have to have time to process information. They have their own timetable, and rushing does nothing but frustrate them. Jim had taken time to process what I wanted done, and decided when was the best time for him to do it. Without theory of mind, he could not have known how important the request was to me.

I joined several community organizations, attempting to integrate fully into Pendleton life. At a Rotary meeting, I sat at a table with several men. One, probably noticing my southwestern speech pattern, said, "Where are you from, and how long have you been in Pendleton?"

"I married Jim Hanks and moved here from Albuquerque, not quite a year ago. How long have you lived here?"

The portly gentleman leaned back in his chair, stroked his white beard, shot looks at the other men at the table, and drew up one corner of his mouth in a smug and tilted smile. "Well . . . I'm the fourth-generation of my family to be born and raised in the Pendleton area, and I've been here quite a while." The others laughed.

That conversation told me I would not live long enough to be anything but a newcomer in this town, and this feeling, coupled with Jim's behavior and the licensure issue, kept me in a state of low-grade depression, unusual for me.

Besides Rotary, I joined the local Altrusa and American Association of University Women (AAUW) chapters, and although I met friends and enjoyed those groups, I continued to feel like a weed in a northwestern lawn.

I began to wonder, *What is the matter with me? I'm never depressed. Maybe I made the wrong decision to move here. Maybe this is not where I'm supposed to be.*

CHAPTER 39

AN OFFICE, BALLOONS, A FIRST ANNIVERSARY

On Labor Day, Dale and Judy, and their pickup, helped Jim and me move the stored office furnishings out of our garage and get the office set up. The sign company put my name on the door of the building. I could start seeing clients! With my usual optimism toward achieving goals, I was sure I would eventually achieve that license. All I legally needed to do was continue to pursue it. I joined the Chamber of Commerce and ordered office supplies.

I was active in the church, serving on several committees, and was even on the church governing board, since Jim was active there and on several committees. Slowly I was becoming involved in this new environment. I had lunch with several other therapists once a month. I volunteered to be on the board of a local retirement community. Together, Jim and I went driving in the little cars, walked together, watched football games, worked both jigsaw and crossword puzzles. We had a full and active life as a newly married couple.

Jim and I finalized our October plans to fly to New Mexico for the Albuquerque Balloon Fiesta, rent a car, and drive around Texas to visit some of my relatives. Jim was looking forward to his first experience at Balloon Fiesta. With Round-Up festivities in Pendleton starting soon, traffic would be unbelievably chaotic, and parking would be a problem, so I decided to delay opening my office until after our trip.

Out my window, I could see the familiar skyline, and the plane landed smoothly in Albuquerque. Jim was glad to have his first prescription sunglasses for the southwestern sunshine. I had suggested he get them at our last eye appointment, knowing experiencing the bright sun in the southwest for an extended time would be hard on him. We checked into the motel and grabbed a bite to eat.

The next morning, we were up before dawn, rode a bus out to Balloon Fiesta Park, and had traditional breakfast burritos and coffee at a picnic table. We watched people scurrying to and fro, some getting their balloons ready to launch, some just wide-eyed at the hundreds of balloons that would take off soon. We dumped our trash and walked onto the field. It was now daylight, though the sun had not yet come up over the mountain. Jim was amazed to be able to walk around on the field among the balloons and talk to the balloonists. He seemed as engaged with the balloons as he was with cars at car shows. After conversations with the pilots, he watched as these voluminous bags of hot air began to rise to the sky with their gondola baskets of pilots and passengers. He learned how the balloons were constructed and how the process of lifting off and landing worked. He continued to wander through the waiting balloons and talked to the pilots about mechanical and technical details. I snapped a great smiling photo of Jim with one of the "zebras," the guys in black-and-white striped shirts, who acted as traffic controllers, dictating when each balloon could begin to ascend. Soon the sky was filled with the colorful balloons, an amazing sight. I was thrilled for Jim to be witnessing this phenomenon for the first time.

Jim was game for another morning at Balloon Fiesta, so once more we were up early, to repeat the experience. He was enjoying it even more than I had anticipated, and this made it even more fun for me! We decided two days were enough, so we plotted our trip to Texas.

After leaving Albuquerque, we drove to west Texas, visiting relatives, some of whom Jim had never met. Jim and I went to the cemetery and placed flowers on the graves of my first husband, our daughter, my parents, and my in-laws. Jim was patient, and I wanted him to realize these plots, all adjacent, were hallowed ground to me. He had taken me to the cemetery in Oregon, where his mother and stepfather were buried, so it was his turn to see my special Texas cemetery.

Heading north, we covered a lot of territory that was familiar to me, and Jim got a taste of my earlier days in Texas. The trip was a balm. Jim and I were relaxed, and besides the brief cemetery visit, we spent a lot of time being with fun people, seeing fun sights, eating great meals, and laughing a lot as we traveled. Jim and my male cousin in North Texas instantly hit it off, and Jim was having such a good time with Bill and his wife, we were both reluctant to leave there. We experienced no troublesome incidents, except a speeding ticket on a southwestern New Mexico highway in the middle of nowhere. We had passed one car in the last forty-five minutes before seeing the red flashing lights behind us. Jim was not happy, but it did not affect him as much as the Illinois toll ticket.

We arrived back in Albuquerque and caught our plane, the day before our first anniversary.

I did not realize it at that time, but Jim was engaging in masking during much of the trip, and we often retired to the motels early, giving him time to recuperate and get ready for the next day. Long, leisurely baths, and/or hot tubbing, enabled him to relax between events. When we got home, Jim spent a lot of time playing Spider Solitaire, as well as an inordinate amount of time soaking in our hot tub. What an effort he must have put forth without my realizing it, to make our trip special!

On October 18, 2010, we celebrated our first anniversary, twelve months of many adjustments and trials, but we made it. Jim gave me a dozen long-stemmed red roses and a sweet card. We had dinner at Plateau, the fine rooftop restaurant at Wildhorse Casino. Their peppercorn steak was legendary. We sat side by side in the curved, rich maroon-leather-upholstered booth, and held hands while we had our drinks.

Jim turned to me, squeezed my hand, and said, "Happy anniversary, Mary Muffin. I'm the happiest I've ever been in my life."

My heart beat a bit faster, hearing this smiling man I loved say this. *Had I been too sensitive to his bluntness and other annoying behaviors?*

Even though at times he seemed verbally rude and could hurt feelings, both mine and others, he could also be charming, loving, and thoughtful. I was shored up for days by his dinner comment. I hoped his annoying behaviors were behind us.

I held an open house at my new office in November, with a ribbon cutting by the Chamber of Commerce Ambassadors and many congratulations from the community attendees. Jim said he was so proud of me, and he mixed and mingled with the townspeople, most of whom he knew well. I was in business as a counselor, still pursuing Oregon licensure. My file labeled "Application for Oregon Licensure" was several inches thick, with copies of everything I'd sent them, along with their replies. I wouldn't give up, and kept communicating with the board, hoping for a breakthrough.

Jim went around before the open house at my office, straightening any pictures he thought askew. I had noticed his doing that at home, too. At the time, I smiled, because I thought it smacked a bit of OCD (Obsessive/Compulsive Disorder), but I appreciated his making sure all was prepped for the open house. Aspies have a preference for symmetry, and this may explain the affinity of some for appreciation of architecture (Attwood, 2008, p. 286).

One weekend, Jim and I planted tulip and daffodil bulbs, and it snowed three consecutive days, giving our bulb beds a blanket of warmth in which to develop for spring. I hoped our lives would also continue to develop a consistent warmth, with no more odd, unexpected episodes.

CHAPTER 40

HEARING, DRESSING, AND STRESS

Jim mumbled. We were driving one day on an errand, and I asked him twice to repeat a sentence.

I said, "I'm sorry to ask you over and over, but it seems to me that you mumble a lot."

His jaw tensed, and he said, "You need to have your hearing tested," implying a denial of any imperfection on his part.

So, the next day I made an appointment with the audiologist, realizing maybe my hearing wasn't as good as I thought. I told her I had trouble hearing my husband, and I thought he mumbled, but I wanted to know how my hearing stacked up and whether I might need hearing aids. After a thorough testing session, the audiologist said my hearing was excellent for my age, with only a 3% loss.

"You're certainly not a candidate for hearing aids." She handed me printouts of the testing results. She did not say anything about my husband's mumbling, but it was implied.

I took the paperwork home and reported to Jim. I suggested he might want to speak either a little louder or enunciate more clearly.

He had little comment. He had a hard time being proven wrong – about anything.

As has been discussed, many Aspies feel they are too smart to be wrong, and are defensive about being proven wrong. Their brain is wired for them to think they are right about everything, and many of them rarely apologize for anything (Carley, 2008, p. 83).

Judy and Dale invited us for dinner and to watch a Ducks football game on their big-screen TV. Jim was excited, because he liked watching a bigger picture than our small TV. I was ready to go.

"Is that what you're wearing? It's too formal for a football game," Jim said, dressed in his jeans.

So, I changed, but then I was in no mood to go visiting. The atmosphere was still tense between Jim and me when we arrived. I hoped it was not evident to Judy and Dale. I felt Jim was oblivious, as always, to the hurt and tension I felt. As the evening progressed, the Ducks won, things eased up, as they always did, and we enjoyed the evening. Judy and Dale were gracious hosts and served a delicious dinner after the game.

Would Jim's criticisms never end? I was tired of his bluntness and critical words. The lack of a filter causes Aspies to be blunt and honest, and while I did not like it, it did not occur to me to attribute it to anything except rudeness and his wanting to be in control.

Another time I was dressed for church, and Jim pointed out that the dress I had on showed my "pudgy roll" on my midriff. I changed, but had not thought of the dress as making me look fat.

I was asked to give a talk on stress management to a group at Pendleton's St. Anthony Hospital. My own stress level was like a ship in a storm, depending on Jim's behavior surprises. I could not predict when he would say something thoughtless to hurt my feelings or insult a friend. I gave the talk and got applause, with no one apparently able to detect my personal stress.

I kept thinking we were just in our second year, and sometimes adjustment between couples took longer.

CHAPTER 41

BIRTHDAY CELEBRATIONS

In January, we were invited to Michigan to grandson Henry's first birthday celebration. We flew to Chicago first, and took a limo to Nancy's house in Wheaton (no more toll tickets!). We had a good visit with Nancy, Wes, and family before flying to Michigan for the birthday party. Jim looked forward to this trip, as my kids and grandkids embraced wholeheartedly his joining our family, and demonstrated their affection. He and baby Henry entertained each other with grins and giggles. Jim cheerfully played Candyland, and Chutes and Ladders, with Chloe and Jack, although I knew he disliked board games. The birthday party was fun – a small crowd with only three other adult couples, plus four little kids, and Jim appeared to enjoy talking to the men while having a couple of gin and tonics. It was one of our most enjoyable trips. Everything went well, and I sensed our love was deepening.

Oh, good! We're adjusting to marriage.

Jim's 77th birthday was a cold, dark, blustery day in Pendleton – and we celebrated another year of life. He came up behind me while I was baking his favorite cake, and put his arms around me. "You're my best birthday present."

This was a highly unusual demonstration of affection. Okay, reader, go ahead and roll your eyes, but his act pleased me, because his behaviors sometimes made me wonder about my importance to him. His behavior was unpredictable, sometimes a nice surprise, sometimes not so much.

We had his favorite cake, white with chocolate filling and frosting, and Cherry Garcia® ice cream. He was a young-acting, strong, and vigorous 77-year-old. We were both grateful for our good health.

A few days after his birthday, Jim and I and two other couples went for an afternoon tour in our little British cars. Despite our gratitude a few days earlier for good health, Jim fell on our driveway when we got home and wrenched his right knee. He was sidelined from work for a day or two. No doctor visit, of course, but resting it by alternate stints in the hot tub, and ice packs in his easy chair, seemed to be the home remedy.

Jim had some annoying repetitive habits, like stirring his coffee long after the sugar had dissolved. I hesitated to bring these things to his attention, because they weren't harmful, just annoying. I was sure I had habits that irritated him, too. Some of our coffee cups were black on the inside from the excessive scrapes of the spoon. He tapped his feet on the kitchen linoleum while we ate lunch every day. He fiddled with his silverware at every meal, arranging and rearranging the order of the pieces; he folded and unfolded his napkin, rarely laying it in his lap. He incessantly crinkled empty pop cans. I wondered what habits I had that irritated him.

Repetitive actions are common among persons with Asperger's, with their not realizing how those actions annoy others – possibly a form of stimming (Falk & Schofield, 2018, pp. 35,41; Silberman, 2015, p. 196). Arranging things carefully, lining them up, is also a trait of some Aspies, including Jim. To me, at this time, these were simply annoyances, but not annoying enough to mention, and not realized as traits of

Asperger's. Actually, some of his repetitive habits were amusing, like spinning on the breakfast table a tiny top that came in a box of cereal, or spinning a coin on its edge, over and over. Sometimes he spun a lid he'd removed from a jar, making me laugh.

Some of his idiosyncrasies were cute and amusing, but some could be hurtful. Neither of us could imagine that a few months later information would surface that would change both our lives.

CHAPTER 42

TRIP, DONUT HOLES, A PUMP, AND BILLS

In mid-April, Jackie Downie and I drove to Portland to attend a conference for therapists. After the conference was over, Jim met me there. We planned a trip to Astoria, on the coast, for a few days of rest and relaxation.

As we walked to the car, Jim remarked, "You walk very deliberately." His statement took me by surprise, but I had noticed over the months that he was exceptionally observant.

I asked him what he meant, and he said, "Just deliberate. Not like other women your age." I took it as a compliment, since I felt I walked with confidence. I found his statement odd, but as far as I could tell, not critical.

Intense observation is a trait of some Aspies (Finch, 2012, p. 51; Grandin, 2006, p. 153; Grandin & Panek, 2014, p. 120; Higashida, 2016, p. 59; Hollands, 1985, p. 11; Stanford, 2015, p. 209). Their observation and memory skills are sometimes off-putting to people.

Another time, I had been vacuuming our dining room, and Jim stood in the doorway watching me. I asked him what he was doing, and he said, "Just observing." I knew he was meticulous about housekeeping, so I felt he was making sure I was doing it correctly, the way he wanted it done. Aspies like to have things done their way (Aston, 2001, p. 69). He also wanted the baseboards wiped down with a damp sponge. I did that once. If he noticed I never did it again, he didn't say anything about it. I thought life was too short for such things, and I was ready to defend my position.

All the way to Astoria, in pouring rain, I gripped the armrest. Because of my car wreck in the rain years ago in Louisiana, I disliked being on a highway in the rain. Jim couldn't understand why that long-ago event still triggered my nervousness about riding in the rain. I tried to relax, but I saw every approaching vehicle as a threat, and sometimes I gasped.

Jim said, "You're ruining the trip."

To me, the heavy rain was ruining the trip, not me.

By the time we got to Astoria, the rain had stopped. We went to a deli and got carry-out: sandwiches, chips, salsa, and a bottle of wine to take to our room. We were given a large, comfortable room at the inn. We spread our food on the table beside a window, and looked out on the wet street and yard. We ate and talked, and nothing was said about the drive. The air in the room seemed damp and chilly, and it was close to bedtime, so I put on my warm flannel gown.

Jim looked at me and said, "You wear old woman clothes," even though I often wore that gown at home when the weather was cold. This was the first comment he'd ever made about it. I felt unattractive and hurt. I had a hard time going to sleep.

The next day everything seemed normal. We climbed the 164 steps to the top of Astoria Column, and the mood was one of adventure – a little breathless, but adventurous! Jim drove us around the town and showed me where he used to work, and Tongue Point, where he was discharged from the Navy.

We drove down the coast, stopping at Fort Stevens State Park, where Jim pointed out the Peter Iredale, an old shipwreck. Farther on, we came to Cannon Beach, where I was introduced to Haystack Rock, a landmark just off the coast. We stopped at Tillamook for lunch, and toured the Tillamook Creamery. All in all, the trip to Astoria and along the coast was fun and interesting – some light rain, but mostly clear – and I learned a bit about Oregon history. I tried to ignore his failure to understand my nervousness in the rain and the unusual and hurtful things he had said. When we were having fun, it was easy to forget the hurt and focus on my love for him.

If I had been looking for signs of Asperger's, I would have recognized a lack of theory of mind, and this was an excellent example. He could not put himself in my place and imagine the trauma of the wreck years ago and my fear of its happening again.

Also, if I had been attuned to the Asperger's traits, I might have realized Jim had spent a lot of the day driving in the heavy rain from Portland, coping with my nervousness, and getting us settled into the motel. Although I didn't recognize it at the time, he was having a meltdown of sorts, being grumpy and irritable, and needing time to relax. He may also have been feeling somewhat abandoned, by my going to the several-day conference in Portland and leaving him alone, triggering his constant abandonment issue. "Frustration issues can often result from a buildup of little things over the day that lead to becoming upset over what seems to be something trivial" (Christian, in Attwood et al., 2014, p. 73).

"There can be a buildup of tension due to experiencing an overload of minor irritations, disappointments, exhausting social occasions and unpleasant sensory experiences" (Attwood, in Attwood et al., 2014, p. 83).

After some food and wine and a good night's sleep, Jim recovered. The mood lifted, and the rest of the trip was pleasant.

One Sunday in May, it was our turn to provide refreshments for the coffee hour after church. Jim had spent long hours during the week installing a part to repair our hot tub, and it still wasn't working properly. Also, there had been a meeting at Westminster Woods that week about building a deck on the north side of the kitchen/dining building. Jim did not agree with the way the majority of committee members wanted to do it. He had experience in construction and maintained the materials they planned to use were not appropriate. I could tell he was out of sorts.

On Saturday, we went grocery shopping, and Jim picked up two packages of donut holes. I knew he liked them, and I did, too, so I said, "Yum, yum!"

Jim said, "They're for tomorrow at church."

"What else do you want to serve?"

"Nothing. That's enough."

I thought he was joking. "So what else are we serving?"

"Nothing. That's enough."

"Jim, those will be gone in an instant."

"We're not required to provide a meal. That's enough."

There was no changing his mind. I even tried to inject levity.

"We could always serve liver and onions as a side. I'll go pick up some liver now," as I turned toward the meat counter. He kept walking and was not amused.

I did not know why he was so stubborn and was buying so little. It was another surprising behavior. Money was not a problem.

Sunday after church we went into the fellowship hall, and I went to the kitchen to make coffee. Jim put the donut holes out on a platter. I knew they would be gone quickly, and I couldn't understand Jim's reasoning.

It was Jim's church, and had been, long before it had become my church, so, as the newbie, I didn't interfere. Instead, I continued making pot after pot of coffee and stayed in the kitchen. In the process, my nerves reacted, and I spilled coffee down the front of my blue wedding dress.

One of the church members came into the kitchen, looked around, and said, "Where are the rest of the goodies?"

The strong smell of coffee permeated the kitchen.

I said, "Jim put them out on the table."

"Those are gone."

I was at a loss to justify or comment. Making refills for the coffee urns kept me busy and out of the dining area, hiding my embarrassment.

As we drove home from church, I said, "I will never again let you dictate what we are to serve at coffee hour. Two packages of donut holes was a pathetic decision. Since it also involves me, I will buy or make whatever we need from now on."

A person with Asperger's often has a difficult time transitioning from one event or thought process to another. He will get something in his mind and can't, or won't, let it go. I have to assume this was the case for the insistence on such a small amount of food for a crowd Jim knew could be 30-40 people, some of whom were children who liked donut holes. He was still frustrated about the hot tub, plus his words, "We're not required to provide a meal" [for church people] might demonstrate that he was still feeling at odds with the church committee's decision about building the deck at the campground. What upsets an Aspie may not always make sense to neurotypicals, but may signify that he feels misunderstood (Ariel, 2012, p. 86).

Jim did not have the emotional capacity to deal with providing refreshments after the week he'd had. Another clue I failed to recognize.

In late May, my Albuquerque house sold, and I happily signed the papers. The next day, we began another trip in the MGB with the other owners of British cars. On our way to Canada, the group stopped for lunch in downtown Leavenworth, Washington. Just as we parked, I saw water spewing out from under the hood. Jim got out and looked. The water pump had gone out. Jim called around and found a foreign car repair shop in Wenatchee, less than 25 miles away. He was agitated and grumbling about having to spend money to have the car towed and about missing part of the trip. I told him I had my AAA card with me that would cover the towing cost, and we could rent a car for the rest of the trip.

We had the MGB towed and rode to Wenatchee with the tow truck driver, so Jim could talk to the mechanic when we arrived with the car. We rented a red Toyota sedan for the rest of the trip. At least it was red, like our MGB. We were disappointed, but made the best of it and joined the group that night in Anacortes, to catch the ferry for Vancouver Island the next morning.

Jim had a chance to sleep and recover from the frustrating experience. The few days on the island were fun and relaxing, even to Jim, and I hated to see them end. I had been to Vancouver Island, but during this trip, I saw different areas. Except for having to deal with our car breakdown, the Canadian trip was delightful, one of the high points of my northwestern experience.

We drove back to Pendleton, and a rainbow welcomed us home.

Grumbling about the towing expense was not about money. Lack of money was never an issue to us. His plan for the trip had been interrupted, we were with a group of his car buddies, and I believe he was upset to have the water pump go out on our car and not have a replacement with him. He may not have recognized that emotion, so placing an emphasis on the cost of towing was an acceptable focus of his irritation. This is common for anyone, to transfer an emotion to another object (have a hard day at work, so kick the dog, etc.), but an Aspie has trouble even identifying the causative emotion, much less coping with it in a realistic way. Lipsky, an Aspie, says, "No matter how visibly distressed, upset, or anxious the person may be, your focusing on what they are feeling will not deescalate the situation. They are in need of a solution before anything else can be dealt with" (Lipsky, 2011, p. 74).

Without realizing it at the time, my concrete, logical solution to the problem, given in a straightforward manner, away from the other group members, gave Jim an acceptable alternative plan. The overnight in Anacortes allowed him to recover.

I sat at the kitchen table paying my bills from my separate bank account. Jim paid his house payment, utilities, and credit cards one at a time, as they came in. I collected my bills in a stack on one end of the kitchen table and paid them all at once, but before the first of the month, knowing they'd arrive before the end of the grace period. None had ever been late, and I had done it that way for years. My credit rating was excellent.

I worked through the stack – no more mortgage payments nor utilities on an empty house but a few other assorted bills, and payments on my credit cards. Jim often offered to pay off my credit cards, but even though he rationalized (correctly) that it would save the interest, I insisted the debts were mine, and I'd pay them off. It was a point of pride to me.

He was observing me as I wrote my checks, and began criticizing my method. "If your bill is due on the first of the month, and you don't pay it until just before the first of the month, then it will be counted late."

I assured him there was a generous grace period before it would be considered late and incur a late charge. I couldn't anticipate when he might focus on something to criticize. I let it go, because I felt it was my business how I paid my bills, but I was irritated. Perhaps he didn't like my independent streak. I looked at this episode as a small blip on the screen of life with Jim. At least the blips seemed to be getting farther apart, and perhaps would eventually go away.

Aspies like to do things their own way, and often consider any way but their way to be wrong. Usually inflexible about how they perform certain tasks, they expect others to perform them in the same way. Kind of like rules that are to be followed. Aspies' perfectionism causes them to become agitated over trivial matters (Attwood, in Murray, Ed., 2006, pp. 38-39).

I saw this incident as Jim's being critical, and I attributed it to his wanting to control me. I saw this, as I said, as a minor blip in our lives, compared to more major ones.

After the bill-paying session, Jim and I took the envelopes to the post office and went out to Wildhorse Casino to celebrate the sale of my house, by having dinner and seeing a movie. *The King's Speech* was the story of England's King George VI, how he worked to overcome his stuttering, a trait thought to be, at least in part, genetic. Movies were spot on for celebrations.

Later we would have reason to be more interested in genetics.

CHAPTER 43

A FUN VISIT AND A LICENSURE DEVELOPMENT

In mid-June, Nancy and Wes arrived from Illinois for a long-awaited visit. Jim took some days off from work, and we packed a lot into those few days. We showed them Westminster Woods, the Oregon Trail Interpretive Center near La Grande, the Pendleton Underground Tour, the Pendleton Woolen Mills, and my office. Jim took them for rides in the MGB, and cooked delicious meals. We all had fun and enjoyed being together.

Jim didn't feel he could miss more work, so when their time was up, I drove them to catch their plane. I hated to see them go.

When I got home from Portland, I found my day's mail in a neat pile on the kitchen counter, and beside it, a yellow rosebud in a tiny glass vase. Jim smiled and said it was for his "yellow rose of Texas." He could blow me away with his thoughtfulness.

Jim had not had a single bizarre behavior during the visit. His effort always to mask around my family showed me he loved me, even though neither of us realized that's what he was doing. Sometimes I held my breath, because Wes is intelligent, with a scientific bent, and Jim could have been tempted to engage him in one-up-man-ship on several topics. But he didn't. I was relieved.

After the fun visit, the licensure saga dragged on, and I was beginning to think I might never be licensed in Oregon, threatening my practice, but I decided to make another attempt. I called the board and asked if I could possibly do anything more to gain licensure. I figured the worst they could say was no.

The woman I spoke with did not say "no," but said, "Well, you will be required to take another graduate course."

What? Another graduate course, after already having a doctorate? I was shocked, but was so intent on getting that license, that after the initial shock, I saw her reply as a glimmer of hope!

I asked where, and she said, "Online, at one of two universities." I asked which course, at which university, and she told me which course they wanted, and gave me the names of two acceptable universities.

I thanked her and got online to look at the courses offered. I picked one, and verified with the board that the specific course and the specific university were acceptable to them and would lead to licensure. They replied in the affirmative. I still had a chance!

Yes, I would take the course, if that is what would give me licensure. The cost for the several weeks' long online course was $1,800.00, which I hated to spend, but licensure in Oregon was important to me, and if I had to take one more course, I would do it. The course would begin with an introduction to the professor, on Monday, July 11th. Licensure seemed to be in sight.

PART VI

AN ADVENTUROUS RESOLUTION

CHAPTER 44

IT HITS ME!

I'm doing laundry in the middle of July. The dryer buzzes. I unload warm bath towels, toss them onto the bed, and start to fold one. As I carefully put the edges together, a mind-blowing realization causes me to stop.

With my hands still in the air, immobile, I feel a powerful force similar to walking out of the house years ago, in hot, humid Houston, when the heat would hit me like a blast, almost take my breath away, and cause me to stand still, waiting for my body to adjust.

This time I need to let my mind adjust.

I . . . have . . . missed . . . the . . . obvious. How could I have failed to see? How could I be a counselor and not realize the truth before now?

Jim has Asperger's Syndrome! The pieces of the puzzle bounce around in my head.

"Jim has a multitude of the classic traits of Asperger's Syndrome," I say out loud, as if I need to examine the idea and let myself absorb it.

I abandon the towels. I walk into the kitchen to make a cup of tea. The tea bag goes into my Life is Good mug, and I heat water in the microwave.

The revelation has a visceral effect. I need to let my

thoughts catch up. Drinking my tea, I reflect on many clues I've missed. After all, I've not been looking for them – I'm in love.

I begin to cry. The release of emotion comes with a flood. The events are assembling in my brain, falling into place, and making sense of the last months. A heavy weight is being removed from my body, and perhaps my marriage and my life. What should be an easy diagnosis, one I have made for many clients over the years, has been delayed because of my love for Jim. The old song, "Smoke Gets in Your Eyes," comes to mind.

Another factor occurs to me. Our courtship was mainly by email, providing a distance between us, interspersed with short in-person visits during which Jim could mask, making it difficult to read him accurately until we started living together (Aston, 2001, p. 47; Carley, 2008, p. 206; Falk & Schofield, 2018, p. 141; Grossberg, 2015, p. 66; Hendrickx & Newton, 2007, pp. 43-51; Kupferstein, in Attwood et al., 2014, p. 181; Moxon, in Murray, Ed., 2006, pp. 222-223; Silberman, 2015, pp. 257-258; Solomon, 2013, p. 278; Stanford, 2015, p. 198).

My mind leaps forward. Jim will be home from work soon. How am I going to tell him? How can I explain it? How will he respond? What if he already knows? He said he has been to counselors several times for various issues. Surely a competent counselor would objectively pick up on the traits of a client presenting in person. After taking a history, asking pertinent questions, and possibly having input from a family member, in a few sessions a diagnosis would be clear. If he has been diagnosed, why hasn't he told me?

I must tell him of my discovery. If he accepts the diagnosis, there may be hope for our marriage; if not, the only answer may be divorce.

CHAPTER 45

THE REVELATION

I pull myself together and hurry to have lunch ready – ham sandwiches and RUFFLES®, a normal lunch for us. I make fresh coffee for Jim, make sure the sugar bowl is full, and pour iced tea for me. I greet him with a hug, he washes his hands, and I put our food on the table. My hands are trembling.

"How was your morning?" I ask.

"Same old, same old. Mopping, vacuuming, wiping down bookcases, cleaning toilets. Really exciting. At least everyone was there today, so I didn't have to do anyone else's work."

I hope he isn't too tired to hear what I'm going to say. I wait, gathering my courage and giving him time to take in some food and coffee.

Halfway into lunch, I decide the time is right. I get up and get him one of the cherry Pop-Tarts® for his dessert, something I know he likes.

As I lay it on the table beside his plate, I begin, trying for a casual approach, "You have Asperger's, don't you?"

Jim looks up at me with wrinkled brow and says, "What?"

He looks as if he is being spoken to by an alien in an unknown language.

"You have Asperger's, don't you? Have you been diagnosed?"

"I don't know what you're talking about." He looks confused, but not annoyed, and continues eating – by now, the cherry pastry.

"Did any of the counselors you saw mention Asperger's to you?"

He shakes his head. "What is it?"

I will interject here that many professionals do not understand Asperger's and do not know how to diagnose it. Robison was not diagnosed, even after seeing several professionals, until later in life (Robison, 2008, p. 90), and I personally know many counselors and psychologists who are not familiar enough with Asperger's to diagnose competently. If the reader suspects they, or someone they love, has Asperger's, seek a mental health professional who has a thorough knowledge of Asperger's and feels confident diagnosing it.

By this time, Jim is staring at me as he is stir, stir, stirring his second cup of coffee. I think of what my high school chemistry teacher taught, about how to dissolve substances in a liquid – either heat the liquid, or stir until the substance is dissolved. In a cup of hot coffee and with constant stirring, the sugar in Jim's coffee dissolves quickly and doesn't need endless stirring.

I clear my throat. "Well, you have it, and it's not a deficiency, but a difference. The brains of people with Asperger's are wired differently from most other people's brains. It's true from the time you're born. You learn to cope, but you never outgrow it. But, I repeat, and I emphasize – it's not a deficiency, but a difference. It causes behaviors that seem quirky to people who don't understand it."

Jim stares at me. I can almost see and hear his brain's wheels turning. The stare morphs into a look of surprise and interest, and he leans forward.

At least he hasn't tuned me out.

"You mean . . . there's a name for it?" he says. He pauses and turns his head in slow motion, gazing out the window beside the table, as if pondering my words and processing what he is hearing.

I wait, giving him time to absorb what I've said.

"Yes, it's called Asperger's Syndrome. A high-functioning form of autism."

Seconds go by.

Still looking out the window, he says, "I always wondered...why...I felt...different."

I get up, walk to his side of the table, put my hands on his back, and start kneading his shoulder muscles, something I've learned he likes. I wait a minute before giving more information. I know he is still thinking.

"I've diagnosed quite a few people," I say, "and this morning I realized you have it. I've tried to put up with some of your behaviors, and even though we also have a lot of fun and good times, I have at times been very unhappy living with you. Now it all makes sense."

The shapes of his face and its features are changing before my eyes – quizzical, then intense, then relieved – as in one of those funny-mirror houses at carnivals. What a lot for him to take in, all at once!

I'm glad he doesn't appear angry or resistant. I can see every muscle of his face loosen and feel his shoulders soften.

He looks at me. "That explains a lot." His relief is palpable. "Tell me more about it."

Many Aspies report feeling intense relief at being diagnosed. It serves as a discovery, as well as being labeled a diagnosis. They say they are glad to know about Asperger's, having always known they were different, and, knowing it has a name, having validation of their life-long feelings (Fisher, in Grandin, 2012, p. 125; Lesko, in Attwood et al., 2014, p. 12; Robison, 2008, pp. 237-238; Stanford, 2015, p. 53).

And so the explanations begin, at Jim's invitation . . .

CHAPTER 46

JIM IS A SPONGE

I tell him that because of his charm and our relationship of love, I have been blind to his Asperger's until today. I begin explaining why I know he has it, and that people with Asperger's sometimes like to be known as 'Aspies.' He smiles at that term.

Although somewhat embarrassed at overlooking the clues, I must accept my blindness, as apparently, I'm not alone in being slow to put pieces together, blinded by love. According to Ariel (also a therapist), "When you first get to know your partner, the symptoms of Asperger's can be subtle and hard to recognize" (Ariel, 2012, p. 56).

Finch's wife said, "Slowly the condition revealed itself to us, one confusing situation at a time" (Finch, 2012, p. 230).

Hollands (also a therapist) said, "There are indicators for problems available to us, though. Usually, we just don't want to see them!" (Hollands, 1985, p. 33).

Robison says, "In the first sixteen years of my life, my parents took me to at least a dozen so-called mental health professionals. Not one of them ever came close to figuring out what was wrong with me" (Robison, 2008, p. 90).

In fact, Aspies are good at masking during the courtship period and finally, after marriage or cohabitation, they begin to be themselves, and that's when trouble begins. When expectations are for normal, and idiosyncratic behaviors are exhibited, frustration, disappointment, and resentment result (Solomon, 2013, p. 279).

As has been mentioned, courtship may be shortened by the Aspie's eagerness to secure a partner. I think about mine and Jim's courtship, mostly by email, with a few visits, and the energy he must have expended at masking during our pre-marriage time together.

I begin, wanting to break the explanations into bite-size bits. I say, "Going back to the first times my feelings were hurt – by your throwing a log in the fire and stalking off upstairs on our first Christmas Eve, and by your telling me I talked too much when I was excited about my library card and the prospects of licensure. Most Aspies don't have a natural filter that examines thoughts before they leave their mouths, and they say things and do things that unintentionally hurt other people's feelings. Aspies don't realize they are offending, because most don't have what is known in psychology as theory of mind, or the ability to see things from other people's perspective. They can be unintentionally offensive to family, friends, or co-workers, with no intention to be rude or hurtful" *(Ariel, 2012, p. 29; Stanford, 2015, p. 185).*

I remind him of the time his friends stopped by unexpectedly, and he couldn't imagine why I didn't like being surprised by people he knew well, but I didn't know yet. Another example was when I asked him to call the telephone company again about the listing in the phone book. He did not understand my feelings about wanting his ex's name removed, balked at my request and answered with irritation, and I decided to give him the silent treatment. He had no idea why I wasn't conversant.

I tell him it is difficult, if not impossible, for Aspies to put themselves in someone else's shoes and realize how the other person feels or what they are thinking.

I remind him of times when I asked him what he thought about why people had done things, and his response was always, "I don't look at motivation. I have no way of knowing that."

"You were so right, and you were describing your lack of theory of mind without realizing it; and without my realizing it at the time. At other times you said hurtful things to me, when I know you to be a loving, kind man, and I was puzzled that you would want to hurt me or be rude. The answer, I now know, is that you didn't want to – you did not realize what you said was hurtful."

After a bit of time for him to process, I go on. "When you interrupted people, and I called you on it, you said it was your opinion, and you felt what you had to say was more interesting or important than what they were saying." I explain to him that being interrupted is annoying to most people, and it is considered by neurotypicals to be rude behavior, but is a common trait of Aspies. They lack awareness of the social rule of taking turns in a conversation (*Attwood, 2008, p. 209; Grandin & Panek, 2014, p. 7*).

Jim is attentive, listening, and waiting to see what I will tell him next. I ask him if he wants time to digest what I've said so far.

"No, I want it all now." He is like a sponge.

I continue, "An interesting anomaly about Aspies and sex – they either want it often, or they aren't very interested in it at all. In the couples I counseled, if intimacy and sex were issues in their relationship, and they often were, it was because the partner with Asperger's either wanted a lot of sex, or, on the other hand, rarely was interested. Either extreme was problematic for the spouse or partner. Some complained that their spouse would wake them several times a night, but some complained they couldn't remember the last time they were intimate. You and I are fortunate and early settled into an arrangement that works well for both of us, so that is not an issue for us, but it is for some couples" *(Ariel, 2012, p. 130-136; Attwood, in Attwood et al., 2014, p. 175-176; Weston, 2010, p. 155).*

At this bit of information, his eyes are bright, and he is grinning and nodding.

I talk about his repetitious sayings, and that even though they are cute and funny, it is typical of the repetitious habits of Aspies. Some of his favorites are, "I'll keep it up here in my kidneys," pointing to his head, meaning he'll remember something; "I'm a legend in my own mind"; "There you have it, sports fans"; "Get'er done"; "If I didn't want to do it, I wouldn't"; "I'm just a piece of driftwood in the wake of life"; "If times are hard, we eat stewed tomatoes on light bread"; "It just doesn't get any better than this"; "Presentation is everything"; and "The church is the world."

"Those are examples that come to my mind, because I hear them again and again. They are just things you say, and they are not annoying, just a part of you, but I point them out because they relate to Asperger's."

I tell him many Aspies calm themselves by repetitive actions called stimming. He squeezes and crinkles a soda or beer can longer than most people do, or stirs his coffee much longer than it takes to dissolve the sugar. With a cold drink, he jiggles and shakes the glass interminably, making noise with the ice. When he taps his feet on the floor at the meal table, drums his fingers on a surface, taps on the table with a utensil or pencil, or keeps rearranging the silverware during a meal, those appear to be some ways of stimming.

I say, "You have a habit of opening and closing your hands repetitively, spreading your fingers wide and then making a tight fist. When I asked you why you did that, you said it was to relieve your arthritic joints. That may be true, but it is also a common form of stimming, called 'hand-flapping.' You told me in an email that playing Spider Solitaire is calming, but I failed to pick up on that, which I now see is one of your forms of stimming" (*Falk & Schofield, 2018, pp. 35, 41; Hendrickx & Newton, 2007, pp. 35-36; Higashida, 2016, p. 68; Lipsky, 2011, p. 122; Stanford, 2015, p. 144*).

He is leaning forward, listening intently, arms now on the table. I get up and refill his coffee cup and hand him another toaster pastry. He sugars his coffee and begins stirring.

He says, "Go on."

I speak of our tradition to have hamburgers every Saturday night, made by him, and they are constructed a certain way – no deviation, although he acquiesces to my request to have a slice of cheese and an occasional bit of mustard on mine. Many persons with Asperger's tend to be perfectionists and enjoy a common trait, with a fixed routine, some to the point of appearing obsessive/compulsive. "To you, everything has a place, and it needs to be put back in its place as soon as it is no longer being used. This applies to utensils or tools, either in the house or in the garage. You are meticulous about the lawn. You spend hours mowing, trimming, and weeding these four levels, that have lots of trees, shrubs, and flowers; and you're determined to do it all yourself. No hired help can please you. Even your wife can't please you with yardwork!"

He laughs at this last comment. "Did I say that?"

"Yes, you told me one day to go on into the house, because you would eventually get all the weeding done. I knew why – I was not doing it to your satisfaction!"

"You keep your desk neat and orderly, with everything in place and not much on it. My desk is a mess and jumble, and you told me soon after we married that you wished I would keep my desk orderly. I didn't pay attention, because I know where everything is, and I like it that way. I know just looking at my desk annoys you and makes you uncomfortable, but, after all, it is *my* desk. I think you tested me once. You asked for some paper that was a few months old, and I produced it from a stack in about ten seconds. You were amazed. I don't think you complained about the condition of my desk anymore."

He does not dispute the statement that he tested me. And I know him well enough to know he would correct me if I were wrong!

I say, "Another trait of many Aspies is their sensitivity to touch. This includes the feel of materials next to their skin. You like to wear only very soft fabrics – no starched or coarse clothing. You want no socks with seams. You wear the same blue-striped or pink-striped, long-sleeved, WearGuard™ shirts and Wrangler™ jeans to work every day, and even when we're just lounging around at home or running errands. You have several shirts and pairs of jeans to rotate, and they have been washed so many times, they are super soft. Much of your clothing I've never seen you wear, only the few items that feel good."

I then add, "The touch sensitivity also extends to having people touch you. You told me you were uncomfortable at our wedding reception in Albuquerque, because of all the touching and hugs. At first your idea of hugging me was a sideways, one-armed hug, not what I am used to. I started putting your other arm around me, and now you've learned to hug me with both arms, and you don't seem uncomfortable doing so. Are you?"

Jim answers, "No, now that kind of hugging seems good to me. But only with you. I don't think I'd want to hug anybody else like that."

"Are you tired of listening? Want to rest a while?" I say.

I know Aspies need time to process new information, and this is a lot of information for Jim to process at once. I also know they need to have things stated in a straightforward way. They are not likely to interpret oblique statements or sarcasm when receiving information. Jim commented in emails about how he appreciated the way I communicated. Aspies like for specifics to be stated, not merely alluded to.

"No, keep going. Get'er done! I can always ask you to repeat things later, but I want to hear everything now."

He, like many Aspies, wants the complete details, all the pertinent information *(Hollands, 1985, p. 38)*.

"Most Aspies have certain topics that interest them a great deal," I say. "You like to discuss cars, as well as other things mechanical; politics, especially Obama; and space with its black holes, as well as nature and the universe in general. You enjoy being with and talking to people who love cars – your friends at the body shop and the people in the vintage car shows and runs – they speak your language. Aspies are usually good at taking things apart and putting them back together. You built an intricate model airplane at one time. Sometimes you help other Brit car owners with mechanical problems. You restored two vintage British cars from scratch, and built a Geiger counter. I know you like to discuss politics, to the point of making people with opposing views uncomfortable. You read many books on physics, space, and the universe. You spend many hours at Westminster Woods – felling trees and doing general maintenance of the grounds and buildings. In your earlier years, you were a logger, so you are good at it. You love the outdoors – the sunsets, the clouds, and all aspects of nature, feeling very content in Earth's space and the universe The Man has created. Did you know some other Aspies say they feel 'grounded' and stabilized by their connection with nature? Do you share that feeling?"

"Yeah," he starts. "I'd never thought of it that way, but there is a contentedness that almost overwhelms me when I engage with nature. Interesting!"

"You're also good at drafting and construction, having worked at that in your earlier days, so you are handy around the house, installing faucets, repairing the lawn sprinkler system, building decks and stairs, installing a hand rail on our steep front stairs outside, repairing the hot tub, installing additional memory in my computer, and you finished the brick fireplace in this house. These are other examples of your knowing how to put things together, and many Aspies are very good at that and enjoy it."

Jim remains attentive and doesn't interrupt. So far, he hasn't raised an objection to anything I've said.

I explain that social cues, like whether a person's facial expression indicates they are happy, angry, frustrated, or sad, or recognizing people's readiness to engage in conversation or to have it end, seem difficult for him, and he nods.

I say, "Remember the day I got a letter from my cousin that touched my emotions, and I cried? You thought crying meant sadness, so you asked what was the matter. When I said I was happy about something in the letter, that puzzled you. After that, when I cried about something, which was more often than you were accustomed to, you would ask, 'Are you crying because you're happy, or because you're sad?'"

I pause, feeling he has probably had enough for one session.

He says, "This all makes so much sense to me. How can I learn? Will you help me?"

I say, "Of course I'll help you, if you want me to. I also have some books about Asperger's you can read that may be interesting to you."

After diagnosis, "there can be a new sense of personal validation and optimism, at last not feeling stupid, defective or insane" (Attwood, 2008, p. 31).

"For some, diagnosis spearheads a new sense of purpose, which is driven by the desire to find out everything that there is about the condition" (Georgiou, in Murray, Ed., p. 233).

"It is a label that at least offers the comfort that one is not an alien, that there are others out there encountering similar problems in this puzzling world" (Murray, in Murray, Ed., 2006, p. 16).

I tell him he can learn some things, but he may never get the hang of how other people think or feel, that his brain is wired in a way that doesn't allow it. However, I can inculcate him with some social cues that will be helpful to him.

I feel very proud of Jim. I did not know how he would handle my diagnosis, and it took great courage for me to unload all this on him. He could have been resentful, resisting what I was saying. Some Aspies, when diagnosed, become angry and don't want to believe there is anything different about them. I took a risk with Jim, because of my deep love for him; fortunately for me, and for him, he identifies with everything I tell him, and says he is so relieved.

"There can be intense relief: 'I am not going mad'; . . . at last discovering why they feel and think differently to others; and excitement as to how their lives may now change for the better" (Attwood, 2008, p. 30).

What relief I feel, too! By now, I have a few tears, both because of relief, and because of my love for this man.

He says, "I'm so lucky to have you."

He begins to spend time studying Asperger's, both in the books I give him, and online, and we begin to outline some ways I can help him.

One day he says, "I can now just be me, no trying to be someone else."

After diagnosis, an Aspie is free to choose whether to change or maintain his current sense of self, which has worked for him for years (Stanford, 2015, p. 159). It must be liberating to be able to "just be yourself," after years of trying to be something else (Finch, 2012, p. 211). Diagnosis helps adults put their experiences into context, increases self-awareness, and improves self-confidence (Georgiou, in Murray, Ed., 2006, p. 241). He is relaxed; he can be himself. It is comforting to know someone close to him understands and accepts him (Hendrickx & Newton, 2007, pp. 70-76).

On this day, our lives change; a turning point in each of our lives and in our life together. Jim is relieved to know why he has felt different all his life; I am relieved that he has accepted the diagnosis so readily and is optimistic about the future.

Can you imagine the rage that builds up in a person restraining his innate traits all his life, trying to fit in? No wonder he walks away from conflict. He has learned to ignore it and walk away, so afraid that if he lets out his anger, he might not be able to control it. He now has an explanation, and it will take him a while to process it. His relief is something he will have to get used to. I can now point things out to him as we go along, knowing he is receptive and eager to learn. I no longer resent his behaviors, knowing they are not aimed at me, or at anyone. They are just the way Jim is made. I can accept them and become a guide, at his request.

We forge a stronger bond this day. During our courtship by email, Jim said a couple of times, "I win, I win," when we'd exchange our views on a topic. I would reply, "A relationship is not a competition, but a collaboration."

We have been living a competition, but now we are experiencing a collaboration. A true win-win!

CHAPTER 47

DISCLOSURE

In a few weeks, Paul visits us again. One day at lunch, Jim says to Paul, "Your mother tells me I have Asperger's."

Paul listens with interest as Jim tells him some of the reasons I have given. Paul has two master's degrees in different areas of education, so Asperger's is not foreign to him. He asks Jim how he feels about learning he has Asperger's.

Jim says, "I'm relieved. I have felt different all my life. I now know why." Paul says he is glad Jim knows about the difference and feels relief. To my knowledge, Paul is the only person Jim ever told. Jim may have been reluctant to disclose to relatives, because it might concern them about genetics.

Disclosure involves trust – trust that people will not react negatively (Carley, 2008, p. 134; Georgiou, in Murray, Ed., 2006, pp. 237-238; Lesko, in Attwood et al., 2014, p. 236).

Because of twin studies and family studies, there is no longer any doubt that autism and Asperger's are heritable conditions, from one or both parents. The chances of another sibling having it is about 5-10 percent, and males with it outnumber females about 10:1 (Baron-Cohen, 2008, pp. 92-93; Falk & Schofield, 2018, p. 85).

Lanier reported, "Dr. Calhoun [her daughter's doctor] said, 'Chromosomes don't get passed down in their entirety.'" The doctor explained that one might have a bit from this person, and bits from another person, and bits from another. "The chromosomes copy themselves to become chromatids – exact replicas." They tangle up with others and exchange genetic material, then they part (Lanier, 2020, pp. 168-169). Even Dr. Hans Asperger said Asperger's was "undoubtedly polygenetic," rather than transmitted by a single gene (Silberman, 2015, p. 99).

A day or so later, we drive Paul back to Tri-Cities to catch his plane. On our way home, we stop at Great Pacific for dinner. Life is immediately different for us. Our love is richer now that I *understand* why things seemed hurtful and inappropriate. I tell Jim I will not talk to anyone about his Asperger's, except I will tell our doctor at my next visit, if that is okay with him, because I feel the doctor needs that information. Jim agrees. If he wants anyone else to know, he can tell them himself *(Carley, 2008, p. 140; Willey, 2015, p. 142).*

Life is sweet. I look forward to living with this man forever.

CHAPTER 48

THE GUIDING AND LEARNING BEGIN

At an appointment with our doctor, I tell him about Jim's Asperger's and his reaction to the diagnosis. I report how relieved I am that there is a good reason for Jim's seemingly odd behaviors. The doctor is interested, and I believe he notes it on his pad – I had mentioned at earlier appointments that at times I was stressed and unhappy. He says he is glad to see my relief.

I mention Jim might enjoy watching TV's Sheldon on *The Big Bang Theory,* a CBS series, where Sheldon is a classic, overdrawn case of Asperger's. While the show never mentions the term, Sheldon displays many Asperger's traits. We begin watching it every week. Jim loves the show. He records the episodes, and we watch them over and over. We watch Sheldon's blunt statements, lack of empathy, failure to read facial and social cues, all done for comic effect, and Jim says, "That's me," as we both engage in hip-slapping laughter. Our eyes water, and we are out of breath. Jim especially enjoys Sheldon's facial contortions, and he mimics them, opening his mouth and drawing one side into an overdrawn sideways rictus grin. He calls it his "Sheldon face." He also adopts Sheldon's pet word, "Bazinga!"

"If you've never watched this show [The Big Bang Theory], do so. The four main characters all have social challenges in various ways, and this series can be used to discuss social problems and solutions with a spectrum individual" (Grandin, 2015, p. 335).

I also recommend it. The original show, with Sheldon as an adult, is available in reruns.

Jim's whole demeanor is different since he learned about Asperger's. He knows he can be himself, and I will understand. He wants help. The minor things, we agree, like repetitive behaviors and stimming, I may occasionally point out for teaching purposes as he does them, but I will not expect him to change these calming behaviors. They are harmless, and if they help, I am glad.

We agree I will bring any major inappropriate social behaviors to his attention as they occur – like interrupting, or talking too long about his favorite topics, or being blunt and saying hurtful things, or not reading social cues about when to end a visit. I will help him interpret people's facial expressions and what they are feeling, when it is obvious he isn't interpreting them correctly, by saying to the person speaking, "Oh, that's too bad!" or "Oh, that's nice!"

We work out a code system so that only he and I will know what I mean. For interrupting, I will raise my hand at the wrist, palm facing him, as my signal that he has interrupted, and to let the other person speak and quit monopolizing the conversation. When he has been blunt and hurtful, I will call it to his attention and help him learn that some things are better left unsaid. When we are visiting people, and I can tell by their body language they are ready for the visit to end, I will initiate our departure and gently take Jim's hand or arm and say, "We've enjoyed the visit, but it is time for us to leave." He agrees that these codes will be helpful.

While we are both relieved about the Asperger's diagnosis, I still have licensure on my mind. My final class paper is due, and as I understand from the board, a passing grade on the course will ensure my license will follow.

The class ends, and I make a final grade of A+. The university is to send the grade to the counseling board. I am exuberant. A reasonable time passes, still no word from the board.

A few days later, I take an envelope from Salem out of the mailbox, and I hop down the steps to the house to share with Jim, as I know it contains my license. He, like I, will be so glad the waiting is over, although he is much more supportive since his diagnosis.

I hurry to open the envelope. There is no license.

Instead, a letter saying the board notices it has been over ten years since I took the National Counselors' Exam, so in order to be licensed, I will have to take it again.

I cannot believe it. In New Mexico, you never have to repeat the national exam. My initial urge is to crush the letter in my fist and give up, but I toss the letter across the table to Jim, fold my arms onto the table, lay my head into them, and sob. I am disappointed, resentful, angry, and feel at the mercy of, and defeated by, a powerful bureaucracy.

Jim waits until I can tell him what this last requirement means. He does not criticize my reaction as negativity, but is supportive and patient. I tell him how much that means to me.

I am not going to let them win. Determination takes hold once again. I raise my head, wipe my eyes, blow my nose, and tell Jim I will take the exam. Surely that will be the last requirement.

The exam is scheduled in Tri-Cities in six months. I load up on current exam materials − CDs, books, and practice exams. I took it when I was fresh out of school, in Albuquerque, and it was difficult, but I did well. That was years ago. I will be well-prepared again.

We celebrate our second wedding anniversary. We are grateful for our love, which is enriched in so many ways by our understanding of Jim's Asperger's, the changes that understanding makes in our day-to-day interactions, and the possibility that I may eventually get my Oregon license. I can continue my counseling practice, which is full, while I prepare for the exam. We toast each other with our glasses of Riesling at our Raphael's dinner, with loving and joyful hearts!

We spend Thanksgiving in southern Oregon with Jim's sisters and brother-in-law. The dinner is a feast, and we have a great time with Jim's family. Nothing is said about Asperger's, but I think everyone can see how much more relaxed and jovial Jim is. Jim attempts to interrupt speakers a few times, but I employ our "code" for that: My raised hand, at the wrist, palm facing outward, so he can see it, but it isn't obvious to others. That is his cue to finish his sentence and let the other speaker continue for a while. He is watching as we visit, and it works. After dinner, as we drive to visit Jim's son and family, Jim says, "Thanks for the help. I can learn to wait and let others talk."

While Jim was learning, he still had a ways to go. Some can learn from one experience, others take a lot more practice (Grandin & Barron, 2016, p. 115). Weaknesses can be helped by supportive people (Stanford, 2015, p. 44).

I was happy to be that supportive person for Jim.

In mid-December, Jackie and Bob Downie go to Westminster Woods to cut their Christmas tree, and they stop by our house to bring us a tree they picked out and cut for us. We appreciate their thoughtfulness. Jim and Bob stow the tree on the deck, next to the house, and we invite them in for lunch. I fix lunch while Jim sets the table, making sure the plates and silverware are meticulously placed. His precision table-setting Aspie trait is quite nice.

We work a jigsaw puzzle in the afternoon, and as usual, Jim picks one piece and puts it into his pocket, assuring he'll be able to put the last piece in and finish. Always competitive!

I have to cue him only once about interrupting, but he catches on, and it works. Jim and I are a team! The visit is fun, and I get better acquainted with Jackie.

None of us can imagine what lies ahead for the Downies.

CHAPTER 49

A TRAGEDY AND A LEARNING EXPERIENCE

In January 2012, Jackie Downie experiences a sudden, catastrophic loss. She finds Bob unresponsive in his recliner one evening when she comes in from feeding her horses. I grieve, both for the loss of Bob, and for Jackie, whom I know, from experience, has a long, hard road ahead. We are thankful for that last visit with both of them, a few weeks earlier. We are reminded of the fragility and brevity of life.

Jim wonders why so many people from church are planning to go visit. I explain to Jim the emotional, mental, and physical effects of grief, because even though he has experienced the loss of several family members, his understanding of how grief affects most neurotypicals is lacking. He is amenable to hearing the differences in how he feels while grieving and how most others feel, and although he can't manufacture feelings he doesn't have, he at least needs to have an intellectual knowledge of the devastating loss of a spouse through death.

I say, "Grieving people often want people around them, showing support."

"I don't. I want to be by myself," Jim says.

"That's what I mean when I tell you your brain is wired differently. You experience things differently from people who aren't Aspies."

In the next few days and weeks, Jackie asks Jim for various kinds of help repairing some things around her house and barn, and I am glad he is cued into the common aspects of grief. I believe it is a sobering learning time for him.

Aspies are many times "loners," meaning they like to spend a lot of time by themselves. Plus, having a lot of people around them tends to overload their sensory circuits, so to speak, causing a desire to get away from the crowd. Jim needed to be aware that his reaction to grief is different from most other people's, who are comforted by having people around to give them emotional support.

CHAPTER 50

EVIDENCE OF LEARNING

Jim turns 78, and his sister and brother-in-law arrive for the weekend. Jim gets a subscription to Mad Magazine from my kids, a gift that causes his face to contort with laughter. His laughter comes so much more easily now. I wonder if our guests can tell the difference. He is mellowing and blossoming. He is more at ease with himself, with me, and with life.

"A late diagnosis might lead to a flowering of social development and relationships as the person finds the courage to move forward in work and life, no longer blaming themselves, afraid of making mistakes and learning how to interpret other's (sic) behaviour" (Moxon, in Murray, Ed., 2006, p. 222). Porges suggests a sense of safety causes relaxation, and a person becomes more receptive to engaging with others in the world (Porges, 2009, 2011, cited in Siegel, 2015, p. 316).

The National Counselors Exam is upon me, and I dread it, because even though I have studied for many hours, I remember it as a tough one. I drive up to Tri-Cities the day before, and stay in a motel, as I don't want to take a chance on the weather or any car trouble. Jim is to meet me at Starbuck's in Columbia Mall after the exam.

The exam lasts three hours, and I am trembling when I exit the soundproof room. The proctor hands the results to me. I not only pass, but make a higher score than I made years before, fresh out of my doctoral program. I burst into tears of both relief and joy, and the proctor puts her arms around me and says, "Congratulations!"

I drive to meet Jim. He is hunkered in an overstuffed chair in Starbuck's, facing the door and drinking coffee. When I walk in and see him smiling at me, I begin to cry again. The long study hours are over, and he has been supportive though it all. Jim sees I am crying, so he gets up to greet me, puts his arms around me in a bear hug, and says, "It's okay, it's okay. Can't you take it again?"

I look up at him, hold up my hand with palm facing him, dab my eyes with a Kleenex, and say, "No, no, let me tell you! I passed it. I passed it, and I'm so relieved it's over." I break into sobs again. I know Jim doesn't care what people think, and at that point, neither do I. My victory tears taste sweet.

Jim holds me close, then pulls back, looks into my face, and says, "Are you through telling me?"

"Yes," I say.

"Then it's okay if I tell you I'm proud of you?" We laugh at his noticing my hand and letting me finish. Collaboration, not competition!

During lunch at the Mexican restaurant around the corner, Jim says, "Let's go around to that clothing place you like and look at some spring clothes for you. This calls for a celebration."

Jim again picks out several outfits, and I try them on for him. I notice the items he chooses are not only lovely colors, but soft textures. He even likes for *me* to wear soft clothing! We walk to the car with bags of new items. What a day!

I don't think I could have persevered through all the studying before Jim's diagnosis. My stress level would have prevented the necessary concentration and retention. The studying paid off. One of the best parts was Jim's "I'm proud of you!"

We take the MGB on a road trip to Ukiah one sunshiny day, through Pilot Rock. Spirits are high, and the ride is lovely – interesting puffy white cloud formations in a clear blue sky, a white church with a spire high on a hill, a logging mill, multiple cattle grazing, a pretty little redbud tree blooming in someone's yard, and beautiful horses in a field. A deeper understanding and connection between Jim and me is a contrast to the misting picnic trip near Ukiah a few months earlier.

We get home, Jim puts the little car to bed, we eat dinner, then he puts *me* to bed . . .

CHAPTER 51

WORDLESS

The end of May 2012, my Oregon counseling license arrives in the mail. I cradle it in my arms and hold it to my chest. Never has a license been desired and fought for more fiercely, and now earned.

I cry a few tears of relief and gratitude. My heart overflows. The Oregon licensing ordeal is over. I show the coveted paper to Jim, and he gives me a hug and a kiss. It is an awesome event, and few words are necessary.

Jim makes me enchiladas for dinner. The evening is delicious . . .

CHAPTER 52

A WINNING SURPRISE

At the Walla Walla Balloon Fest Car Show, vendor booths are set up around the perimeter of the show area. Jim goes to the registration booth to register the MGB and picks up our complimentary T-shirts, while I walk around and peruse the items for sale. I decide on a beaded zebra coin purse. The balloons are rising, a miniature version of the Albuquerque event.

We enjoy visiting with other car owners and looking at their cars. After the car judging, we leave our cars and gather around the canopy to hear the winning names. I hear *my* name called. I look at Jim, raising my eyebrows.

Jim looks at me, grinning, and says, "Go on up and get your trophy." He has secretly entered the MGB in my name. My first time to win a car trophy! What fun, and what a winner of a husband!

Over the weeks, Jim gives me more driving practice in the MGB and Sprite. I am getting better at anticipating the little cars' quirks, just as I am getting better at anticipating and understanding Jim's quirks. Some of Jim's become amusing to me, now that I understand where they come from; others, as you will see, are more serious.

CHAPTER 53

WEDDINGS

Jim's daughter calls to ask him to escort her down the aisle at her wedding in a few weeks. We both like the young man she is marrying. I offer to let Jim go to the wedding by himself, as I don't want my presence, as his new wife, to make anyone uncomfortable.

Jim says, "No, we're a unit. Where I go, you go. If that makes anyone uncomfortable, that's their problem."

Jim buys new khakis, a new white shirt, and new brown loafers to wear at the wedding, all according to his daughter's suggestions. Jim takes his time shopping for a white shirt that feels soft enough. None pleases him, but he picks one. He helps me shop for my wedding attire, a beige suit and a zebra purse, which he picks out and holds up to me from across the store, grinning, knowing I collect zebras.

We stay at a rustic lodge near the wedding site, where Jim and Mrs. Davidson (the cat) quickly make friends. Other relatives are staying there, and we have several meals together as a family.

Friday afternoon, at the rehearsal, the moppet flower girl cries, because she tilts her basket and loses most of the petals. Jim stoops down and helps her pick them up. I observe that sweet act, and I am thankful he is my husband. He has a good heart. He is different, but certainly not deficient. We rehearse, and are told what we're supposed to do.

As the outdoor wedding begins, a handsome young groomsman comes up to me, and with a cheerful smile, gives me his crooked arm. I take it, and he escorts me to the chair beside the empty one reserved for Jim.

As Jim and his daughter come down the grassy aisle, my heart swells with pride and love for him. His daughter is beautiful in her long white gown, carrying a lavender bouquet. Jim is handsome in his new wedding clothes, including the white shirt. He never wears it again, because he says the collar is stiff, even after I have washed it several times, trying to soften it.

After the wedding, Jim and I run to our car in a blinding cloudburst and drive to the reception. The bride and groom roar up on a motorcycle, to the delight of the guests. Beautiful bride, good-looking groom, lovely wedding, the promise of a nice reception. As people gather, we mill around on the grounds of the community building, visiting with the few family members and friends Jim and I know. Soon dinner is served.

Not long after we finish dinner, Jim turns to me and says, "Let's go."

"What? Go where?"

"Back to our room."

"Jim, they haven't cut their cake yet."

"I'm ready to go."

I know not to try to persuade him, as when he feels a meltdown coming, he wants to get away. He hates small talk, as do most Aspies. It has been a long day, and he is tired of socializing. I feel we owe the couple an explanation, so at my insistence, we walk over to tell the bride we are leaving. She is surprised, but Jim is not to be deterred. I feel the exit is Jim's decision to make, not mine, since it is his daughter's wedding, but I am sorry he is disappointing her. I know he is tired of masking, and all the hubbub is overwhelming to him. It may be that witnessing his daughter's start on a new life journey might also be affecting him and taking a toll, though not acknowledged, and perhaps not realized, by him.

We walk over to the lodge, about a football field away, and get comfortable in our room. I don't question Jim, but allow him to lie down and relax. We have brought Riesling, so I pour each of us a glass. The quiet and the wine are calming.

After the reception, some relatives come by our room to check on us. They wonder why we left before the reception was over.

Jim tells them, "My feet and legs hurt."

That is true, because he has stood for long periods of time during the day and done a lot of walking. The people don't stay long, and are apparently satisfied with his answer.

After the relatives leave, I tell Jim I know he is experiencing his Aspieness and aversion to crowds, small talk, and overstimulation. He says he is glad I understand and did not make a fuss. We are a unit.

Aspies dislike small talk, and would rather have silence unless the conversation is geared to one of their interests (Dubin, 2009, p. 124; Goleman, 2007, p. 134; Robison, 2008, pp. 191-192). Because they are often reticent unless they have something they feel is worth saying, they are often perceived as selfish, arrogant, and/or aloof (Robison, 2008, p. 194; Silberman, 2015, p. 26; Wylie, 2014, p. 32). One Pendleton friend told me she viewed Jim as aloof and arrogant, almost a snob, before she got to know him better.

Aspies are known to detach themselves from social situations with conversations going on all around them, go to their computer or begin to read a book or magazine, or just leave (Bogdashina, 2010, p. 177; Stanford, 2015, p. 182; Willey, 2015, p. 183).

One summer weekend, Jim and I drive to Prineville, Oregon, to my niece's wedding, on her grandparents' estate on Lake Ochoco. The grounds are breathtaking, and there is a lighthouse on the grounds, at the end of the point near the lake. The bride's grandfather built it to enclose a water pump. Before the wedding, Jim corners and converses with the grandfather, pointing to the lighthouse and questioning him about how the pumps and lights work.

I observe this interaction and think, *Jim, your Aspieness and comfort zone are showing. Mechanical things are much more interesting to you than wedding festivities.*

The grandfather is cordial and gracious, but I can tell he is darting looks toward the house and is antsy to be doing other things right before the wedding. I walk over, take Jim's arm, smile, and say, "I'm sure this grandfather has last-minute details to attend to. We need to find our seats." Another example of Jim's failure to recognize social cues.

We have an arrangement that when he fails to notice body language or facial expressions indicating it is time to make a change, I will take his arm or hand and say something appropriate, making a smooth transition for him.

The bride is beautiful, the groom handsome, the wedding lovely, and after a small, brief reception with dancing, cupcakes, and punch, Jim and I leave to drive home. As we drive, I explain to Jim some of the grandfather's body language and facial expression that alerted me he needed to do other things – the way he shifted his body weight from one foot to the other, and kept looking back at the house to see what was going on there. Jim said he didn't notice. I encourage him to see if he can notice those kinds of things in other situations.

We stop for dinner at The Tavern in Bend, and afterward drive through Malheur National Forest near Mt. Vernon, and along the John Day River. The scenery is new to me, and as the terrain changes toward the approach to Pendleton, it seems comfortable and homelike. The trip has been fun, and Jim has been a trooper. Our coding system is working well, and Jim is learning, little by little. I believe he is proud of himself, though he never says so.

CHAPTER 54

TV, DANCING, AND A VISIT

On a beautiful afternoon, we drive to Tri-Cities to look at big, high-def TVs. Jim has been researching them online, but is having trouble making up his mind about the kind to get, and is having trouble deciding to spend the money, even though we can well afford the purchase. I leave the decision entirely up to him, but am supportive, as I know how much he will enjoy the fall and winter football games on a new TV.

We come home empty-handed.

The next afternoon we go to Walmart in Pendleton to look at TVs, and Jim is still hemming and hawing around about the money. The salesman can hear parts of our conversation. He comes up and tells Jim about a Walmart credit card that will let him pay the TV out over 12 months, with no interest. Conservative Jim falls for that deal; we bring home a 46" TV. Jim gets it hooked up, and now fall football can be watched in all its close-up, high-def glory. In the first Ducks game of the season, they beat Arkansas State, and Marcus Mariota thrills us on the huge screen.

We go to Raphael's for a dinner of salmon with huckleberry sauce and wine, to celebrate our third anniversary. When we get home, Jim puts on a big band CD, and we move together rhythmically in front of the fireplace's dancing flames. Our actual anniversary will not be for several days, but the real day happens to be a Ducks game night. Priorities, you know, and now we even have the big, new TV!

We attend our monthly Dinner/Dance Club event at the Pendleton Country Club, with cocktails, dinner, and dancing to a live 50s band. Jim has some smooth moves, and I am kept on my toes (literally) following him in my felt-sole dancing pumps. As he twirls me, and we dance to the romantic music, he lays his cheek next to mine, and I count my blessings. Life is, indeed, good!

One Sunday, during the coffee hour after church, a bunch of us ladies stand around chatting. One says, "Look at that smile on Jim's face. I think you are good for him," and another woman says, "I've never seen Jim look so happy." Now when he smiles or laughs, his eyes crinkle at the outer edges, the sign of a sincere smile. The ladies do not know about his knowledge of Asperger's that has led to his relaxed and smiling demeanor. I don't say anything, but am pleased.

Often, after a diagnosis, a more relaxed state causes Aspies to let go of some of the tension that is always with them. They loosen up and are much less anxious, and, experiencing understanding, they don't work so hard at holding in their emotions (Dubin, 2009, p. 200).

On Jim's 79th birthday, he is in his happy place! He has worked for days getting a new top installed on the MGB. He has disassembled, stripped, painted, and reassembled the bars that will hold the new top in place, and today he is putting the top on. What an appropriate way for him to commemorate his birthday – spending energy on his little cars!

He successfully finishes the project and cleans up in time for a birthday salmon dinner at Raphael's. We toast another year!

At a fund-raising event for St. Anthony Hospital, I bid on, and win, a large, embroidered, framed floral piece that reads, "Welcome." Jim hangs it high in our entryway to welcome guests. I think I am attracted to it because I am feeling more at home in Pendleton, especially now that Jim is not having episodes of his hurtful behavior as frequently. He still cannot read social cues well, but depends on me to give him signs, when I'm with him. He welcomes my help, with never an indication of irritation or resentment – in fact, he often thanks me. I believe having a partner who understands him and lets him be himself is calming to him and reduces his quirkiness somewhat.

Can you imagine the discomfort a person holds within himself all his life, trying to fit in, but knowing he is somehow different? Just letting go of that feeling, even at home, must make a difference in his whole being. However, as you will see, he still sometimes exhibits Asperger's traits. Just because he knows about it doesn't change the way his brain is wired.

One night Jim is in his bathroom getting ready for bed. He calls, with an unusual urgency, "Mary, come look at something."

He has his undershirt raised. I see a sprinkling of red, blistery bumps around his right side and abdomen. I look farther and see that they spread all the way around his waist. I worked in assisted living and nursing homes years ago, so I know what I am seeing.

"You have shingles."

"Are you sure?"

"Yes. No doubt."

It is a weekend, so on Monday, Jim goes to our doctor and says, "One doctor has already said it was shingles, but I want a second opinion."

The doctor says, "She's right," and gives Jim some ointment for the pustules.

Shingles is a synonym for pain and misery. It will be a while before Jim's pain is diminished and his energy is restored. He spends much of the next few weeks on the bed or in his easy chair watching TV. Thank goodness for the big TV! Work is out of the question, so he applies for all the vacation time allowed.

Memorial Day weekend, Jim's son and family arrive from southern Oregon for a visit. In spite of the shingles discomfort, Jim seems to enjoy being with them. His son and one of the grandsons mow the big, multi-level lawn for us, which is a great help. Jim will not be able to mow for a while, and I will not tackle it. The large lawn is getting to be a chore for Jim to take care of, even before the shingles. I'm not sure how much longer he will be able to take care of the landscape.

Our company leaves Monday morning after breakfast. Jim pushes himself during their visit and is tired after they leave. He obviously is masking much of the time, and needs time to be alone and recuperate. To my knowledge, Jim says nothing to them about Asperger's. It is a memorable first visit from them since I've lived in Pendleton, and though we don't know it now, it will be their last.

CHAPTER 55

FUN TIMES

Paul arrives for another brief visit. The next morning, I wake a little later than usual and walk into the kitchen to see two happy guys with their cups of coffee. My version of happiness is listening to my husband and my son exchange one-liners and laughter. Paul goes to the Pendleton Woolen Mills and buys us a Chief Joseph blanket – an exquisite surprise. I think it is a reward for our "down time" with the shingles.

This town, with its woolen mills, wheat fields, underground tours, rodeos, parades, and Native American reservation and casino, now seems like "my town," and I consider the blanket a symbol of warmth that covers all my feelings about Pendleton. I work on my book every chance I get, and after Paul leaves, I get another chapter organized.

Our doctor finally gives Jim a clean bill of health about his shingles; the lesions are healed. However, the prognosis is that Jim may have recurring pain for a long time. The bout with shingles has convinced him that he might as well quit working. He turns in his resignation letter and officially retires from his job with the City of Pendleton. Decision made; deed done. I am delighted, as we don't need the money, and he will have more time to devote to his cars and the lawn, at his leisure. He enjoys both, although the lawn is getting to be more a burden than an enjoyable activity. That night, we toast his decision with gin and tonics. No more 4:30 a.m. alarms.

To celebrate his retirement, the next weekend we drive to Wallowa Lake and rent a cabin, cozy and rustic, at Wallowa Lake Resort. Jim's energy is gradually returning. We take walks, talk a lot, read some, and relax.

As we walk up the main road, I see a miniature golf course. It reminds me of the fun Mother and Daddy and I used to have. It is relatively new and has a windmill, some clear streams, and a sand trap.

I point to it, and say, "Oh, miniature golf! Let's play!"

Jim says, "I don't know how. I've never played."

I say, "Really? Then let's do it. You'll never learn any younger."

We have a hilarious time, and Jim almost beats my score. He is so proud of his new skill.

This romantic and luxurious time together is a high point among our fun times. Squirrels and deer roam the yard of our cabin. We have a picnic in Wallowa Lake State Park, a chipmunk joins us, and birds congregate for our crumbs. A doe and her fawn stand at a distance. Jim and I are relaxed and happy. Jim crinkles his soda can and chips bag. He smiles at me as he does it, and makes his "Sheldon face." Conflicts are rare. Understanding rules our relationship.

We walk down to the marina and see mallards on the shore. We look up at the Eagle Cap Mountains. Jim puts his arms around me and says, "Glad we could have a great vacation! It has been fun. Next time I'll win at miniature golf!"

Some of my friends from New Mexico, who attended our wedding reception, are on their way home from Seattle and stop with us for dinner and overnight. We are happy to share our home with these full-of-fun people.

Jim fixes his famous spaghetti for dinner, and the spicy, delicious odor fills the house. The husband is from Japan, and at dinner, Jim, making a connection, talks on and on about living in Japan and going to high school there. Jim is monopolizing the conversation. I surreptitiously give my hand signal, and he stops soon to let our friend talk about *his* life in Japan – an opposite view, eye-opening, told by a Japanese citizen who lived there during the MacArthur era. Our friend tells it with grace, and Jim doesn't interrupt, but listens attentively.

After dinner, Jim takes our guests to the garage to show off our little cars, and the male guest tries on the Austin Healey for size. He is taller than Jim, so finds it a tight fit, and we are amused. Of course, Jim shows him what is under the hood of each car and goes over to the workbench and shows him multiple car parts. Anyone who shows the slightest interest in cars gets the whole routine.

Later, as we are in our bedroom getting ready for bed, Jim says, "Was I hogging the conversation?"

I say, "Yes, I think so. Thanks for taking my cue. And I'm proud of you for not interrupting him once!" Jim is learning, and life is much less stressful.

After they drive away the next morning, Jim comes up to me in the kitchen, puts his arm around me, and says, "Hello, beautiful!"

My heart beats faster. Since the Asperger's diagnosis, he is much more demonstrative, and expresses his emotions verbally more often, which pleases me. At intervals since the diagnosis, he says, "I love you for letting me be me." I think he feels freer and more at ease in general.

A word about an Aspie's words. Being literal, if they say it once, they assume it is still true. Many are reluctant to keep saying, "I love you," and say they've already said it once and nothing has changed, so that's enough (Attwood, 2008, p. 307; Hollands, 1985, pp. 66-67; Stanford, 2015, pp. 205-206, 218).

After the diagnosis, I found Jim's verbal expressions of love even more precious. He knew it pleased me to hear the words, even if nothing had changed since he said them once, so he began using them more freely and brought joy to my heart.

In October 2013, Jim is well enough to make a trip to southwestern Oregon. We return home in time to celebrate our fourth anniversary. On our first anniversary, three years ago, I wondered if we would have any more. Now I look forward to many, many more.

I am thankful Jim is feeling better. For months I have worked on my first book. Jim affords me the silence and time cheerfully, and most evenings he prepares our dinner, so I'm not interrupted. More later about finishing the book.

CHAPTER 56

A MAJOR DEVELOPMENT

One Sunday in February 2014, while we are getting ready for church, Jim puts his arms around me in a bear hug. I love these hugs. I snuggle into his chest and feel safe and secure and loved. *I had to stop for a moment after writing this last sentence, overwhelmed with the memory and feelings of those hugs.*

He says, "I think we should sell this house and move to Albuquerque."

My ear is pressed against his chest, and I feel the vibration of his voice. I cannot believe I heard him correctly. I pull back slightly to hear better.

"What did you say?"

"This house is old and needs work, and the yard is big and is getting to be too much for me. I think we should move and buy a newer house with less maintenance, and a smaller yard. I know you love Albuquerque, and I know I would love the weather there.

Jim goes on, "When we began talking about marriage, we talked about where we would live. You were flexible and said you would be happy to move to Pendleton. I said maybe we should take turns and live five years in each place. You've lived in Pendleton several years, and I think it's time for us to live in Albuquerque for the rest of our years."

I still can hardly believe what he is saying. I become tearful. I enjoy many things about living in Pendleton, but there have been adjustments of many kinds, to be sure, and Albuquerque means a lot to me.

I look up at him and say, "I hope you're not teasing me. Don't say that if you don't mean it."

"I'm serious. I think we should start getting this house ready to sell."

I can tell he is letting me in on something he's been thinking about for a while. Jim does not make snap decisions, so I know he has been waiting to tell me until he feels sure.

Moving to Albuquerque. A newer house. Less snow and ice. Old friends. My mind races. It seems I am dreaming.

While this may seem a strange decision for Jim, since he loves the northwest, even turned down a promotion years ago that would have required his moving to Arizona, Jim has changed in many ways. This decision is made logically, the way Jim makes his decisions, such as the one about working, when he said, "When I can't work anymore, I'll quit."

Word gets around that Jim and I are moving to Albuquerque. People meet the news with raised eyebrows and "Really?" and "When?"

At the coffee hour after church, I overhear someone say, "Jim, are you sure you want to leave Pendleton?"

Jim's reply, "Yes, this is Jim and Mary's excellent adventure!"

He beams as he says it, and he looks happy about the prospect. He never wavers or shows any sign of regret about his decision. I am delirious with joy.

The attic has to be cleared of an accumulation of thirty-five years. I hear Jim clomping around up there, gathering boxes. He spends many days dragging boxes to the opening above the pull-down stairs in the laundry room. He hands boxes to me, and I put them into the spare bedroom. We shred papers and sort old clothing and mementos into piles for Jim's relatives, Goodwill, and trash – back-breaking work. We occasionally take a weekend off to do something fun, like going to see the movie, *The Secret Life of Walter Mitty*, relieving the monotony.

In early March, Jim turns 80. Time for him to stop working so hard on a house and yard. Getting the house ready to sell is a lot of work, but soon that will be over.

-hard Oregon Ducks fans, we have an early in-
drive into town, go home, and watch the Ducks
shington Huskies 45 to 20. We laugh about our
m for the Ducks that causes us to temporarily
atch the game. I remember to grab our wedding
e go back to our hotel room for our champagne

rning, we have room-service brunch and later
at the penny slots. In the afternoon, back home,
nd ready to start another week of preparation
o Albuquerque.
htfulness has given me the princess treatment,
ul! Where have these five years gone? Seems
we were saying our vows in my back yard!

so much about each other and about life. My
finished, and we expect the house to sell soon.
ll . . .

CHAPTER 57

NEW BABY, CONSTRUCTION, AND A MEMORIAL

In late spring, Jim's daughter and her husband present the world with a beautiful baby girl – Jim's first granddaughter. When she is eleven days old, we drive up to northern Washington to meet her. Such a sweetie! We have a great visit, and I get some nice photos of Jim holding the baby and looking proud.

No tour with the MGB group this spring. We are too busy working on the house, and Jim says he is getting too old for long trips in the tiny car.

However, the annual car show in downtown Pendleton in June is not to be missed. We enter both our cars. I win the raffle for a $1,000 gift certificate for car services, including new tires. I give it to Jim to get tires for his Buick – mine are new, but he will need tires for our eventual trip to Albuquerque.

In the middle of June, we have a fire in the fireplace. The air is still chilly. We are tired, and use that cozy evening to sit and read. Julie and her family sent Jim a subscription to *Architectural Digest* for his birthday in March, and the first issue has arrived in the mail. He devours it. He was a good insurance adjuster, but what an architect he would have been!

Since I introduced Jim to Pop-Tarts®, they have become a household essential – at the head of every grocery list. We come home from Safeway and unload boxes of every variety. Jim plays architect and stacks the boxes to make a pyramid on the kitchen counter. When one box is emptied, he re-designs the pyramid. Always into design and construction!

Jim and I take time off from the moving tasks, and fly to Salt Lake City to my niece, Jan's, memorial service. She was a talented artist, and her works are displayed all around the area where we gather. Jan's mother, sisters, daughter, and I exchange memories. Jim seems engaged and interested. Two of my nieces attended our wedding, and Jim meets some family for the first time. After the service, we all meet at Jan's favorite restaurant for a lovely dinner hosted by Jan's mother. Jim experiences a group of grieving family members gathered to comfort one another. Jim is a calm, comforting influence to all of us, just being himself.

CI

A FESTIVI

Fall arrives, and we'r anniversary is on Sat assume we will go restaurants to celebra

On Friday afterno the day.

I say, "But it's ear

"Not now. Just pt and hang on for a ri

We drive up to t "We're here!"

He has arranged top-floor corner ro meals. His card says wonderful years wi our room, includin and crème brulé surrounding area. I we relax together.

The next morr breakfast in our r to watch the Du disappointment tl

Being die room dinner, defeat the Wa intense fando run home to v goblets, and w five-year toas

Sunday m go spend time we are rested for our move t

Jim's thoug and I'm gratef only yesterday

We've learned book is almost Life is good. W

CHAPTER 59

THE BOOK, A CANCELLATION, AND A BRIEF VISIT

We are working in our home office. My book is done, edited, and ready for publication with Amazon. They will format it for an extra charge, which I am glad to pay, knowing I have no experience doing that. When I mention to Jim the book is ready to be formatted, and that I am going to let the company do it, he disagrees.

"I can format the book for you."

I don't know how to format a book for publication, and I know Jim has no experience doing that, either.

I say, "No, I want it professionally done."

The discussion becomes heated, and I'm not willing to give an inch. Our desks are positioned so that we are back-to-back in the room. I try to ignore Jim as I work at my desk. He will not be put off.

"There's nothing to formatting a book. I can do it," he says.

I'm tired of listening to him, so I get up from my desk and start down the hall toward our bedroom, escaping from his annoying insistence. He gets up and follows me, continuing to harp about the formatting, that he can do it.

"No, I'm going to have it professionally done." There are a few repetitions by the time we walk the length of the hall, and I get to the bedroom door.

I turn toward him and say, "Jim, this discussion is over. I'm going to have the book professionally formatted. It's my book, and it's my decision."

"But I can do it for nothing."

Aspieness is rearing its head once again. Money is never an issue, but he seems reluctant to spend it in certain ways – like snacks for church coffee hour, like a TV, and now for formatting my book.

I make fists and shake my arms, elbows bent, while I stomp my foot, and my voice has a firmness that surprises even me.

"Jim, you can't control me. Maybe you've been able to control some people in your life, but you can't control *me*. I said the formatting discussion is over, and I *mean* it."

I turn to go into the bedroom. He is silent, and I can tell he isn't following me. I look back to see his reaction.

His head is bent. He looks up and says, "Please don't leave me."

I say, "I'm just going into the bedroom to get something."

"No, I mean don't leave me." His posture and voice are childlike.

His fear of abandonment is trumping his insistence on formatting. I again assure him I have no intention of leaving him. I have never mentioned leaving him. I say I understand that his behavior is because of his Asperger's, but I reiterate that he cannot control me. I know he dislikes confrontation, but I am determined to stand my ground, Aspieness or not.

The next morning the manuscript is on its way to the publisher for professional formatting. I spend some time talking to him about the Asperger's trait that is evident in that situation. I tell him it accounts for his being certain he can do

CHAPTER 57

NEW BABY, CONSTRUCTION, AND A MEMORIAL

In late spring, Jim's daughter and her husband present the world with a beautiful baby girl – Jim's first granddaughter. When she is eleven days old, we drive up to northern Washington to meet her. Such a sweetie! We have a great visit, and I get some nice photos of Jim holding the baby and looking proud.

No tour with the MGB group this spring. We are too busy working on the house, and Jim says he is getting too old for long trips in the tiny car.

However, the annual car show in downtown Pendleton in June is not to be missed. We enter both our cars. I win the raffle for a $1,000 gift certificate for car services, including new tires. I give it to Jim to get tires for his Buick – mine are new, but he will need tires for our eventual trip to Albuquerque.

In the middle of June, we have a fire in the fireplace. The air is still chilly. We are tired, and use that cozy evening to sit and read. Julie and her family sent Jim a subscription to *Architectural Digest* for his birthday in March, and the first issue has arrived in the mail. He devours it. He was a good insurance adjuster, but what an architect he would have been!

Since I introduced Jim to Pop-Tarts®, they have become a household essential – at the head of every grocery list. We come home from Safeway and unload boxes of every variety. Jim plays architect and stacks the boxes to make a pyramid on the kitchen counter. When one box is emptied, he re-designs the pyramid. Always into design and construction!

Jim and I take time off from the moving tasks, and fly to Salt Lake City to my niece, Jan's, memorial service. She was a talented artist, and her works are displayed all around the area where we gather. Jan's mother, sisters, daughter, and I exchange memories. Jim seems engaged and interested. Two of my nieces attended our wedding, and Jim meets some family for the first time. After the service, we all meet at Jan's favorite restaurant for a lovely dinner hosted by Jan's mother. Jim experiences a group of grieving family members gathered to comfort one another. Jim is a calm, comforting influence to all of us, just being himself.

CHAPTER 58

A FESTIVE ANNIVERSARY!

Fall arrives, and we're still working on the house. Our fifth anniversary is on Saturday, and Jim is secretive all week. I assume we will go out to dinner at one of our favorite restaurants to celebrate, as we usually do.

On Friday afternoon, Jim says it's time to stop working for the day.

I say, "But it's early – I can still get a few boxes sorted."

"Not now. Just put some undies and a toothbrush in a bag and hang on for a ride!"

We drive up to the Wildhorse Casino Hotel, and he says, "We're here!"

He has arranged a festive weekend, staying in a luxurious top-floor corner room, and having room service for all our meals. His card says, "Looking forward to at least twenty more wonderful years with you." We have a sumptuous dinner in our room, including our favorite peppercorn steak, Riesling, and crème brulé for dessert, and enjoy the views of the surrounding area. I shower while he takes a long tub bath, and we relax together.

The next morning, we wake with smiles, and order a full breakfast in our room – eggs, pancakes, fresh fruit. We plan to watch the Ducks game that night, but we find to our disappointment that the hotel doesn't provide that channel.

Being die-hard Oregon Ducks fans, we have an early in-room dinner, drive into town, go home, and watch the Ducks defeat the Washington Huskies 45 to 20. We laugh about our intense fandom for the Ducks that causes us to temporarily run home to watch the game. I remember to grab our wedding goblets, and we go back to our hotel room for our champagne five-year toast.

Sunday morning, we have room-service brunch and later go spend time at the penny slots. In the afternoon, back home, we are rested and ready to start another week of preparation for our move to Albuquerque.

Jim's thoughtfulness has given me the princess treatment, and I'm grateful! Where have these five years gone? Seems only yesterday we were saying our vows in my back yard!

We've learned so much about each other and about life. My book is almost finished, and we expect the house to sell soon. Life is good. Well . . .

CHAPTER 59

THE BOOK, A CANCELLATION, AND A BRIEF VISIT

We are working in our home office. My book is done, edited, and ready for publication with Amazon. They will format it for an extra charge, which I am glad to pay, knowing I have no experience doing that. When I mention to Jim the book is ready to be formatted, and that I am going to let the company do it, he disagrees.

"I can format the book for you."

I don't know how to format a book for publication, and I know Jim has no experience doing that, either.

I say, "No, I want it professionally done."

The discussion becomes heated, and I'm not willing to give an inch. Our desks are positioned so that we are back-to-back in the room. I try to ignore Jim as I work at my desk. He will not be put off.

"There's nothing to formatting a book. I can do it," he says.

I'm tired of listening to him, so I get up from my desk and start down the hall toward our bedroom, escaping from his annoying insistence. He gets up and follows me, continuing to harp about the formatting, that he can do it.

"No, I'm going to have it professionally done." There are a few repetitions by the time we walk the length of the hall, and I get to the bedroom door.

I turn toward him and say, "Jim, this discussion is over. I'm going to have the book professionally formatted. It's my book, and it's my decision."

"But I can do it for nothing."

Aspieness is rearing its head once again. Money is never an issue, but he seems reluctant to spend it in certain ways – like snacks for church coffee hour, like a TV, and now for formatting my book.

I make fists and shake my arms, elbows bent, while I stomp my foot, and my voice has a firmness that surprises even me.

"Jim, you can't control me. Maybe you've been able to control some people in your life, but you can't control *me*. I said the formatting discussion is over, and I *mean* it."

I turn to go into the bedroom. He is silent, and I can tell he isn't following me. I look back to see his reaction.

His head is bent. He looks up and says, "Please don't leave me."

I say, "I'm just going into the bedroom to get something."

"No, I mean don't leave me." His posture and voice are childlike.

His fear of abandonment is trumping his insistence on formatting. I again assure him I have no intention of leaving him. I have never mentioned leaving him. I say I understand that his behavior is because of his Asperger's, but I reiterate that he cannot control me. I know he dislikes confrontation, but I am determined to stand my ground, Aspieness or not.

The next morning the manuscript is on its way to the publisher for professional formatting. I spend some time talking to him about the Asperger's trait that is evident in that situation. I tell him it accounts for his being certain he can do something he's never done before, because Aspies sometimes get in their heads they can do something, and won't give up about it. It is hard for them to let things go.

I say, "If it were your book, you could try it, but it isn't. It's *my* book, and it isn't appropriate for you to keep insisting that you be allowed to format *my* book. Your insistence is similar to interrupting people's conversations. You are encroaching on my territory. I'm glad you finally gave up, but we could have avoided a scene if you had taken my word about it from the beginning."

Jim listens, and without saying he is sorry, says, "I'm still learning. I didn't realize I was doing anything wrong. I was just trying to help."

I reply, "As I've said, if it were *your* book, you could have done it, and I wouldn't have tried to stop you. You need to learn the difference between your business and my business. As an example, what if I insist I can build the steps in front of the house? What if you say I don't know how, but I keep insisting I can do it? And you might say I've never done it before, but I keep saying I can do it? If you want them built correctly, you will tell me you are going to build them, and that will be that. We are wired differently. I know not to try to convince you I can build steps, but you are not aware that it is inappropriate for you to insist on formatting my book. Maybe you can't see that, but that's why I'm telling you, trying to teach you."

I can tell Jim is processing this information. Each instance needs to be explained, because it is hard for him to extrapolate from one specific situation to another. He is truly trying to learn.

Transitions are hard for Aspies. I'm sure he really felt as if he could format my book, but I knew he could not do it as well as a professional. It was hard for him to give up. Some Aspies, to compensate for their feelings of inadequacy, can come off as stubborn. It was impossible for him to see the situation from my point of view. To deal with his lack of theory of mind, it was necessary for me to use a concrete, specific example to explain my annoyance. "If you employ logic, concrete and controlled language, specific examples and an objectively open mind, you will be far more likely to keep the channels of communication between you and your AS [Asperger's Syndrome] friend open and meaningful" (Willey, 2015, p. 181). Jim knew I had no experience building steps, and I think he saw my point.

The next week, his annual physical is scheduled. When he gets home, I say, "What did the doctor say? How are you?"

Jim says, "I told him about the place on top of my head that never heals, and he said it looks like cancer and should be taken off." This is something he's never mentioned to me and I've never noticed. I ask to see the place.

In the afternoon, at my urging, Jim agrees to call the surgeon for a pre-op consultation, and he makes an appointment. The next day he demonstrates his aversion to medical treatment by calling both the surgeon and our doctor, telling them to cancel the appointment, that he doesn't want surgery. I am not happy when he tells me what he's done, and I tell him he is being unreasonable. He says he is a grown man and can make his own decisions, so I let it go.

Jim's daughter and husband bring the little granddaughter, now a toddler, by for a short visit on their way home from a trip. The spring weather is pleasant. We visit on our front deck, Jim plays with his little granddaughter, and I take some sweet photos of them. Jim and I wish the visit could be longer, and we could become better acquainted with the little one. This is the second time we've seen the baby, none of us realizing it will be Jim's last.

CHAPTER 60

A TOP HAT, A CAR SHOW, AND HONESTY

One afternoon, we drive to Tri-Cities to look for some materials Jim needs for house repairs. On the way, I see a sign pointing to Hat Rock State Park. We always turn left onto Highway 730 to reach I-82, but the sign points to our right. We have already turned left, but since I see the sign often on our trips to Tri-Cities, but have never been to that park, I ask Jim to turn around and drive by, so I can see it. It is only a few miles out of the way, and we're not in a hurry.

He says, "You've been there," and keeps driving.

"No, I've never been there."

"Yes, you have. We'll go, but when you see it, you'll realize you've been there."

Reluctantly, Jim turns around and drives to the park. It is on the south bank of the Columbia River, east of McNary Dam, and I know I have never been that direction on Highway 730. I do not recognize anything about it. He drives through the winding road. I take a picture of the large rock formation that looks like a top hat. There are lovely shady picnic areas with tables, and we see a couple of deer.

I say, "I would remember this if I had been here. Thanks for bringing me. It's so pretty. Maybe we can come here for a picnic sometime."

He keeps insisting I have been here.

I say, "Jim, I have not been to this park. You have obviously been here, but I haven't. You're demonstrating an Asperger's trait, and I understand that. Aspies don't like to be wrong, and I know it's hard on you to admit it, but you are mistaken. I have not been here."

Whether he believes me or not, I have no way of knowing, but to his credit, he does let go of the topic.

Jim could be stubborn and did not like being wrong. Aspies think they are always right, never wrong. I spoke in concrete terms, with a logical presentation, and he had no rebuttal.

One morning, Jim gathers a fresh cup of coffee, the manual for repairing the Sprite, a ruled tablet and pen, and sets himself up at the dinette table. I know better than to interrupt as he spends time deep in thought, studying the manual before overhauling the Sprite's brakes – heavy reading. We don't drive the green car much lately, because he is afraid it isn't safe.

A few hours and many cups of coffee later, after lunch, he goes to the garage and repairs the brakes, as if it were a simple thing, just following the instructions. He is an amazing mechanic.

I don't realize it at the time, because he hasn't mentioned selling the Sprite, but he is getting it ready to sell before our move. He wants it to be safe for the buyer. He is unable to sell anything in shoddy condition – even our house. When people come to look at the house, he points out what needs paint, how he's always meant to replace the upper windows, etc. I think he jinxes several possible sales this way. I tell him to let them look, not to comment unless they ask a question, but he says he doesn't want them to overlook anything that might give them trouble.

Jim's Aspieness causes him to be completely honest about everything. He is ethical to a fault. Aspies are hardly capable of telling a lie or being dishonest. "Adults with Asperger's syndrome can be renowned for being honest, having a strong sense of social justice and keeping to the rules. They strongly believe in moral and ethical principles" (Attwood, 2008, p. 118).

Later in May, we go to the Blue Mountain Community College car show, enter the MGB, and after the show, all the cars cruise through town with police escort – by the Pendleton Round-Up grounds, past the City Hall, past the First Presbyterian Church, the post office, and the courthouse. We don't win any trophies that day, but we see lots of people we know and have fun honking the horn and waving wildly from our little red convertible.

Jim again gives me a heartfelt compliment, laughing and shouting over the roar of the cars and the wind, "I love you, because you let me be me."

He has developed a free and easy style, since he knows why he has some idiosyncratic behaviors, and he knows I understand. Sometimes his judgment about acting with abandon is questionable, as you will see weeks later.

CHAPTER 61

A DREAM COMES TRUE

The final proof of my book comes. I open the box, hold the book in my hands, and feel as if I've given birth. I am amused by my editor's comment, "I feel like the godmother of your book." And it is true. Without her encouragement and motivation, I might never have finished the book. And Jim has allowed me all the time needed to work on it for hours at a time, while he cooked for me and tended to household chores.

To celebrate, Jim and I have dinner at Raphael's. Raphael is interested and excited to hear about my book.

She says, "Oh, let's have a book signing here. Get with me and let's plan it."

The evening of the event, I am apprehensive that few people will show up, and it will be embarrassing to have so much empty space in the large room. People begin streaming into the doorway and greeting Jim and me. The room fills, and I am overwhelmed. In this, my adopted town, people are eager to hear me read from my book and celebrate my success. I can never forget this warm feeling. What a satisfying celebration of my years of labor on the book!

Jim and I are both relieved that the event goes smoothly, and we feel like a couple of kids. The next night, we have a "date," at Jim's suggestion – he easily falls into childlike behaviors and fun. That's one of the things I love about him. We have ice cream cones at Dave's teen hangout and survive the stares of the teens, as we sit in a booth, laughing and reveling at the good things that are happening. I've written a book, but now I am acting like a teenager, encouraged by my husband. After our ice cream, we two old people drag up Main Street in our MGB with the top down. Our silly, bizarre behavior keeps us young. When we get home, we are exhausted, but happy. Once again Jim says, "I love you, because you let me be me."

CHAPTER 62

HOUSE HUNTING, FRIGHT, AND HILARITY

Jim accepts an offer on the Pendleton house, and we fly to Albuquerque to look for a house there. We are giddy with excitement about this new chapter in our life adventures. It seems we are living a dream.

We meet with our realtor, and look at many houses over a two-day period. We narrow our choices to two – they are in the same nice neighborhood. Jim wants to inspect each house thoroughly before we make a decision. He is detail-oriented, meticulous, and will make his decision about the houses based on logic and practicality, not emotion.

Jim, the wannabe architect, who has experience in construction and insurance adjusting, arrives armed the next day with pen and clipboard, ready to make his inspections, and I tag along. By the time he is through, a few hours later, we are both exhausted. Jim has filled a sheaf of papers with his findings. We discuss the results and make our choice.

Jim deems one of the houses "very well constructed and well maintained," and luckily, it happens to be my choice as far as floorplan and landscaping. Mine is the emotional component, and it is lovely that we agree. He likes the nuts and bolts, I like the ambience, and we make an offer. It is accepted. We celebrate at a steak dinner that night and toast to our success at house-selling, -hunting, -finding, and -buying! The next day we head back to Oregon to tie up loose ends.

Jim's Aspie penchants for fact-finding, practicality, logic, observation, and processing, plus his early experience in construction and insurance adjusting have made his choice of a house solid and wise. We look forward to many happy years in it.

The couple in front of us in the long, crowded check-in line at the airport is younger and possibly foreign, judging from their conversation. The woman kisses a man who walks up outside the boundary tape to tell them goodbye. Then she throws kisses at him as he walks away. We are close enough to smell her perfume, a sandalwood blend.

Jim leans over me, toward her, keeping a respectable distance, smiles at her, and says, "Can I have a kiss, too?"

I turn to look at him, astonished, and say, "Jim!" not believing what I'm seeing or hearing.

The woman steps back, and she and her male companion are obviously surprised and taken aback.

She appears confused and says, "What?" with an accent unlike ours.

Jim repeats, with a twinkle in his eye, "Can I have a kiss, too?" and, thinking she doesn't understand English, acts as if he is throwing a kiss in front of him – not *at* her, but off to one side, demonstrating what he means. The male companion puts his arm around the woman, and they turn away from us.

I am shocked. Jim knows it. I'm hoping for silence until we are through checking in. I'm thinking we don't know the couple's culture, and they may have taken Jim's apparent joking gesture as an insult. The line moves, and I stay in front of Jim, ensuring we stay some distance behind the couple.

As we walk to our gate, Jim says, "Did that embarrass you?"

I say, "It was totally inappropriate. You're lucky the guy didn't deck you." I am still shocked – very, very out of character for Jim.

We are on our plane, and I'm hoping the couple doesn't board. They don't. The plane's door is closed. I breathe a sigh of relief and say, "Jim, you could easily have put us in a dangerous spot, and I hope you won't ever do something like that again."

He says, "I was just playing."

I say, "They didn't like it. Maybe because of your age they ignored it, but another time you might not be so lucky. Asking a strange woman for a kiss, even a blown one, especially in front of a male companion, could be dynamite. I'm hoping you will learn to monitor your thoughts before you speak, especially to strangers."

Jim was being his silly self, not taking into consideration the intimate nature of his gesture or request, not understanding that the woman and her male companion might take offense. His impaired judgment appalled me. His lack of theory of mind could have involved us in a serious incident.

We change planes in Salt Lake City, and have time for lunch. Jim doesn't want all of his ham sandwich, and I tell him I don't want the rest of it, either.

He scrunches his eyes, gets a mischievous look, and says, "Maybe I'll offer it to that little boy over there," pointing across the aisle. I sense his mischievous mood, and I dare him to do that, not thinking he will.

But he does. He leans over the aisle to the woman sitting next to the boy, apparently his mother, holds out the almost-eaten sandwich, and says, "Would your little boy like the rest of my sandwich?"

The woman looks confused. I cringe. *He's really doing it!*

Jim says, "I'm doing this on a dare from my wife." The mother catches on that it's a joke, and we all smile about it, all except the little boy, who is about four, and who looks up from playing with a toy. Even at four, I think he realizes this man's behavior is odd.

I laugh, as I always do with Jim's silliness, making it difficult to talk, but I tell the little boy, "This man is really a nice man, but he's joking about the sandwich. Of course, you wouldn't want his sandwich after he has eaten off of it. He is playing a joke on me." The boy looks down, pulls at his Mickey Mouse tee shirt, and says, "We're going to Disneyland."

I say, "Oh, have fun! It's a magical place!"

Jim rolls the rest of his sandwich up in the bag it came in. He tosses it into the trash bin as we leave the lunch area and make our way to our gate, laughing.

"You're nuts," I say, "but I love you."

We never forget that incident, and often we mention it and go into a laughing fit. I wonder if the little boy and his mother remember "that strange man in the airport in Salt Lake City."

This was probably Jim's way of lightening the atmosphere after the incident with the foreign couple. A lack of humor is common to many Aspies, because they tend to take words literally, but Jim definitely had a great sense of humor. I go back to my explanation of the Asperger's traits – not all Aspies have all of the traits. A common saying is, "When you've seen one Aspie, you've seen one Aspie." Often Jim was funny, slapstick, joking, making me laugh. It was one of his most endearing traits.

CHAPTER 63

THE MOVE AND
A SORE BACK

When we get home, Jim closes on the Pendleton house. In a couple of days, we close on the Albuquerque house remotely. The move to Albuquerque is on the horizon.

Jim sells the Sprite and arranges for the MGB to be transported to Albuquerque. The van arrives, and the movers load our furniture, while Jim carries boxes up from the basement. He works as hard as the movers.

We drive in tandem to Salt Lake City, then on to Albuquerque. After a long two-day trip, we are glad to get to the motel in Albuquerque, get checked in, have dinner, and head to bed.

Jim says his back hurts. He says it is from lifting and carrying heavy items during the move. I don't doubt it – for weeks he has hoisted boxes clearing out the attic, then carried boxes from the basement for the movers to load. Jim is not one to sit idly by and let others do the work.

The moving truck arrives, ready to unload. Jim says his back is still hurting, and he keeps saying he must have pulled a muscle moving. In spite of that, he helps the movers unload, much to my regret. I want him to rest that sore back. The movers finish and leave, leaving us with a house full of boxes.

A truck arrives with the MGB a few days later. Jim gets onto the truck and slowly backs his red prize out onto the ramp, and pulls it into our driveway. Several neighbors are standing out watching the action. They come over and admire the little car, and Jim is happy to show it off. Neighbors up the street bring us a note of welcome and a bottle of wine that evening.

One afternoon, neighbors invite us for shrimp cocktails and wine. I start telling a story, and Jim begins interrupting. Not wanting to embarrass him in front of our new friends, I let him interrupt, but languidly raise my hand. He stops.

"I'm doing it," he says.

I smile and nod. "Now may I finish?"

I hope the couple do not notice the learning taking place.

We come home, and Jim decides to mow the lawn. He is pleased with our two grassy lawns, divided by decorative native rock – enough to be green and pretty, but manageable. He is accustomed to spending two hours mowing four levels, and now he can do it all in about 20 minutes on a level lot. The ease of the yard work is already a relief to him.

We enjoy sitting on the shady patio each day, watching the birds in the crabapple tree and a lizard Jim named "Fred." We see Fred dart here and there, and Jim tries to keep up with the lizard's whereabouts. I'm sure it is several lizards, but Jim likes to think Fred is his pet.

Jim makes the first batch of his famous spaghetti sauce in our new home. After dinner, he complains about his back, and asks me to massage it with lotion.

Our sixth anniversary is our first anniversary in Albuquerque, just a month after we move in. Jim says he'd like a steak dinner, so we go to a steakhouse and have filet mignon and baked potato with all the trimmings. Jim raves all through the meal about how good the food is. We make plans to celebrate anniversary number seven at the same restaurant in another year, since he enjoys it so. Six years have flown by, and we look forward to many more.

CHAPTER 64

SETTLING IN

We register our cars for New Mexico plates and get set up with a primary physician. After our first appointments, I ask Jim if he told the doctor about his sore back.

"No, it's just from the move. It'll get better."

On Thanksgiving Day, I prepare a traditional turkey dinner, and we watch football. The day after, we do little except watch football again all day and eat leftovers. I note on our calendar, "A <u>most</u> relaxing day!"

In early December, we go to a Christmas party. Jim doesn't feel good, but says he wants to go. Standing is painful for his back, so he sits down before the cocktail hour ends. We sit at a table with friends, some of whom were at our wedding reception. The dinner is good, and friends seem glad to see us. We leave soon after dinner. Jim is still attributing his back pain to the move.

A friend hosts a book reading and signing for me. A small, but interested, group attends, and Jim is my cashier, elegant in his coat and tie. He moves as if in pain, and as he cashiers, he tells some buyers that he feels he pulled a muscle in his back during our move, lifting heavy things. He is functional, but I know he does not feel good. He is relieved when the signing is over, and he can come home to his favorite chair.

We put up two Christmas trees, one small, in the living room, and one large, in the family room. Jim enters into the festivities of tree decorating with gusto. "New home, new traditions," he says. I think his back must be better, as he does not mention it. On Christmas Eve, we set out the luminarias, and Jim helps me light them, his first experience with the lighted candles in sand-filled paper sacks that light the way for the Christ child to New Mexican homes. We spend time that night planning for things we'll do after New Year's and when Jim's back is better: the Roswell Alien Museum, the Very Large Array, White Sands, Ruidoso, Cloudcroft, Bosque Del Apache National Wildlife Preserve, La Posta Mexican Restaurant near Las Cruces. So much to see and do in this "Land of Enchantment," no end to our anticipated adventures.

Albuquerque has its first snow of the winter, but with our gas fireplace, we feel cozy and warm. No more need for carrying wood in – another benefit for Jim. Also, little need for shoveling snow. I know it will be gone in a day or two. We look forward to a good 2016.

We cannot know what this new year will bring . . .

CHAPTER 65

EVERYDAY STUFF
AND HEALTH

Texas Christian University (TCU) beats the Ducks, 47 to 41, in the Alamo Bowl. At the end of the fourth quarter, the score is 31-31. The first overtime ends with a score of 38-38, second overtime ends with a score of 41- 41, and it goes into 3rd overtime, with TCU finally making a touchdown for the win. It has been a nail-biter! Jim and I are exhausted and disappointed.

Eager to get all our health issues taken care of, we arrange back-to-back appointments with my dentist, to whom I've gone for years. After we both have been seen, on the way to the car, I ask Jim how his appointment went.

"The guy thinks I need a lot of work. I don't want to do that now."

I later read copies of the notes from Jim's visit, which say in part, "Patient is very jumpy. Scared of treatment. Extractions in future. Return as needed, or check in 6 mos." Jim did not like any medical procedures, and avoided them when he could.

We hope some of our kids and grandkids will visit and enjoy Albuquerque, so we plan for additional sleeping space. We decide a comfortable futon for the family room will fit the bill.

Jim and I go shopping, and he is actively engaged in choosing the right piece. He spies a Frank Lloyd Wright prairie-style wooden frame with a thick mattress covered in a tan, brown, and turquoise southwestern pattern, and immediately likes it. I like it, too, but it is more expensive than we've planned. Jim doesn't seem to mind, says it will last forever, and he and the furniture man complete the paperwork. Jim seems to feel energetic, is happy with our purchase, and there is no mention of his back pain.

Long-time friends of mine invite us for dinner. All goes well until after we visit a while after dinner, and I can tell we've stayed long enough. I reach over, put my hand on Jim's leg, and say, "We've had such a nice visit. The dinner was wonderful, and it's so good to see you all again. We must be going." Jim takes the cue, and we get up to leave.

Our friends walk with us to the front door and open it. I'm walking out, Jim is behind me, and he starts a new topic of conversation with the husband. Our friends are captives by the open door!

I can see Jim is in it for the long haul, so I say, "You'll need to tell them about that next visit. We're on our way out." I reach for his hand and arm and gently lead him out the door, while saying again to our friends how much we enjoyed the time together.

On the way home, I explained to Jim how I knew it was time for us to leave by noticing our friends' body language. He never did seem to get the hang of that, but depended on me to cue him. Fortunately, he was receptive to my guidance.

When the futon is delivered in several days, I suggest putting casters under each leg to prevent marring the wooden floor, but Jim says that won't look good. Instead, he cuts pieces of felt exactly to fit the bottom of each leg and glues them on, to prevent its scratching the floor when it is opened and closed. He is meticulously preserving our floor and making sure the felt fits so that none of it shows.

Many Aspies tend to be perfectionists, and Jim is no exception. Even though conservative about purchases, Jim obviously has fallen in love with this particular futon, and price is no object. His perfectionistic nature motivates him to spend the effort to prevent scratches on our new floor.

One night, my crazy husband makes me laugh so hard I am breathless – and still, every time I think of it, I start laughing again. When I am sorting a load of freshly-dried clothes, I find only one of Jim's socks. I tell him I can't find the other one.

He says, with little facial expression, and without taking his eyes off the TV, "Well, one had holes in it, so I threw it away. Just put the clean one in my drawer, and I'll wear it on one foot 'til noon, then put it on the other foot."

I'm laughing again now, as I write this.

He surprises me after dinner with this remark, "Thanks for dinner. It was a really good meal. And the asparagus was really tasty." This, from a man who six years ago would not have touched asparagus, and this night he eats ten spears and likes it. His food tastes are widening, but I notice in the last few weeks his appetite is not good, so I am glad to see him eat and enjoy a big meal.

On my birthday, Jim makes enchiladas for dinner and gives me a beautiful card. The card and the dinner bring tears, and the realization of how blessed I am. The note on the card melts my heart, and I am glad he is mine. His back seems to be better – at least he isn't saying much about it.

The next evening, Jim's brother is in Albuquerque, and we meet him downtown for dinner. Jim is not feeling good, is having some digestive distress, and doesn't feel like going, but pushes himself. He orders something easy to eat, but doesn't eat much. He has hardly any appetite at all. After a brief visit, he is ready to go home.

Jim has a birthday and looks and acts young for 82. At dinner that night, he says he doesn't feel good. He says, "I'm hardly ever hungry, and I don't think I eat much, but my jeans are getting too tight around the waist. Can we get some that are a size or two larger?"

We do, and he says the new jeans feel better, put less pressure on his belly. I urge him to talk to our doctor about the way he feels, but he says he doesn't want to, that he will feel better before long.

Even though Jim has not mentioned his back pain for a while, he tells me he has digestive problems, stomach discomfort, continuing back pain (still from the move, he says, although the move was six months ago), and very little appetite. He self-medicates with Pepto-Bismol™ and begins to feel better. We are both encouraged.

CHAPTER 66

VISITS AND A ROADRUNNER

Julie, John, and the kids arrive for a visit. Jim is glad to see them, and it seems to be a boost for him. The two boys are the first users of the new futon.

My whole family – children, grandchildren, and cousins, have enveloped Jim with love from the time they met him. One grandson was two when husband Paul died, and the other one was born after Jim and I married, so Jim is the only maternal grandfather they've ever known.

One night, Jim says Mexican food sounds good, and we all agree. I'm glad he seems hungry. We go to El Pinto, our favorite New Mexican restaurant. He eats tacos, and says they are tasty.

The grandsons ask Jim questions about the ship he was on and what he did in the Navy. He gets out a photo of the ship, and they listen intently as he tells them about the ship and his duties as a young sailor. He gets out his Navy blues to show the boys. Jack, who is 12, tries on the uniform's top, and it fits him well, showing what a slender young sailor Jim was. Jim says he used to have a white dress uniform, but something happened to it, so he is sorry he can't show them that. Jim seems pleased that the kids are interested in his Navy experiences. His back seems to feel better, and he is obviously enjoying the interaction with the kids.

One day while they are visiting, I notice Jim has his lightweight outdoor jacket on in the house. I ask if he is planning to go somewhere. He says, "No, I'm cold." It is normal spring weather to the rest of us, not jacket weather. I raise the temperature on the thermostat, hoping he'll be more comfortable.

The visit is coming to an end. Before they leave, we take pictures in our back yard. It is sunny, but Jim still wears his jacket. It is as if his internal thermostat is malfunctioning.

One sunny day, Jim gets out the shears and trims some shrubs in the back yard, but I notice he periodically sits in a lawn chair to bag the twigs and branches he cuts – very unusual. I holler out the sliding glass door, "You seem tired. Why don't you quit and come in and have a drink of water and rest a while?"

"I'm almost done with this bush. After that, I'll quit."

Later, we're having a snack, and he comments, "This yard is so easy to keep. I'm glad I don't have four levels to mow, and all the bushes I had to trim in Pendleton. This one is a snap."

I think, *Yes, this house and yard are so much easier on you than the maintenance on the Pendleton house and the expansive yard there, especially the way you've been feeling.*

Later I see him slouched comfortably in a lawn chair on the patio, arms raised, and hands clasped behind his head. He is watching Fred and the birds. His back is to me, and I snap a picture of him. It's a favorite of mine, illustrating his contentment with our new home and yard. I have not seen him do anything like that while enjoying the yard in Pendleton. I take it he is relaxed and pleased about the lighter workload.

I am working in my home office early in May, when Jim comes running down the hall.

"Look! I saw what I think is a roadrunner racing along our side wall. It hopped down into our back yard, and ran toward the front yard."

He is right! We watch from the front window as the bird takes off down the street. Jim stares as it runs out of sight. The roadrunner became New Mexico's official state bird in March 1949. Jim is experiencing our state bird in person for the first time, and I am happy to see that Jim was running down the hall in his excitement! He seems to be feeling better.

Jackie Downie comes for a visit. We three have dinner on the patio at El Pinto. Jim does not seem to feel bad, at least he is not saying so if he does. The weather is mild, the evening is pleasant, and we enjoy being together. Jackie comments that Jim looks as if he's lost some weight. I agree his face looks thinner, but I've not noticed it day to day.

When Jackie leaves, a tree crew works their magic in our back yard. I am glad Jim has hired them to do the hard work. I remember not long ago when he single-handedly sawed down and dismembered the cherry tree in the Pendleton back yard. He used to stand precariously on a stepladder by the large evergreens in the Pendleton yard and trim one limb at a time, while I braced the ladder for him. He is now ready to quit the hard and potentially dangerous work and pay someone else to do it. *About time.*

I have the piano tuned. It sounds so much better, and I enjoy playing again. Jim sits down and tries his hand at the better-sounding instrument. Later we try a guitar and piano session, which ends up in hilarious laughter and a snuggle on the futon.

Paul arrives with his wife, Sepi, to be in New Mexico for part of the summer. Jim meets Sepi for the first time. Paul and Sepi bring dinner in, as Jim says he does not feel like going out. His physical ailments seemed better for a while, but are reappearing. I can see that Jim is glad Paul is in town, and I sense he feels secure having Paul around. After dinner, we move out to the patio.

Paul and Sepi talk about their experience living in New Delhi, and Sepi speaks of her love for the eastern culture. Jim gets up and goes into the house, and I assume he is going to the bathroom. He comes back out carrying two large Japanese scroll paintings his family had obtained when they lived in Japan in the late 1940s. I think he is bringing them to show Paul and Sepi. Instead, he ceremoniously presents them as gifts to Sepi. She is overwhelmed, and thanks him profusely for his generosity in honoring her with the scrolls.

After they leave, Jim says, "I didn't know what to expect when I was going to meet Sepi. I was impressed with her. Her smile lights up a room, doesn't it?"

Sometimes Jim's generosity is boundless. An admirable trait that endears him to many.

The next night, Paul and Sepi bring dinner in again, and we have a pleasant time visiting on the patio. Jim eats small amounts, but says he isn't very hungry.

In mid-June, Jim again comes down the hall, saying, "There's another roadrunner."

A roadrunner hops from our front yard onto our neighbor's low wall. This is the second one we've seen in our yard. We also see woodpeckers on our crabapple tree, and hummingbirds flock to our feeders. We love watching the birds, but Jim is especially excited to see real roadrunners, not the cartoon variety! I think he's had an idea they are only cartoon characters, similar to my idea about huckleberries. If the cartoon character Chicken Little were real and intuitive, it would likely be running through our house shouting, "The sky is falling, the sky is falling . . ."

PART VII

ADVENTURES INTO
THE UNKNOWN

CHAPTER 67

THIS TIME HE'S RIGHT

We've been married six years and eight months. We've lived in our new home nine months. On Father's Day evening, June 19, 2016, the moon is almost full. What happens after dinner chisels an unforgettable image into my memory.

I fix Jim a Father's Day dinner of things he likes and that are easy to eat – baked chicken in mushroom sauce, green beans, and mashed potatoes with gravy. He doesn't eat much, says he isn't hungry. We finish the meal and go sit on the patio to watch the birds and clouds and wait for the moon to rise so we can see it above the neighbor's tall trees. We both enjoy these kinds of evenings.

Suddenly, Jim bolts from his chair, runs out into the grass, and loses everything he's eaten. It happens so fast!

I say, "I'm so sorry dinner didn't agree with you. Do you want to go inside and lie down?"

"Yes, I feel worse than I ever have." This is an unusual admission for Jim.

I say, "I'm making a unilateral decision to call the doctor and get an appointment for tomorrow morning. You haven't felt good since the move, and this is a new symptom. We need to see about it."

He doesn't argue with me this time. His resignation frightens me. I expect a refusal – something like, "It's just a stomach bug," or "I'll be okay tomorrow" – the same refusals I've heard from him before. I know he must mean it when he says he feels worse than he ever has. He looks pale, and worse than I've ever seen him.

The next day, we drive to the doctor's office. The doctor checks for anemia, liver function, and kidney function, as well as bacteria in the intestine. Jim weighs 150 at this appointment, down from 180 in February, four months earlier. It has come off gradually, day by day, so Jim hasn't noticed that big a change, and neither have I. He even got larger jeans, because his abdomen is larger. Now we know that is not an increase in weight.

During the hands-on examination, the doctor finds a mass, bulging a bit underneath Jim's sternum. The mass was not there at his appointment a few months ago. I am sitting beside the examination table, and the doctor motions for me to look at and feel the growth he is palpating. I can see it when the doctor points to it, barely visible to an untrained eye. I reluctantly feel of it, but I would not be able to tell it is a mass if the doctor were not pointing it out. The doctor says this is definitely something new. He sends us to the suburban hospital for tests, saying with the weight loss and symptoms, he feels it may be cancer. As we leave his office, he puts his hand on Jim's arm and says, "You're a very sick man."

Jim is weak, and we are both in shock. We are at the hospital in 15 minutes. After a brief verbal evaluation, the nurse takes Jim into an examination room, and an IV is started with hydrating solution, as well as a med for the nausea. The attendant puts a half-gallon pitcher of contrast fluid on the bedside table, and Jim is told to drink the entire amount before his CT scan. He makes a valiant effort, and in about 15 minutes manages to down most of it, part of which he loses. He is taken down the hall for a scan. The nurse provides an emesis basin for him to hold. I don't like anything that is going on.

When Jim is brought back into the examination room, the attendant says the doctor will be in shortly with the results of the scan. Jim is pale, and his eyelids droop.

He says, "That was awful. It was a real mess. I'm surprised they even did it."

He says he vomited intermittently throughout the ordeal, all over the floor and the technicians. Probably all in a day's work for them, but something to which Jim is not accustomed, and he is upset about it.

Soon a female doctor, in her mid-50s, comes into the small room, greets both of us without a smile, and puts the films onto the reader screen beside Jim's bed.

She says, "Mr. Hanks, I hear you are in a lot of pain and distress, and you have lost a lot of weight recently. Here's why."

She points to areas on the film, and begins, "The scan shows a very large mass on the pancreas, with spots indicating metastasis to the liver. You will need to be taken to the downtown hospital for further tests and to begin immediate treatment." Without uttering the "c" word, she thrusts literature toward me with the heading, "PANCREATIC CANCER."

I feel frozen. I see the date on the whiteboard behind the doctor, June 20, 2016. My stomach churns and my mouth is dry, as I know what that diagnosis means. Jim does not yet realize the full import, both because he feels so bad, and because he has not seen the paperwork.

Jim is stoic, and tells the doctor, "I don't want to go to the downtown hospital."

The doctor looks at him with raised eyebrows, and then shoots a look to me, as she has not put it to him as a question, but as a matter-of-fact statement. She has a stunned look on her face when he refuses.

I say, "It's his decision."

She urges Jim to relent and be taken downtown, but he says, "No, I need time to think about this. I want to go home." As is normal for Jim, he needs time to process what we've been told, and he is stubborn enough not to do anything he doesn't want to do.

The doctor continues to insist that Jim let an ambulance take him downtown. He continues to resist and decline. Reluctantly, the doctor leaves, but comes back and gives discharge orders, with meds for pain and nausea, along with two fresh emesis basins, and slowly shakes her head.

I drive us toward home at midnight. My cell phone rings. I pull into a parking lot to take the call. Our family doctor has already received the report from the hospital. I put the phone on speaker, and he urges us to go directly to the downtown hospital.

I look to Jim for direction, but he is adamant about wanting to go home. As anyone who knows him knows, Jim makes his own decisions. Disappointed and confused at Jim's resisting, the doctor gives up and says he'll call us in the morning. I understand and respect Jim's need to think about everything, so we drive home. Jim needs time to process all of the information we've been given. He has not yet seen the paperwork about cancer.

When we get home, I go over the paperwork with Jim, and the words "pancreatic cancer" don't seem to make the same impression on him as they made with me. Jim asks for a cup of Earl Grey tea, not coffee. I offer him yogurt, which he refuses, and I drink tea and eat a cup of yogurt. We are in a limbo-like state. Jim is glad to be home, and reiterates that he doesn't want to go to the downtown hospital. I email all of our kids that night – rather, it is early in the morning. Neither of us sleep. Jim is up and down to the bathroom, and I am helping him as I can.

The next morning, Paul, who is in town, emails, "So sorry to hear this news. I'm ready to do anything you need me to do."

I call him and give him a grocery list: Boost®; Jell-O® – cherry, strawberry, lime; apple juice; chicken broth; cherry Popsicles®; tonic water; and Sprite® – things I feel Jim may be able to keep down.

As we look at the paperwork given us at the hospital about pancreatic cancer, we realize Jim has had many symptoms – weakness, diarrhea, loss of appetite, indigestion, back pain, weight loss, dark urine (of which I was unaware), and now nausea and vomiting – yet he doesn't agree to see the doctor until the last symptoms. His standard response, when I often suggest going to the doctor, has been, "I'm afraid they might tell me something I don't want to hear."

Sound familiar? This time he's right.

CHAPTER 68

JIM IS STOIC; I'M TERRIFIED

In a few short hours our lives have been not only turned upside down, but sent tumbling sideways, as if off a mountain highway without a guardrail, into a bottomless abyss. Our family doctor calls, as he said he would, again urging Jim to go to the downtown hospital. Jim again refuses, saying he needs time to think about things. I know the doctor is frustrated, but I know Jim, and I know he is going to do it his way.

Jim asks me what I think the treatment would be. I tell him I think he would be hospitalized and undergo tests. That is why he is being encouraged to go there.

He thinks for a few minutes, and says, "I don't want to go to the hospital. I don't want to die with lines and tubes in me."

I know he is fearful of doctors and hospitals, so his pronouncement does not surprise me. I tell him I'll be with him every step of the way, but that I can't be the one to undergo the tests or treatment, so I will respect his decision. I can insist he fight it, because I want him around for a long time, but I also respect his right to make his own decision.

Both Jim's son and daughter call and talk to him. Jim seems remarkably composed, and I hear him say, "I've had a good life."

Jim's stated feelings are that he has had a good life, and rather than submit to a plethora of tests and treatments, he'd rather stay home and enjoy the remaining days. He is noticeably weaker, and Paul picks up a walker and wheelchair from my friend's homecare agency. This makes me feel more secure, even around the house, as I don't trust myself to be enough support for Jim as he walks, and I don't want him to fall. Paul is impressed with Jim's outlook about this situation and his courage to take whatever is in store.

I'm sure it has not sunk in fully for either Jim or me. One day it's Father's Day with a pretty card and nice meal, the next day it's cancer day with an ugly report from the ER. A fast, confusing and unreal transition, not quickly processed.

I begin emailing Jim's siblings and keeping them informed. Jim is not eating anything, and I offer Jell-O®, all kinds of juices, chicken broth, Boost®, and Popsicle®. He refuses it all. We discuss the importance of nutrition, to no avail.

I email Judy and Dale, who are planning to come to the Balloon Fiesta in October and stay with us. They need to know that we cannot host, no matter how things play out. Judy asks permission to put Jim's name on the church's prayer chain, wording it, "asking prayers for his health concerns." Jim and I give our permission for that benign information, but ask for confidentiality about the diagnosis. We don't want a lot of details spread among the Pendleton church members yet. We know Judy and Dale can be trusted.

The oncology nurse calls late in the day. Jim is asleep, so I talk with her. She tells me Jim will need a battery of tests – another CT scan, more blood work, and an endoscopy. She says we will get calls for several days scheduling the various tests. The first test can be as soon as twelve days from now.

I say, with some irritation, "Jim is not able to go to test after test and endure that, and he doesn't want to. He is weak and walks with a walker. He weighs 150 pounds from 180 in

February, and is very, very sick. I don't think you take into account the energy and stamina it will take for him to go on this round of tests in two more weeks. When he wakes, I'll talk to him about it, but I have heard him say he doesn't want any intrusive tests."

She says, "What is his performance level?"

"Very poor, and not taking any nourishment at all."

"When was his last solid food?"

"Four days ago – Father's Day dinner, and he lost it right afterward."

Now she seems to "get it."

She says, "I doubt he needs these tests at all, and I think he should already be on hospice."

I am glad to know she is seeing the accurate picture. She encourages me to get a hospice lined up. That is the most helpful medical opinion we've had yet – I want people who understand, who are responsive and caring and helpful, and I want Jim to be as comfortable as possible.

When Jim wakes, I tell him about the call, and the tests required. He concurs that he doesn't want to do all that. He and I cry together (well, not stoic Jim, but me) and talk about the situation we are in. He says he wants me to find another companion so I won't be alone – I tell him I can't even think about that and don't want to talk about it. I want *him*.

I'm trying to be brave, but it is hard. We still make little jokes to each other, and we still smile, but on the inside, I, at least, am melting into sadness. Jim continues to be stoic and matter-of-fact.

Sometimes, now, years later, I have a flash of regret about not insisting that Jim get treatment. He might not have done it, even with my insistence. I could have asked him, and he might have done it, for me. However, as soon as those images flit through my mind, I imagine Jim in the hospital, going through all kinds of exams and treatments, and I know how miserable he would have been. Treatment for pancreatic cancer is rarely successful for long, and I would have felt guilty if I'd cajoled him to do that against his will. As Jim used to say about various decisions, "Make your decision and never look back."

I mention this feeling I have of regret, only to say it is fleeting, because if I follow it through, I realize Jim knew what was best for him. One friend in Pendleton, after hearing of Jim's diagnosis, wrote, "I think it was divine intervention that got both of you to Albuquerque before this was diagnosed." Did Jim have a premonition? We'll never know.

CHAPTER 69

GATHERING DATA

One morning, Jim's ex-wife calls. We are still in bed. The phone is on my side of the bed, so I answer. She says something like, "I hear Jim is very sick."

"Yes, he is."

She asks to speak to him. He is still groggy. I reach over to his side of the bed and tell him who it is and that she wants to speak to him.

"Do you feel like talking?" I ask.

He whispers, "Yes," and I hand him the phone.

He says only a few words, and I don't know what is said on the other end of the line, but it is a brief conversation, and it is nice of her to be concerned. The threat of death is a leveler.

In an email that same day to the kids, I say, "I have no problem with Jim's ex-wife calling, or coming to see Jim, if she would like to, for a short visit. Nothing has been said between Jim and me about this, I'm just saying how I feel about it."

Jim and I have not discussed this possibility, but I feel if I am okay with it, he will be, too. I know that at one time there was a great deal of love between them.

I help Jim into our home office, and he is on his computer for a short while. I think maybe he is sending emails, though I don't know to whom, or what he is saying, and I don't ask him. I feel he needs privacy. For all I know, he is playing Spider

Solitaire to calm himself. When he calls that he is through at the computer, I help him back into the living room.

Afterward, he sits on the couch, going over all the papers from the hospital. He asks if I have a medical dictionary. I do, and I get it for him. I feel I can almost hear the wheels turning as he methodically looks up some terms and enters all the information into his brain for processing.

He is drinking only water, no nutrition. I'm sure he has lost at least a few more pounds. He is weaker, and the walker is a great help. Even though we have grab bars in the bathrooms, he is now too weak to use them, and I'm not able to support him safely and help him out of the tub. He is now resigned to sitting on a shower stool and taking showers instead of his beloved long, soaking, tub baths. I watch him carefully. I don't want him to fall. He smiles and says, "I never thought it would come to this – you helping me shower."

Jim's brother arrives from out of town one morning and visits until a little after noon. During his visit, Jim's younger sister calls. I answer. She asks about Jim, and wonders if she can speak to him. I hand Jim the phone. Months before, when we started talking about moving to Albuquerque, Jim told me she said, "You'll probably die down there," to which he replied, "Well, we all have to die sometime." At that time, none of us could have dreamed of this current scenario.

After his brother leaves, Jim is tired, and he takes a long nap on the couch. After he wakes, we decide we'll spend the weekend relaxing and not talk too much about sickness and sorrow. We enjoy some TV and conversation, and go out onto the patio with the walker in the afternoon when it is cooler. We watch the multitude of birds that come to feast on our feeders. We watch the plane contrails and try to guess where the planes have come from and where they might be going, a pleasant pastime of ours. Fred, the lizard, is a constant attraction.

Jim is easy to care for – appreciative of everything, and he tells me how lucky he is to have me. He isn't grumpy or difficult, as some patients might be under these circumstances. He says the bedspread is too heavy, so I take it off and leave our prized Pendleton blanket on, and he says that is much better.

He is no longer safe in the shower, even with the grab bars, so I wash his face and sponge his arms and legs, dry them thoroughly, and he says he feels better. He gets up and looks at the Sunday paper, and watches TV. He is interested in the History Channel's program on Trump's life. Neither of us is a fan of the guy, but look on him as an entertainment item. Jim says he doesn't like either candidate, so he's going to vote for Homer T. Hoop-de-doo. His humor is intact.

I am emailing all our kids every day with updated reports, and soon begin emailing Jim's siblings daily. I feel they must be sorry they are so far away from what is happening. I know Jim's children want to visit. Jim says he doesn't want company yet.

Jim asks about hospice, says he doesn't know anything about it. I explain to him that they have a doctor and a nurse and aides who will visit him at home and keep him comfortable. I say I'll call, if he wants me to, and ask the nurse and social worker to come out and explain to him what they do. There will be no obligation for him to sign up. By now he is having trouble walking, even with the walker.

He agrees to a visit from hospice. "Just to get information," he says.

On a Monday late in June, the nurse and social worker come and explain what they can do, and will do, if he is under their care. The nurse asks Jim, "What sounds good to you to eat or drink?" His answer, "A beer!" produces laughter. She says he can have beer, and wine if he wants, and really anything that sounds good to him.

He is impressed with the women and their manner and knowledge, and the fact that they are not pressuring him. He says he is "just gathering data" and is not ready to sign up yet. He asks many questions, repeatedly telling them he is just gathering data. They begin to be amused by that. One of them says she can see he has a scientific mind, and asks if he is an engineer.

He says, "No, but I have to have all the data to be able to make a good decision." One comments on his well-worn and comfy-looking fuzzy slippers. Both say for him to take his time and think about it, and to call them if he decides he wants their help.

After they leave, Jim asks for and sucks on a Popsicle. I ask him if he wants some beer, but he says, "Not now," his usual response to my offers. We watch his favorite Fox shows, and he naps on the couch. He is spending a lot of time and energy trying to formulate the plan that makes the most sense to him.

A box arrives from Nancy and Julie and families, full of small, wrapped gifts. He opens one package, a rubber duckie that lights up, and he smiles and puts it on the table by the couch. The kids are calling often to check on us. Paul is close by, and is running errands for us.

That night Jim makes many trips to the bathroom.

CHAPTER 70

WE GET HELP

When he wakes the next morning, he turns to me in bed, and his first words are, "Call hospice. I'm ready to sign up."

He has approached the problem in his usual pragmatic, problem-solving manner, gathering all the data available, weighing the options, and has made his decision. I call, the nurse and social worker come back, and he signs the paperwork. He immediately appears relaxed, relieved, and confident of his decision. In the afternoon the hospice doctor arrives, and he tells her he doesn't want tests or treatment. She is with us three hours – gives him an examination, questions him, and pores over the hospital report. Jim likes the physician right away. She is soft-spoken and gentle, and very thorough.

The doctor is sitting across the room; Jim is sitting next to me on the couch. He turns to me and asks, "How long do you think I'll live?"

I look across at the doctor for verification, feeling Jim could have addressed the question to her.

I say, "Well, if you're not eating, and only drinking water, my education and experience tells me about a month to six weeks."

Somehow, I am able to get the words out without breaking into tears. The doctor nods in agreement, and comments on the close bond Jim and I project and the trust he apparently has in me. Jim does not seem surprised at the time he has left, and appears resigned to live a short time at home, rather than any time in a hospital.

This man, after all we've been through, and on the cusp of our new adventure in Albuquerque, is going to die. I try to let my brain absorb that reality.

Jim and I both feel relieved and confident that his symptoms will be under control and well-monitored. I am careful to administer the dosages exactly as the doctor has written them, and I document each dose with the time and amount administered, not trusting that to memory. I had hospice experience with my mother and with husband Paul, so I have no problem being Jim's "nurse."

Jim is spending most of his days on the couch now, sitting up, but sometimes lying down to nap. We are often watching our favorite show, *The Big Bang Theory*, with the Sheldon character, and Jim can still laugh at it. Jim says for me to tell his children they can visit whenever they want to. This is more evidence of his relaxation after his decision has been made to be cared for by hospice.

I email Jim's siblings that he has enrolled in hospice. Jim says his relatives might not understand. He wants me to send them some booklets the hospice gave us. I put them into brown envelopes and have a friend mail them to Jim's children and siblings.

I cannot imagine life without Jim. He and I sit together on the couch and talk, and I cry some, but he is stoic and says, "I've had a good life, and we all have to go sometime. I want you to find another companion so you won't be alone."

I sob, look at him, and say, "I'm not interested. I want *you*."

We both are in another realm, like an alien adventure, hoping we'll wake up.

The hospice is getting things under control, but Jim may have lost another ten pounds – he is skin and bones. He mowed the lawn on June 18th, the day before Father's Day, and now it is only the 29th. That's how fast things are progressing. However, he still has his cute sense of humor.

Jim and I are talking freely about plans for the end, and we set a private code word, as I had done with Paul. I'm convinced Paul communicates with me, and I believe Jim will also be able to do that.

I ask him what kind of service he wants. He says something simple, without participation from the audience, and no congregational singing.

I say, "Where?"

"I don't care – here in Albuquerque is fine."

I say, "I would like to have a visitation here for our Albuquerque friends, but I think a memorial service in the Pendleton church would be nice, so your relatives and long-time friends can attend."

He opens his eyes wide, raising his eyebrows, creating furrows in his forehead, and says, "Do you want to do that?"

"Yes, I will do that for you. I think a Pendleton service will be appropriate."

"I think it will be hard on you."

I say again, "I will do that for you."

He says, "If you have it there, I want you to give the eulogy. I want you to tell people about my Asperger's and apologize to them for anything I've said or done that seemed rude. Tell them I didn't mean to be rude or hurtful. And you're a good writer – I want you to write a book about our life together, so someone may read it and see themselves in it and feel the relief I felt when I found out about Asperger's." I promise with watery eyes that I will do these things.

CHAPTER 71

TOLL TICKET, VISITS, AND BETRAYAL

The hospice nurse comes by, with an aide to give him a shower and shave. Although he is tired afterward, I think he is refreshed.

In fact, he is refreshed enough to tell me, "I'm still sorry I paid that toll ticket in Chicago. I should have challenged it in court."

Same old stubborn Jim – it's on his mind, even though he's dying, and he's reluctant to let it go.

The hospital bed is delivered and positioned in the living room so Jim will have access to the TV – that is a requirement of his, for Fox Channel shows and Sheldon. He isn't ready to sleep in this bed yet. Says he is more comfortable in our big bed. The hospital bed is a constant reminder things are not going to get better.

He lies on the couch watching the news about the Bangladesh terrorist attack in Dhaka. I suggest he might want to watch something more uplifting, but he has the remote and doesn't want me to change the channel.

We are sad together some of the time, but mostly we are trying to enjoy the days when we can, and cope with our topsy-turvy life. Sometimes, we are still our silly selves. He occasionally still makes his "Sheldon face" and says "Bazinga!" to make me laugh.

Twice, his wedding ring slips off his once sturdy, now thin, ring finger. I tell him he can take it off if it bothers him, but he frowns at me, and says, "No, the ring stays on." I wrap narrow strips of adhesive tape around the back of it, and it fits more snugly. We estimate his weight at about 140. It would be difficult to get him on the scale.

Paul and Sepi drop by for a brief visit. Jim comments again on Sepi's beautiful smile. He is quite taken with her. He isn't commenting on much at this point, but he is comfortable and in no pain.

I learn that daughter Nancy has undergone serious emergency surgery. I feel so helpless in so many ways. My stress level is over the top of the scale – with a dying husband here and a daughter who is seriously ill 1500 miles away. I long to be a clone.

Paul and Sepi pop in periodically to do whatever we need done. Another roadrunner is in our back yard while they drop by – the first time Sepi has seen one, and always exciting for all of us. Paul tries to get a photo, but the bird is F-A-S-T! Like, beep-beep!

Jim likes the large, soft, fuzzy, gray and brown throw my girls sent. He is sitting on the couch, wraps himself in the throw, and smiles a satisfied smile, knowing he is loved by many. I take his picture, the last picture I have of him. When I look at it, his face looks hauntingly skeletal. I never show it or send it to anyone.

At 4:00 a.m. on the 4th of July, I am instantly awake when Jim sits up in bed, is confused, and becomes rigid, with a wild look in his eyes. He says nothing, but falls back onto the pillows and gradually relaxes again. Later he doesn't remember doing this.

Jim is quite a bit weaker that day. Early in the morning, he is non-communicative – not unconscious, but non-responsive when I ask him to sit up or hold out his arm. He looks at me, but he is not with me. He has a dizzy spell and seems in another world. Today is the first day he's shown no interest in TV.

Everyone is helpful and kind, and the support we have is amazing. I am eating well, mostly frozen dinners, and getting enough sleep, with breaks in my sleep, but overall doing okay. Jim's kids are planning visits. I warn them to be prepared for many changes in their dad.

I receive news that Nancy has been discharged from the hospital and is feeling better – a huge relief to me.

Jim takes a turn for the worse – more vomiting and can hardly stay awake. The nurse comes by. Jim's daughter is to arrive the next day, and his son is due in another few days. I see Jim's condition going downhill by the day, sometimes by the hour.

His daughter arrives in the early afternoon. They visit on the couch, with her showing him pictures of his granddaughter and telling him about the little girl. Jim musters enough energy to enjoy the visit, but is totally exhausted by bedtime. He wakes at 11:30 p.m., nauseated, and we are awake until 3:00 a.m.

He doesn't wake again until 6:30 a.m., but is not ready to get up. I remind him his daughter is leaving shortly. He wants the covers straightened, and he goes back to sleep. I rouse him at 9:00 a.m. to tell her goodbye. He is groggy, says, "Goodbye," and goes back to sleep. He is still asleep when I check on him at 2:20 p.m., and wakes only when the hospice nurse arrives at 3:30 p.m.

Jim is losing ground. I feel if I start to cry, I might never stop. He is so thin and frail, but still so sweet, never complaining. He is contending with a vicious enemy.

The next day, he watches his favorite Fox shows at 4:00 and 6:00 p.m., then the news about police killings of Black people, and the shooting of police officers, in Dallas. I am ready to turn it off, feeling we have all the sadness we need, but he wants to watch – so we do, until almost 11:00 p.m., when I say it is time to turn it off and go to bed. It has been a fairly normal day, with no nausea and no pain, for which I am thankful.

Jim doesn't want the doorbell or phone to ring. I post a sign on the door: "Illness here – Please do not ring the bell, just knock gently." I have the ringtones on the phones set on low.

The next morning, Jim wakes at 4:00 a.m. I help him use the bedside commode, and he becomes rigid – like he is frozen. In a few seconds he becomes limp, unable to help me transfer him from the commode back to the bed, and he can't sit up. I manage to hold him up. I'm not sure how I manage to do this, but I do, because I can't let him fall. He eventually becomes more "with it," and after a great deal of time and effort, he and I work together to get him safely onto the bed. I am exhausted, as is he.

This is a turning point – I can see I will no longer be able to transfer him safely from the bed to the commode and back. When the nurse comes in the afternoon, she brings disposable undergarments. Jim does not protest, and I think he feels more secure this way. He does not remember the scary part of his rigidity and then limpness, but he trusts me when I tell him we cannot do a transfer in the middle of the night anymore. Together, we can still get him into the wheelchair and go into the living room, but I know that may not be possible either at some point. Each day has changes. I move the commode into the spare bedroom, along with the other items that have become useless – walker, throw rugs, shower bench.

Jim's son arrives one afternoon. He and Jim visit, but Jim is weak, and tires easily. He asks me to get a box of his belongings from the closet, and he finds some mementos and gives them to his son. Jim is exhausted and wants me to help him get ready for bed at 9:35 p.m. I can tell he is confused.

His son and I stay up a while, in the living room. His son is going over Jim's hospital report from the ER, and I'm on my computer, reading the many emails that have come in.

Earlier in the evening, Jennifer, my niece in Connecticut, sent an email that read, "While I've only had the opportunity to meet Jim twice, it was so easy and natural. He is truly part of the family. It was an honor to attend your wedding. There was an aura of joy surrounding you both as you pledged your vows. When you and Jim came to Salt Lake, to Jan's memorial, Jim was a calm and comforting presence. Please let him know how much I've appreciated his becoming a part of our family." I am touched, and tears form in the corners of my eyes.

I become angry as I read the next email. Someone in Pendleton is being fed detailed personal and intimate information about Jim's condition, something we are trying to keep in the family. The details are being disseminated in Pendleton, as well as being posted on Facebook. I am beyond distressed. Without divulging who has sent me the email, I find myself thinking out loud and sharing the information and my feelings with Jim's son, because he is the only one around.

After venting, I realize I have no control over what other people do or say, and decide I have to let it go. I need to conserve my energy to take care of Jim, and I have none to waste on anger.

After this, any emails I send, even to relatives, are less frequent, much shorter, and less detailed, as I have no way of knowing who is sharing mine and Jim's personal information. I feel we are being betrayed and violated. I go to bed, but it is a difficult night, with Jim again becoming rigid and limp and non-communicative.

Jim's son is leaving close to noon. I ask him to help me get Jim from our bed into the hospital bed in the living room, as I feel I will not be able to transfer him by myself anymore. As we lift Jim from the wheelchair into the hospital bed, he has another one of his rigid-then-limp episodes, and I could not have managed him alone. I have padded the mattress with several layers of blankets to make it softer, and Jim says he is comfortable. We have a pile of pillows that can be used in various ways to prop his head at a comfortable level and support his back as he lies on his side.

Jim and his son say their goodbyes, knowing it will be their last time together. Jim sleeps most of the afternoon and apparently is comfortable in the hospital bed. He has a good view of the back yard and the hummingbirds. I make hummingbird food and fill the feeders, so we can watch the fascinating little birds.

The sun sets, dusk comes, and it is the end of another day's vigil. My emotions are often volatile at this time of day – the ending of a day, not knowing what the darkness of night will bring. I am hit with remembering the realia, the small stuff, like Jim's reaching over to catch my hand as we drive along; his running to tell me about the roadrunner; his laughter and facial expressions over Mad Magazine; ice cream at Dave's among the teenagers; his silly walking in Safeway; our choosing Chinese from the deli; his talking back to the self-checkout register. It's all too much. I jerk back into the current reality.

Jim is alert that night. I feel him watching me. I draw the blinds over the sliding glass doors to shut out the darkness and begin to prepare my basket of supplies for the nighttime medications. As I put the vials and syringes and alcohol swabs into the basket, a few feet from his hospital bed, I am overcome with anticipatory grief. I try so hard to be stoic like Jim, and face each day with strength, but he has more experience with stoicism than I.

That night, I fail. I break down. I go over to his hospital bed and lay my upper body across his chest, snuggling up next to his face, wailing, "It's not fair. It's just not fair."

Level-headed Jim takes his arm out from under the sheet, puts it around me, and strokes my back. He does not tell me not to cry. He is long past the earlier years when he had been irritated by my tears. He has lived with me long enough to accept me as I am.

He continues stroking me, and says, "Who ever told you life is fair? You pays your money and takes your chances. We all have to go sometime."

I rise, dabbing my face with a tissue from my pocket, and see his strength. I am ashamed that I have failed to be strong for him. The dying man is comforting *me*.

I say, "Oh, Honey, I'm so sorry," and let a few more tears fall.

He takes my hand, smiling at me, and says, "It's okay. I know this is hard on you."

This will be the last time I allow myself to share my tears. He has always admired my strength and determination, said so when we were courting, and I have let him down, but I will not do it again. From now on, my grieving is silent, but ever present. My pragmatic Jim is my model.

CHAPTER 72

A MOVIE SCENE

Jim sleeps well in the hospital bed that evening. I make my bed on the couch, a few inches from him, so I can hear his breathing and be alerted if he calls for me. He can no longer reach the little bell on the table by his bed, so he calls my name when he needs something – a sip of water, a pad change, or just reassurance during restless times. I administer medications on a regular schedule throughout the night.

Paul comes by that day to tell us goodbye before he flies back overseas. He hates to leave, but he needs to go back to his job. As principal of an American school in another country, it is imperative that he be there to greet and orient the new teachers when they arrive.

In his dark blue suit, crisp white shirt, and blue-patterned tie, Paul comes in smiling, and walks to Jim's bedside. He picks up Jim's thin hand from the rumpled sheet, cradles it in his own, and leans close.

"Jim, I want to tell you how much I appreciate the happiness you've brought into my mother's life. I'm sorry I have to leave. I'm glad I could share some time with you and Mom." He pauses, perhaps to regain his composure. "I love you."

Jim manages a weak smile and says, "Thanks for all you did for us this summer. I've appreciated having you in my life. Have a good trip. I love you, too."

Their locked eyes, liquid pooling, speak wordless volumes. They know with certainty they will not see each other again on this earth. Paul strokes Jim's hand before laying it down.

I sit by Jim's bed mesmerized, as if watching a movie scene. I will never forget the poignancy of those brief moments. I get up, and Paul and I say our goodbyes and hug. When he turns to leave, the knot in the pit of my stomach grows tighter, and tears drop onto my blouse. I hear the car pull out of the drive. He will soon be halfway around the world.

CHAPTER 73

CAN'T YOU MAKE IT
GO QUICKER?

Jim has a restless night, and at one of our wee-hour
"rendezvous" (our humorous name for nighttime medication
times), I inject the medications. I feel him looking at me,
observing. Since he is awake, I fluff his pillows and straighten
his covers. I stand by his bed, smiling, drinking in as much of
this lovely man as I can, knowing time is going to rob me of
that privilege.

He continues to look at me and says, "What do you think
it's like to die?"

He asks the question matter-of-factly, with no more
emotion than he might be asking, "What time is it?"

At times during the days, I ask him if he wants to talk.
Sometimes he does, but most of the time he says he just wants
to think. It is as if he lies there, having plenty of time during
the day to think, and comes up with things he wants to say, or
have answered, during the dark hours. The dark hours are like
a tunnel we have to get through to get to the morning light.

I hold his left hand, the one with the taped ring, and stroke
his forearm. After a few thoughtful moments, I say, "Here's
what I think it's like. I think you will go to sleep and wake up
in a beautiful place."

He has faith in The Man, so there is no need to say more.
A simple question, seeming to express no more than curiosity,

and a simple answer. He smiles, appears content with my answer, closes his eyes, and sleeps well the rest of the night.

The young Native American hospice aide comes to give Jim a bed bath and shave. Jim always looks forward to seeing this young man. He is gentle, kind, efficient, and knows all the right things to say. Jim likes having lotion on his body after the bath. I leave the room, as I always do during these times, to give Jim a semblance of privacy. I can hear them talking softly and occasionally chuckling. Good medicine for Jim!

One night, I email Robin, a niece in Utah, who was also at our wedding, "This is not an email from a strong woman tonight – I am an exhausted, sad, and lonely woman, sitting here on a silent vigil, watching the cover go up and down, knowing it can't be many days before the covers cease going up. I've done this before, but it doesn't make it any easier. My heart is breaking, to think I'm losing another good man, and he's losing everything. I think of all the trips we've planned, to show him the sights of New Mexico – White Sands, the Very Large Array, Pie Town, Carlsbad Caverns, Roswell and the alien museum – all of which he wanted to see. I need a sweet shoulder to cry on, and yours is one of the sweetest I know. Tomorrow will be better. The evening and night hours are always the worst."

The next morning, I email her again, "The day has begun after a night's rest, and the glorious New Mexico sunshine is bright, so things don't seem as dismal as they did in the evening hours last night. Jim is sleeping peacefully, and the vigil begins again. Thanks for listening."

One afternoon, I hear a quiet knock on the door, and a young, uniformed delivery man is delivering an arrangement of strawberries, grapes, and pineapple "flowers" with melon centers, with helium-filled "LOVE" balloons attached. The young man says cheerfully, "Are you Mary?"

"Yes."

Handing me the fruit arrangement, with a big smile, he says, "I hope you're having a nice day."

I say, "Well, not really. I'm caring for my ill husband. Thanks for not ringing the doorbell."

"Oh, what's the matter?"

"He has pancreatic cancer."

The young man's face and manner change immediately, and he says how sorry he is. I think for a minute he is going to hug me. I am touched by his youthful caring.

The fruit is from my children and my cousin. I tie the balloons near the fireplace, where Jim will be likely to see them when he wakes. I recently took the large wedding picture from our bedroom wall and put it above the fireplace. I say periodically, "Look at that handsome couple." Jim smiles.

At 1:30 a.m., Jim wakes to rinse his mouth and get a sip of water. At 6:15 a.m., he is awake and asks for a back rub. As he turns to position himself, he points to the back yard, and says, "You need to get someone to take care of the yard."

Responsible Jim, making sure his duties will be attended to. I assure him I will get someone. After I rub his back, he goes back to sleep and sleeps most of the day.

Then another restless night – he needs back rubs, sips of water, covers smoothed and straightened, pillows fluffed – just generally restless. At 2:30 a.m., when I'm giving him his meds, he says, "I want you to find someone else."

It startles me. He is back to that subject again.

I try to make light of it. "Jim, I can't even think about that. I've had two of the most wonderful husbands a woman could ask for. Don't you think trying for a third would be pushing my luck?"

He smiles, but will not be put off. He reaches up and puts his left hand on my right shoulder and says, "No, I'm serious. I don't want you to be alone." His voice is soft, so I lean closer to be sure to hear each word.

He continues, "What will you do when I'm gone?"

Responsible Jim, again wanting to make sure I'll be okay. He is dying, but worrying about me.

"Don't worry about me. I'm a survivor, and after a long period of sadness and adjustment, I'll be okay. I will always miss you, but I'll eventually be okay."

I need to be factual and real with him. He deals better with straightforward communication. I hear myself comforting him, but it seems a mechanical robot is speaking, because at this time I can't imagine being okay – I'm not sure I even remember what being okay is like.

Sometimes even now, years later, my "okay status" varies, dependent upon the memories that arise.

He is awake again at 3:45 a.m., with a dreamy look in his eyes, and delirium, saying he is hearing noises, like people talking. I hear nothing, and there is no one else here.

The nurse comes in the afternoon and says Jim is in the last stages. The increased restlessness at night is another sign that things are deteriorating.

Jim tells me he wants to be cremated – he said that once on a trip to Tri-Cities, long before he was sick, and he says it again in a recent conversation, when I ask him if that is still what he wants. I ask the nurse to verify that with him, so it will be in his chart. I go to another room, but can hear her ask him whether he wants to be buried or cremated when the time comes, and he whispers, "Cremated." I want everything to be done according to his wishes, and I want the hospice record to show his wishes, coming from him.

We are up several times in the early morning. At four a.m., I prepare the syringes, trying to ignore the alcohol smell as I wipe the port, and hoping to get the meds administered without waking him. I carefully pop open the opening in the port and begin the first syringeful. Half of it in. Jim wakes, and looks over at me.

"I'm sorry I woke you. I was trying to be quiet and gentle, so you wouldn't know I was doing this." I continue the slow squeezing on the syringe plunger.

"Can't you make it go quicker?" Jim asks again.

"The nurse says it does better if I inject it slowly."

Then I realize what he means – not just this dosing, but the whole process! Husband Paul had asked me the same thing, in different words, when he was struggling with the laborious dying process, and my hospice training years ago made me aware that it is a common request of the dying.

"You mean make the whole thing go quicker?" I ask, to verify.

"Yes. I'm ready."

"Jim, I can't do that, and I won't do that. I love you. I'm here to take care of you and make it as easy for you as I can, but I can't hurry the process."

"I understand," and he falls asleep again, as the meds relax his body. I put the used syringes into the hazard box, recap the port, and lie down for a few more hours, hoping I can sleep. *This must be so very hard.*

Jim indicates he needs pain meds by moving his fingers like he's pressing a syringe. He isn't talking by now, but points to his right leg and hip. I give the meds and turn him to his other side. He sleeps most of the day.

I hear a faint knock at the front door. My friends' little six-year-old, Emily, is holding a bouquet of yellow tulips.

"These are for Jim," and as she steps forward, I can tell she is hoping to give them to him herself.

"Honey," I say, "Jim is so sick, and he can't have visitors now. These are so pretty. I'll put them in a vase and put them on the mantel where he can see them when he wakes up. You're so sweet. Thank you."

I take the tulips and close the door, my eyes moist at Emily's (and her mother's) sweet thoughtfulness.

The nurse puts Jim on a regular four-hour schedule for med doses, to keep him comfortable. He begins motioning when he wants a sip of water, by tilting his hand toward his mouth as if he is drinking. He can no longer handle his small water glass, so I hold it for him. When he rubs his hands together, it means he wants a back rub. We are a good team in life, and now in the dying process.

Jim is sleeping almost all the time now, and I keep watching the covers move, to be sure he is still breathing. Surely this cannot be real.

Robin, my niece, emails me, "I am so thankful you and Jim found each other. I know how much joy he brought you, and you brought only joy to him. I have such fond memories of a man I hardly knew. Trading little Oregon Duck jokes with him. Having him with all of us in 2013, as we mourned the loss of Jan. He joined our extended family because of the happiness he gave you, but also because he was a great man. And you are a great woman. Jim is a lucky man. I know he knows this. I know he knew this all along. Those who love you have no right to ask you to be strong. But, if you can, hold on, hold on for those who love you so much."

I respond, "I've just given Jim his meds. At some point, I'll have to pick up the pieces and move forward once again. I will have time for all that. Right now, my post is to monitor this precious person in the hospital bed in front of me."

CHAPTER 74

THE PALM OF GOD'S HAND

At 2:00 a.m., I'm up, getting the two liquid medications drawn into syringes, ready to administer. It's dark outside, of course, but I have one lamp on. Just enough to be able to measure the meds carefully and correctly. Before I administer them, I lay the syringes down and stand beside the hospital bed, taking in the brave man before me. Brave, in that he faces death with grace, the choice he has made after digesting all the facts. He is well acquainted with The Man, so he knows where he is going, although the journey and the anticipation of it are foreign to him.

Suddenly, after several days of silence, and without opening his eyes, he calls out, "God has me, God has me," and trembles.

I'm surprised to hear his voice, but I take his hand and respond, "Yes, God has you in the palm of His hand."

"I want to go, I want to go."

"I'm sure it won't be long, Sweetheart."

His eyes are still closed, and his muscles relax. Who knows exactly what is going on in his dear brain? Perhaps he has a vision of things I cannot see, or perhaps he is hallucinating. In any event, perhaps hearing my voice is reassuring enough to enable him to settle back into sleep. I open the tab that protects the end of the tubular port and mesh the ends of the syringes, one at a time, into the opening. Jim sleeps through it all, and I go back to my nest on the couch, close by, for another few hours of rest before the next medications are due.

Jim no longer complains of any pain, and it turns out to be the best night's sleep either of us has had in several nights. I am awakened by my vibrating alarm underneath my pillow, reminding me every four hours to give his meds. There is no restlessness.

I have word that Nancy is scheduled to have another surgery the next day, her fifth surgery since December. There seems to be no end to the stressful news. I am emotionally numb. I think a toggle switch may have been flipped, and I may have reached my capacity. I have later word that Nancy's surgery was moved up and is in progress.

The aide comes by in the afternoon and bathes and shaves Jim. Jim smiles at him, but there is no conversation this time. Friends deliver dinner to me. Jim has a quiet night.

I am so happy to get a very early text from Nancy herself, saying the surgery went fine, and she slept pretty well during the night. Much relief!

The nurse comes later and takes Jim's vital signs. After she examines him, she motions me into the kitchen to tell me he is very near death. I sob on her shoulder. Even though I know it is coming, I'm not ready.

I wrote Jim's obituary a week or so earlier, when he could still talk, and he gave me input and approved it. I am thankful that is done to his satisfaction. The night is quiet, only giving meds every four hours.

CHAPTER 75

JIM AND MARY'S EXCELLENT ADVENTURE ENDS

On Thursday morning, July 21st, I am asleep on our green leather couch, where I have slept ever since Jim moved into the hospital bed a few feet away. It's a long, comfortable couch, somewhat narrow compared to the king-size bed to which I am accustomed, but I'm not sleeping much anyway. Between the scheduled medicine doses for Jim, I lie back down and allow myself a restless sleep.

I wake to my vibrating alarm at 7:00 a.m. – time for administering meds. Last ones were at three o'clock, before dawn, and Jim seemed okay. He hadn't seemed to be in pain and was breathing normally.

Now I don't like the sound of his breathing. It is labored, then puffy, then labored again.

I get up to look at him and lean close. "Do you hurt? Do you want a sip of water?" No response. I carefully measure the dosages into the syringes and give him his meds, hoping they will help his breathing. His eyes are closed. I kiss him on his forehead and tell him I love him.

Just keep breathing, just keep breathing.

I stand beside his bed, holding his left hand, still adorned with his taped-to-fit wedding band. The next dose of meds is due at 11:00 a.m.

For a moment, a brief but vivid moment, I have an intense, irrational urge to call 911 and have the EMTs come and scoop up this sick, frail, emaciated, much-loved husband of mine, take him to the ER and have the doctors magically make him well. I know that is not a logical thought, but it is a frantic thought that sweeps over me, and for a split second, I imagine myself doing it.

Magic is what I wish for and want. We always said, "I love you," before leaving the house, even to the grocery store. This is the strong, hardworking man with the good, sturdy hands, who used to get up at 4:30 a.m. to get ready for work, and whose goodbye-before-leaving-for-work kisses had become traditional and heartfelt over the years.

His breathing continues erratically. I stand motionless, his fingers interlaced in mine. I peer at his once-stalwart body, now showing the outline of bones. I admire his hands, these strong, talented hands that can, or could, do anything – cook, build, play guitar and piano, repair, drive, lift, carry, and make me feel loved.

The breaths are further apart now. I count – sometimes fifteen seconds between, a few twenty seconds between, a few breaths almost thirty seconds apart.

Keep breathing.

His eyes are closed and his cheeks sunken. I lean over and kiss him on his forehead as I wait for the next breath.

I wait, hoping, but Jim does not breathe again.

I kiss his forehead and lips and tell him I love him. I hope he can hear me.

My dear Jim has gone to sleep and is now waking up in a beautiful place. I feel sure The Man is there, waiting to take Jim's hand from mine and welcome him with open arms.

Jim and Mary's excellent adventure is over.

EPILOGUE

I don't let go of Jim's hand until the men from the mortuary arrive. As I did with Husband Paul, I help wrap Jim's lifeless body in a sheet – my final act of caregiving to him. I help lift him onto the gurney, and the burgundy bag is zipped. I watch as they wheel the gurney out to the van.

I walk out and stand in our driveway, surrounded by friends, as the van pulls out, carrying away the shell of my beloved Jim.

Numbness. Finality.

The friends leave; the house seems cavernous. I wander from room to room, feeling the awfulness of the emptiness. I spy Jim's slippers, and break first into moans, then into deep sobs. "You forgot your slippers, you forgot your slippers," I wail.

In a few days, we have a late afternoon visitation at the mortuary, for our friends here. Julie arrives, and she and I gather Jim's abandoned favorite items to display for the visitation – his guitar; his Navy uniform; his Ducks sweatshirt; several books, including his adjuster's manual, his recently read physics book, his favorite cookbook, and the latest issues of Classic Cars Magazine and Mad Magazine, to be displayed with his glasses. There are also several car trophies, our large wedding picture, plus a montage of smaller photos. The cherrywood urn sits beside a dozen red roses and an 8x10 photo of Jim. Friends greet Julie and me – loving people, lots of hugs, and beautiful flowers.

In Illinois, Nancy went home from the hospital. She still is not well, and doctors say it will be six to nine months before she recuperates, but she has survived. Of course, she cannot travel.

In two weeks, I load the car for the trip to Oregon for the memorial. Jackie meets me in Salt Lake City, and makes the trip to Pendleton with me. Such a dear friend. I invite her to sit with me and the rest of Jim's family at the service.

At the memorial service, a talented female friend plays the piano and sings "Somewhere Over the Rainbow." A string trio, bass and two guitars, play and sing "I'll Fly Away," made famous by Alabama. The pastor gives a homily. Jim was a man of simple tastes, and would not have wanted a big hullabaloo at his "going away party." I give the eulogy, and afterward two of Jim's friends say that doesn't seem like the Jim they knew.

Often friends deny the diagnosis (Carley, 2008, pp. 139, 147; Newport, 2001, p. 7; Wylie, 2014, p. 54).

I share excerpts of the eulogy here:

Jim asked me to give a eulogy at this service, to apologize, and to tell you about a unique facet of our life together, so none of the things I am about to tell you was confidential – we just did not broadcast them. As Jim said many times, his life was an open book, or in his terms, "What you see is what you get."

Many, if not most of you, have known Jim longer than I. But after we married, I became aware that Jim had high-functioning Asperger's Syndrome.

[After giving examples of Jim's traits, I ended with:]

I think it is important to recognize that he did not intentionally hurt feelings or behave inappropriately – he did not realize he was doing so. After he was diagnosed, he became so interested in the traits of Asperger's that we began watching the CBS TV sitcom, The Big Bang Theory. The main character, Dr. Sheldon Cooper, can be described as a classic overdrawn case of Asperger's. Jim began to see similarities in himself and Sheldon and was greatly amused by that. He would act silly and make a "Sheldon face," or if he caught himself being an obsessive neatnik, he would say, "Just blame it on the Sheldon in me." It was a good learning tool for Jim, as well as kept us both laughing. He relaxed and learned to laugh at himself. Before he lost interest in TV in the last few weeks, one of the last things he did was pick up the remote and say, "It's time for a Sheldon."

He said, "I want you to write a book about our life together, so someone may read it and see themselves in it and feel the relief I felt when I found out about Asperger's." I plan to do that.

We operated as a good team – in life, as well as in approaching death. I was holding his hand when he breathed his last breath.

Jim was a good man – loving, generous, honest, loyal, forgiving, and with a keen sense of humor – and I am fortunate to have been his wife. I will always love him and am grateful for the joy and happiness he brought into my life.

On the morning of Thursday, July 21st, the world was diminished by the loss of an amazing man – my husband and very best friend, Jim Hanks.

A FINAL NOTE

In the last few months of working on the book, I won a basket in a charity raffle. Jars of various kinds of jams filled the basket, except for one jar – it contained something different and was labeled with our code word! I had shared that word with no one. I'm convinced Jim was with me as I finished the book.

In CBS's final episode of *The Big Bang Theory,* on the evening of May 16, 2019, the main character, Sheldon, gave an acceptance speech for winning the Nobel Prize. He asked the audience for forgiveness for his sometimes-quirky behavior.

Jim was not around for that episode, which he would have enjoyed, but Jim asked forgiveness posthumously through the eulogy. He may have wished I'd ended the eulogy with, "Bazinga!"

PHOTO GALLERY

My first view of Jim when he contacted me on eHarmony.

We visit the deep blue waters of Crater Lake National Park,
June 2009.

Jim explains some finer points about cars to Nancy's husband, Wes, at a car show in downtown Wheaton, IL.

In Grosse Pointe, MI, my grandchildren, Chloe and Jack, asked Jim to play a board game. Jim hated board games, but he was a good sport.

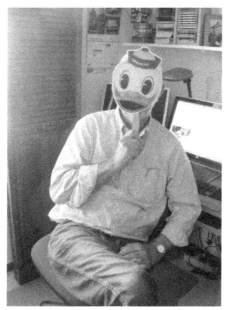

One day Jim asked me to turn around in my desk chair,
and this is what I saw! A rabid Ducks fan!

Waiting for the Round-Up parade in the church yard
in Pendleton.

We marry in my back yard, October 18, 2009
(Photo credit: Jim Myers).

My son, Paul, and Jim clown around, tolerating some
before-dinner photos.

I visit Jim in April 2009, and see this landmark
for the first time.

Chef Jim in his "Ta-Da" pose!

At the colorful Albuquerque Balloon Fiesta, I had to stop and
rest, but Jim couldn't quit roaming the field and talking
to the balloon pilots.

Jim ready to go touring in our beautiful tartan red MGB.

Ever the handyman, Jim installs handrails for the front steps.

An anniversary dinner at Plateau restaurant,
Wildhorse Casino, just outside Pendleton.

My kids sent Jim a subscription to Mad Magazine for his birthday.

At one of many car shows, with our green Austin-Healey Sprite and red MGB.

Jim plays his first-ever game of miniature golf,
at Wallowa Lake.

At a friend's wedding reception in Portland.

Jim serenades me with "Pretty Woman."

Turning the corner onto the living room steps, I found Jim
at the piano. A man of many talents.

Mutual admiration at grandson Henry's first birthday party.

My first-ever car trophy!

Jim hung a spider in the kitchen doorway one Halloween, for me to find when I woke up. He later pretended to feed it a piece of candy.

A sweet, soft side of Jim – making friends with Mrs. Davidson.

Jim takes down our cherry tree because of winter kill.
View from our living room deck, with city of Pendleton
below, and Blue Mountains in distance.

Ready for Thanksgiving in our new Albuquerque home.

ACKNOWLEDGEMENTS

Obviously, I credit Jim with the idea for this book. I hope it serves the purpose he had in mind. The COVID-19 pandemic in 2020-2021 was difficult, and even deadly for many, but I used that cloistered period to finish this book, so the time was a gift to me.

I owe a huge debt of gratitude to my beta readers, many of whom generously read more than one draft: Dr. Wilbur Birchler, Cindy Brown, Jeanne Duggins, Jackie Downie, Dr. Dean Falk, Sally German, Jean Hulbert, Mary Martinez, Dr. Dan Moerman, Joan Moss, Sarah Moulton, Dr. Marythelma Brainard Ransom, and Richard Ransom. They made valuable comments and suggestions, and their perspectives and interest kept me motivated to write a better book with each successive draft.

Encouragers were many – as my first husband, Paul, would have said, "TMTC" (too many to count), as he often said of growth in petri dishes in his microbiological career. Trying to list all those who kept me focused on my goal would be impossible, but I mention a few: My three children, Nancy, Paul, and Julie, always my greatest cheerleaders; my friend, Norm Lindholm in Ohio, who kept asking "How's the book coming along?" and my neighbor and friend, Sally German, who understood when I didn't have time for coffee or to go to lunch. They all knew I wanted to create a book that would honor Jim's request.

The staff at Atmosphere Press have been attentive to my wishes, while making suggestions that have improved the book. I thank and appreciate the expertise of each of those who worked with me.

I hope Jim and The Man are pleased with the finished product. It has been a labor of love, the fulfillment of my promise, and the last thing I could do for Jim.

REFERENCES AND SUGGESTED READINGS

Fiction about Asperger's/Autism:

Carlson, N. & Isaak, A. (2014). *Armond goes to a party: A book about Asperger's and friendship.* Minneapolis, MN: Free Spirit Publishing, Inc. [A charming picture book about an elementary boy with Asperger's/Autism.]

Haddon, M. (2003). *The curious incident of the dog in the night-time.* New York: Vintage. [A novel, also adapted as a stage play, about an adolescent boy with Asperger's/Autism.]

Written by persons with Asperger's/Autism:

Carley, M. J. (2008). *Asperger's from the inside out.* New York: Penguin. [The Executive Director of GRASP (The Global and Regional Asperger Syndrome Partnership) gives valuable information on all aspects of Asperger's/Autism.]

Cooper, R. (2012). Owner of a computer server design and support firm. In T. Grandin, *Different...not less* (pp. 269-291). Arlington, TX: Future Horizons, Inc.

Devnet, C. (2012). Tour guide and lover of history. In T. Grandin, *Different...not less* (pp. 13-42). Arlington, TX: Future Horizons, Inc.

Dubin, N. (2009). *Asperger syndrome and anxiety: A guide to successful stress management.* London: Jessica Kingsley Publishers. [A Ph.D. with Asperger's explains anxiety and how to deal with it. Good for persons with Asperger's/Autism, but also good for anyone dealing with anxiety.]

Finch, D. (2012). *The journal of best practices: A memoir of marriage, Asperger syndrome, and one man's quest to be a better husband.* New York: Scribner. [One of the funniest books I've ever read – really! Finch was diagnosed at 30 and had hilarious adventures.]

Fisher, K. (2012). Senior program manager for Intel and successful "techie". In T. Grandin, *Different...not less* (pp. 99-140). Arlington, TX: Future Horizons, Inc.

Forge, S. (2012). Partner and creative director of an advertising agency. In T. Grandin, *Different...not less* (pp. 357-378). Arlington, TX: Future Horizons, Inc.

Grandin, T. (2006). *Thinking in pictures: My life with autism.* New York: Vintage/Random House. [Grandin shares her experiences with autism, as well as general facts.]

Grandin, T. (2012). *Different...not less.* Arlington, TX: Future Horizons. [A wide range of adults with Asperger's tell their stories.]

Grandin, T. (2015). *The way I see it: A personal look at autism and Asperger's.* Arlington, TX: Future Horizons. [A compilation of articles by Grandin, comprehensive coverage of various topics.]

Grandin, T. & Barron, S. (2016). *Unwritten rules of social relationships.* Ed. V. Zysk. Arlington, TX: Future Horizons. [Dialogue between Grandin and Barron – their experiences with social relationships.]

Grandin, T. & Panek, R. (2014). *The autistic brain: Helping different kinds of minds succeed.* Boston: Mariner Books/ Houghton Mifflin Harcourt. [Scientific information on autistic persons' brain structure, function.]

Grandin, T. & Scariano, M. M. (1996). *Emergence: Labeled autistic.* New York: Warner Books. [Earliest book by Grandin, telling a lot about her childhood. Much of the scientific information on autism is outdated.]

Higashida, N. (2016). *The reason I jump.* New York: Random House. [Written by a 13-year-old boy with Asperger's/ Autism.]

Lawson, W. (2006). Coming out, various. In D. Murray (Ed.), *Coming out Asperger: Diagnosis, disclosure and self-confidence* (pp. 200-213). London: Jessica Kingsley Publishers.

Lesko, A. A. (2011). *Asperger's syndrome: When life hands you lemons, make lemonade.* Bloomington, IN: iUniverse, Inc. [Diagnosed at almost 50, she tells of her experiences and achievement with Asperger's.]

Lipsky, D. (2011). *From anxiety to meltdown: How individuals on the autism spectrum deal with anxiety, experience meltdowns, manifest tantrums, and how you can intervene effectively.* London: Jessica Kingsley Publishers. [Lipsky, diagnosed at age 44, is a highly-trained specialist in how to interpret and manage autistic behaviors.]

Newport, J. (2001). *Your life is not a label.* Arlington, TX: Future Horizons Inc. [Newport was diagnosed with Asperger's Syndrome/High Functioning Autism at age 47. He offers some good advice to his peers.]

Prince-Hughes, D. (2004). *Songs of the gorilla nation: My journey through autism.* New York: Harmony Books/Random House. [An instructor at Western Washington University, diagnosed at age 36, writes about her Asperger's and how it helps her relate to animals, particularly apes.]

Robison, J. (2008). *Look me in the eye: My life with Asperger's.* New York: Broadway. [Diagnosed later in life, tried several things, finally found his niche.]

Selpal, S. (2012). Freelance artist who found success through art. In T. Grandin, *Different...not less* (pp. 159-182). Arlington, TX: Future Horizons, Inc.

Tammet, D. (2007). *Born on a blue day.* New York: Free Press. [Tammet is a savant, a highly successful author, and tells his story in an engaging manner.]

Tammet, D. (2009). *Embracing the wide sky.* New York: Free Press. [Tammet writes engagingly about a number of topics – linguistics, brain development, and numbers.]

Tammet, D. (2012). *Thinking in numbers*. New York: Little, Brown. [This will especially interest mathematicians.]

Taylor, B. (2017). *The hue and cry at our house: A year remembered*. New York: Penguin Books. [A delightful memoir – doesn't dwell on Asperger's/Autism, but includes some references to it.]

Willey, L. H. (2006). To Tell or Not to Tell: That is the Aspie Question. In D. Murray, (Ed.), *Coming out Asperger: Diagnosis, disclosure and self-confidence* (pp. 19-31). London: Jessica Kingsley Publishers. [The pros and cons of disclosure discussed by an adult Aspie.]

Willey, L.H. (2015). *Pretending to be normal*. London: Jessica Kingsley Publishers. [Willey was diagnosed late in life, because of the diagnosis of her daughter. Her life experiences will be interesting to anyone interested in learning more about Asperger's.]

Wylie, P. (2014). *Very late diagnosis of Asperger syndrome (autism spectrum disorder): How seeking a diagnosis in adulthood can change your life*. London: Jessica Kingsley Publishers. [Wylie, who was diagnosed at age 51, gives valuable insights into late-life diagnosis.]

Written by persons married to, or in a relationship with, someone with Asperger's/Autism:

Aston, M. C. (2001). *The other half of Asperger syndrome*. London: The National Autistic Society. [Aston is a trained counselor in the UK. Although she says she has personal experience living with someone with an Asperger diagnosis, the book is about her clients, with no specific mention of her personal experience. The topics will ring true to anyone living with an Aspie.]

Hendrickx, S. & Newton, K. (2007). *Asperger syndrome – a love story*. London: Jessica Kingsley Publishers. [An experiential book about Asperger's traits. Hendrickx, who works in the Asperger's field, and Newton, an engineer who has Asperger's, are a couple, but are not married and don't live together.]

Stanford, A. (2015). *Asperger syndrome (autism spectrum disorder) and long-term relationships (2nd ed.).* London: Jessica Kingsley Publishers. [Stanford, living with a spouse who has Asperger's, uses a pen name, and comprehensively covers situations that have occurred (or may occur). Covers most of the aspects of Asperger's.]

Weston, L. (2010). *Connecting with your Asperger partner: Negotiating the maze of intimacy.* London: Jessica Kingsley Publishers. [Weston somewhat repetitively describes various ways of dealing with a spouse's Asperger's behavior. Some may find it helpful.]

Written by professionals about relationships *between* persons with Asperger's/Autism and persons who are neurotypical:

Ariel, C. N. (2012*). Loving someone with Asperger's syndrome: Understanding & connecting with your partner.* Oakland, CA: New Harbinger. [A psychologist teaching about Asperger's traits and issues with a partner.]

Hollands, J. (1985). *The silicon syndrome: How to survive a high-tech relationship.* Toronto: Bantam Books. [A psychotherapist, without naming Asperger's, and before it was commonly diagnosed, obviously deals with the syndrome between partners.]

Marshack, K. (2009). *Life with a partner or spouse with Asperger syndrome: Going over the edge?* Shawnee Mission, KS: Autism Asperger Publishing Co. [Marshack, a psychologist, says she has unspecified family members with Asperger's. Composite stories of her experiences with clients who are dealing with Asperger's.]

Written by other professionals about Asperger's/ Autism:

Attwood, T. (1998). *Asperger's syndrome: A guide for parents and professionals.* London: Jessica Kingsley Publishers. [Deals mostly with children, with few references to adults.]

Attwood, T. (2006). Diagnosis in Adults. In D. Murray (Ed.), *Coming out Asperger: Diagnosis, disclosure and self-confidence*, pp. 32-52. London: Jessica Kingsley Publishers.

Attwood, T. (2008). *The complete guide to Asperger's syndrome.* London: Jessica Kingsley. [Deals with childhood Asperger's, but offers several helpful chapters that extend into adulthood, such as college, career, and relationships.]

Attwood, T., Evans, C. R., Lesko, A. A. (Eds.) (2014). *Been there. Done That. Try this!* London: Jessica Kingsley Publishers. [Results of study done with Aspies, rating stress levels of various traits, with input from Aspie mentors on how they handle the traits.]

Baron-Cohen, S. (1997). *Mindblindness: An essay on autism and theory of mind.* Cambridge, MA: MIT Press. [A thorough explanation of theory of mind. Research dated, but still insightful and interesting.]

Baron-Cohen, S. (2008). *Autism and Asperger syndrome.* New York: Oxford University Press. [Much historical and research/statistical data on Asperger's.]

Bogdashina, O. (2010). *Autism and the edges of the known world: Sensitivities, language and constructed reality.* London: Jessica Kingsley Publishers.

Falk, D. & Schofield, E. P. (2018*). Geeks, genes, and the evolution of Asperger syndrome.* Albuquerque: University of New Mexico Press. [Falk, an anthropologist, gives a detailed history of the evolution of Asperger's, while Schofield, Falk's adult granddaughter, writes from the perspective of one who has Asperger's.]

Frith, U. (1991). Asperger and his syndrome. In U. Frith (Ed.), *Autism and Asperger syndrome* (pp. 1-36). Great Britain: Cambridge University Press.

Georgiou, D. (2006). Diagnosis in Adulthood and Community Disclosure. In D. Murray (Ed.), *Coming out Asperger: Diagnosis, disclosure and self-confidence* (pp. 230-244). London: Jessica Kingsley Publishers.

Goleman, D. (2007). *Social intelligence: The revolutionary new science of human relationships*. New York: Bantam Dell. [Discussion of the effects of abandonment; chapter on mindblindness (aka theory of mind).]

Grossberg, B. (2015). *Asperger's and adulthood: A guide to working, loving, and living with Asperger's syndrome*. Berkeley, CA: Althea Press. [Helpful for young adults who have been diagnosed, but some newly-diagnosed older adults may find it interesting as well.]

Moxon, L. (2006). Diagnosis, Disclosure and Self-confidence in Sexuality and Relationships. In D. Murray (Ed.), *Coming out Asperger: Diagnosis, disclosure and self-confidence* (pp. 214-229). London: Jessica Kingsley Publishers.

Murray, D. (2006). Introduction. In D. Murray (Ed.), *Coming out Asperger: Diagnosis, disclosure and self-confidence* (pp. 9-18). London: Jessica Kingsley Publishers.

Sacks, O. (1996). An Anthropologist on Mars. In O. Sacks, *An anthropologist on Mars* (pp. 244-296). New York: Penguin. [An interview/visit with Temple Grandin, interspersed with Sacks' independent research on Asperger's.]

Siegel, D. J. (2015). *The developing mind: How relationships and the brain interact to shape who we are (2nd ed.)*. New York: Guilford Press. [Detailed theories of how the brain interacts with others and with experiences. Several mentions relative to the autistic brain concerning theory of mind or "mindsight," sense of safety, and rejection.]

Silberman, S. (2015). *NeuroTribes: The legacy of autism and the future of neurodiversity*. New York: Avery Penguin. [A comprehensive history of autism and Asperger's, well-written and interesting reading.]

Solomon, A. (2013). *Far from the tree: Parents, children, and the search for identity.* New York: Scribner. [Chapter Five, Autism, discusses heredity and traits of autism and Asperger's.]

Other topics of interest:

Ackerman, D. (1995). *A natural history of the senses.* New York: Vintage Books. [Ackerman doesn't mention Asperger's, and this is an older book, but she has quite fascinating discussions of each of our senses, and I had a hard time putting it down.]

Bennett-Goleman, T. (2001). *Emotional alchemy: How the mind can heal the heart.* New York: Three Rivers Press. [Several references to the long-term effects of abandonment.]

Farmelo, G. (2009). *The strangest man: The hidden life of Paul Dirac, mystic of the atom.* New York: Basic Books. [Fascinating biography of scientist, Dirac, who, in retrospect, had many traits of Asperger's.]

Karen, R. (1998). *Becoming attached: First relationships and how they shape our capacity to love.* New York: Oxford University Press. [How attachment issues affect our lives as infants, children, and adults.]

Lanier, H. (2020). *Raising a rare girl: A memoir.* New York: Penguin Press. [Includes references to genetics and stimming, not in regard to Asperger's, but interesting.]

van der Kolk, B. (2014). *The body keeps the score: Brain, mind, and body in the healing of trauma.* New York: Viking. [Deals with the effects of trauma, including abandonment, on the body.]

Diagnostic Manuals and Guides:

American Psychiatric Association (1994). *Diagnostic and statistical manual of mental disorders, IV*. Washington, DC: American Psychiatric Publishing. [Lists Asperger's Disorder as a diagnosis separate from Autistic Disorder.]

American Psychiatric Association (2013). *Diagnostic and statistical manual of mental disorders, 5th ed*. Washington, DC: American Psychiatric Publishing. [Subsumes Asperger's Disorder under Autism Spectrum Disorder, rather than a separate diagnosis.]

Kipfer, B. A., Ed. (2010). *Roget's international thesaurus (7th ed.)*. New York: HarperCollins Publishers.

LaBruzza, A.L. (1994). *Using DSM-IV: A clinician's guide to psychiatric diagnosis*. In collaboration with J.M. Méndez-Villarrubia. Northvale, NJ: Jason Aronson Inc. [Lists Asperger's Disorder as a diagnosis separate from Autistic Disorder.]

INDEX OF SOME COMMON TERMS ASSOCIATED WITH ASPERGER'S

abandon, abandoned, abandonment, 33, 88, 103, 110,121, 172-73, 211, 270, 361-62

alien(s), 33, 36, 55, 58, 74, 234

anger, angry, 37, 225, 233-35

anxiety, anxious, 35, 50, 80, 128, 130, 215, 255, 355, 357

arrogance, arrogant, 27, 124, 252

blunt, bluntness, 84, 201, 204, 238-39

bully, bullying, 27-28, 33, 36, 118

change(s), 1, 35, 43, 47, 55, 92, 117, 136, 141, 171, 191, 235, 241, 253, 256, 358

communicate, communicated, communication, iii, vi, 71, 73-74, 232, 272, 325

compete, competition, competitive, competitor, 43, 118, 235, 242, 246

creative, creativity, 45, 58, 74, 356

cue (see also social cues), 241-42, 250, 288

different (felt), 28-29, 36-37, 225, 234-36, 244, 250, 256, 355-57

emotion(s), emotional, emotionally, 28, 37, 41-42, 45, 54, 58-59, 66, 73, 79, 91, 103, 121, 131, 137, 143, 155, 177, 186-87, 213-14, 233, 243-44, 255, 260, 278, 322, 362

empathy (lack of), 73-74, 177, 187, 238

ethical, 51, 274-75

fantasy, fairy tales, 57, 74, 82

focus, focused, focusing, 1, 41, 59, 214-15

genetic(s), iii, 216, 236-37, 362

honest, honestly, honesty, iv, 51-52, 84, 99, 159, 204, 274-75, 335

humor, humorous, 31, 56, 58, 67, 71, 79, 82, 90, 118, 124, 131, 156, 165, 281, 308, 312, 322, 335

intelligence, intelligent, iv-vi, 38, 43, 56, 66, 361

interest(s) (see also special interests), vi, 29, 40, 49-50, 56, 58, 78, 82, 88-90, 94, 113, 120, 161, 169, 180, 224, 232, 252, 260, 315, 335, 358, 362

interrupt, interrupted, interrupting, 29, 162-63, 194, 214, 228, 233, 239, 241-42, 260, 271, 274, 283

live/living in the now, 69, 89, 102, 130, 369

logic, logical, logically, 41, 54, 58-59, 60, 66, 215, 263, 272, 274, 278-79

loyal, loyalty, 45, 51, 66, 68, 146, 335

mask, masking, 30, 59, 91, 124, 136-37, 147, 162, 200, 217, 222, 226-27, 251, 257

meltdown(s), 28-29, 38, 91, 211, 251, 357

memories, memory, 27-28, 116, 131, 155, 179, 209

nature, 54-55, 66-67, 113, 232-33

observant, observation, observing, 48, 54, 136, 162, 209, 215, 279, 322

obsessive, obsessive/compulsive, 90, 191, 202, 230, 335

organized, disorganized, 170

perfection, perfectionism, perfectionists, perfectionistic, 47, 124, 153, 193, 216, 230, 289

process, processed, processing, 28, 42, 96, 102, 116-18, 196, 213, 225, 228, 232, 235, 271, 279, 300, 303, 307

rage, 37, 235

repetitions, repetitious, repetitive, repetitively, vi, 29, 59-60, 103, 207-08, 229, 239, 270

ritual(s), 47, 59, 103

routine(s), 39, 45-47, 59, 191, 230, 260

rule(s), 38-39, 51, 141-43, 162-63, 191, 194, 216, 228, 275, 356

sensitivities, sensitivity, sensory, 28-29, 48, 60, 85, 111, 134, 211, 231, 244, 360

sex, sexuality, sexually, 61, 228, 361

small talk, 84, 151, 251-52

social, socialize, socializing (see also social cues, social justice), iii, v-vi, 38-39, 45, 59, 90, 124, 129, 142, 147, 159, 177, 180, 211, 228, 239, 245, 251-52, 356, 361

social cues, 233-34, 238-39, 253, 256

social justice, 45, 51, 53, 188, 275

special interest(s), 40, 49, 78, 88, 162

stim, stimming, 60, 103, 128, 207, 229-30, 239, 362

stubborn, 43, 80, 117, 212, 271, 274, 300, 313

tantrum(s), 28, 357

tease(d), teasing, 27-28, 30, 33, 36, 80-81, 118

theory of mind, 73-74, 81, 110, 159, 177, 187, 196, 211, 227-28, 272, 280, 360-61

transition(s), transitioning, 36, 38, 43, 127, 130-31, 213, 253, 271, 303

trust(s), trusted, 110, 236, 303, 311, 317

water, 29, 133-34

wrong, 39, 57, 123-24, 203-04, 216, 226, 231, 271, 274

Photo Credit: SarahLove Photography

ABOUT THE AUTHOR

Dr. Johnson received her B.A. in Psychology from The University of Michigan-Dearborn, and her Ph.D. in Psychological Foundations of Education from The University of New Mexico. She has been in private practice almost 30 years.

Besides her first book, *A Caregiver's Guide: Insights into the Later Years*, she has published in magazines, newspapers, and academic journals, and presented at local, regional, and national conferences and workshops. She is a member of American Counseling Association, and a lifetime member of Psi Chi International Honor Society in Psychology, as well as local groups – SouthWest Writers and Albuquerque Genealogy Society.

Boxes of memorabilia crowd her writing space, as she is working on a family history for her descendants and a memoir about her dad, *Wash Your Face with Cold Water*. She is an avid reader, and having perfectionist tendencies, silently dissects everything she reads! While quite content with single life, she is open to new males in her life, as Jim wished, and is currently dating. She, like Jim, is a firm believer in "living in the now."

She welcomes comments at **MARYABQ@aol.com**, or find her on Facebook at **Mary A. Johnson, PhD, Counselor, Author**, or visit her at www.maryajohnsonphd.com.

ABOUT ATMOSPHERE PRESS

Atmosphere Press is an independent, full-service publisher for excellent books in all genres and for all audiences. Learn more about what we do at atmospherepress.com.

We encourage you to check out some of Atmosphere's latest releases, which are available at Amazon.com and via order from your local bookstore:

The Swing: A Muse's Memoir About Keeping the Artist Alive, by Susan Dennis

Possibilities with Parkinson's: A Fresh Look, by Dr. C

Gaining Altitude - Retirement and Beyond, by Rebecca Milliken

Out and Back: Essays on a Family in Motion, by Elizabeth Templeman

Just Be Honest, by Cindy Yates

You Crazy Vegan: Coming Out as a Vegan Intuitive, by Jessica Ang

Detour: Lose Your Way, Find Your Path, by S. Mariah Rose

To B&B or Not to B&B: Deromanticizing the Dream, by Sue Marko

Convergence: The Interconnection of Extraordinary Experiences, by Barbara Mango and Lynn Miller

Sacred Fool, by Nathan Dean Talamantez

My Place in the Spiral, by Rebecca Beardsall

My Eight Dads, by Mark Kirby

Dinner's Ready! Recipes for Working Moms, by Rebecca Cailor

Vespers' Lament: Essays Culture Critique, Future Suffering, and Christian Salvation, by Brian Howard Luce

CPSIA information can be obtained
at www.ICGtesting.com
Printed in the USA
BVHW030915221121
622224BV00010B/215/J